When Families Made Memories Together

It was a time when families
were close, both emotionally
and geographically, and
children grew up surrounded
with love from parents,
grandparents, aunts, uncles
and cousins who lived nearby.
These are the memories of
people who recall the
happiness, security and
togetherness our families
once enjoyed.

A CELEBRATION OF GENERATIONS. **Whenever there was a family get-together, you can bet that everyone would turn out, including parents, grandparents, aunts, uncles, cousins—even the family pet!**

Publisher: Roy J. Reiman
Editor: Mike Beno
Contributing Editor: Clancy Strock
Assistant Editors: Deb Mulvey, Julie Schnittka,
    Michael Martin, Bettina Miller, John Schroeder,
    Kristine Krueger, Henry de Fiebre
Art Director: Gail Engeldahl
Art Associates: Jim Sibilski, Maribeth Greinke,
    Julie Wagner
Photo Coordination: Trudi Bellin
Editorial Assistants: Blanche Comiskey,
    Joe Kertzman
Production Assistants: Ellen Lloyd, Michelle Paul

©1994 Reiman Publications, L.P.
5400 S. 60th St., Greendale WI 53129

Reminisce Books
International Standard Book Number: 0-89821-124-7
Library of Congress Catalog Number: 94-66341
All rights reserved. Printed in U.S.A.

Cover photo by Harold M. Lambert
Photo above by Archive Photos/LeGwin

For additional copies of this book or information on other books, write: Reminisce Books,
P.O. Box 990, Greendale WI 53129. **Credit card orders call toll-free 1-800/558-1013.**

Contents

This book is dedicated to our parents and grandparents. Without their patience, wisdom and love, we would have never learned life's lessons and the true value of family.

Prologue

By Clancy Strock, Contributing Editor, Reminisce Magazine

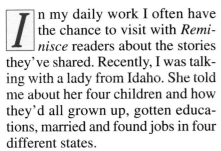In my daily work I often have the chance to visit with *Reminisce* readers about the stories they've shared. Recently, I was talking with a lady from Idaho. She told me about her four children and how they'd all grown up, gotten educations, married and found jobs in four different states.

"It's so sad," she sighed. "Families just aren't close anymore. I doubt my grandchildren would recognize their cousins or aunts and uncles if they met them on the street."

I hear the same thing from friends, and unfortunately, it's true in my own family. My children and grandkids live in California, Minnesota, Wisconsin, Missouri and Texas. We haven't had a family reunion in years.

The Idaho lady's observation inspired this book. I think it's an important book, because it amounts to an oral history of how wonderfully close our families once were.

There's a lot of talk these days about "family values". More and more we hear that if we could just get back to the times when families were close—both emotionally and geographically—a lot of things that are wrong with the world would straighten out.

Trouble is, there's a lot of stammering and foot-shuffling when politicians are pressed to explain what "family values" really means.

To find out, they should read the anecdotes in this book, selected from thousands of wonderful stories sent to us by the readers of *Reminisce*. We asked them to tell us about their families back in the good old days. Did they ever!

Faced Tough Times Together

A number of the stories in this book are from people of my era—the ones born between World Wars I and II. We're the ones who were children or young adults during the Great Depression.

We have warm memories of those difficult years because we knew the love, compassion, warmth, support and joy that were part of belonging to a family. And by "family" I mean the *whole tribe*, right on out to first and second cousins.

In truth, family was about all you could count on back then. If something went wrong, there was precious little in the line of welfare. No food stamps. No Aid for Dependent Children. No government-

---

"How wonderfully close our families once were..."

---

backed home loans. No child-care centers. There wasn't much of anything back then—except reliance on yourself and family.

These days, people in trouble turn to the government. There's a host of federal, state, county, local and private agencies that provide help. As big as welfare has become in the United States, it's interesting to reflect that virtually none of these agencies existed a half century ago.

People in trouble—and at least half the nation fit that description when I grew up—had two places to turn: Their church or their family. The first source of help was family.

My immediate family was small —just Mom, Dad, sister Mary and me. We lived together in a modest farmhouse in northern Illinois. But the four of us weren't "the family", not by a long shot.

Dad's clan was as near as the house across the road. My Grandfather Strock was an easy half-mile

walk away. Mom's family lived in the next town, Dixon. So I was surrounded by grandparents, aunts, uncles and cousins. Through the years we spent lots of time together. My reflections on those days provide my most fond memories.

There was Uncle Wadsworth, who taught me to tell time using a little cardboard clock face he'd cut out from a shoe box. Uncle Howard taught me how to throw a football.

Aunt Florence, who lived in Chicago, told me about the wonders of the big city and spoiled me with gifts she could ill afford. Uncle Earle had lived in San Antonio and had a picture postcard of the Alamo. Uncle Bill was born in Germany and recalled the days just after WWI when it took a wheelbarrowful of marks to buy a pair of shoes.

Grampa Stevens, who'd worked since he was forced to leave school in the eighth grade, introduced me to Dickens, Wordsworth and Thackeray. He also taught me to play chess and pinochle.

In Africa it's said that it takes a whole village to raise a child. In my case, it was a whole family.

Everyone Contributed

If it's the right kind of family, you soon learn that much is expected of you. Grandfather Strock, a gruff and private man who didn't have time for small talk with little kids, had his own way of letting me know when I'd made him proud.

I still remember the day he unexpectedly came in the house with a brand-new pair of high-top boots, with a jackknife in the little pocket. He thrust them into my hands, then turned and left without a word.

Joey Bishop, the comedian, once said that he made a deal with his children when they were young. "I promise never to do anything that ↻

will make you ashamed of me, and I expect nothing less from you."

That's certainly part of the strength of a family. I never wanted to embarrass my family, or make them ashamed because of me. I just couldn't do that to people who clearly loved me so much. Jail was an abstract concept. Bringing shame to my family was easy to understand …and a dreadful thought.

Families provide us with an identity. We're the latest chapter in a one-of-a-kind book begun centuries ago. The cast of characters includes famous figures, ordinary people, statesmen and scalawags.

For every hero at Lexington and Concord, there was a scoundrel. For

---

"The first source of help was always your family…"

---

every gifted inventor, there also was a village idiot.

The marriage license of one of my long-dead relatives contains the handwritten notation, "Married in the home of Captain John Alden". But lest I get too puffed up with my tenuous relationship to a famous woman, it's also true that another relative bought his way out of Civil War service, preferring to cower at home and accumulate wealth.

No matter. They're all *family,* and I'm part of it, writing my own brief chapter in that endless book.

It's not really a case of family values. It's really a case of *valuing your family.* It's a case of wanting *your* chapter in that book to be one your present and future family can talk about with pride.

This book is about the days when family members were closer, both emotionally and geographically. They looked after each other. It wasn't charity—it was just what you did for family. No big deal.

We celebrated holidays together. We worked together. We had fun together, even if it was just gathering around the piano to sing favorite songs. We took aging parents into our homes and tenderly cared for them, the way my Aunt Grace did with Grandmother Stevens.

Children Showed Respect

Cynics say we're guilty of romanticizing a time that never was. I think they're wrong. I don't think an age when children respected their parents and revered their grandparents needs any romanticizing. I don't think a time when families cared about each other needs to be viewed through rose-tinted glasses.

It was a time when kids knew their cousins and even "first cousins once removed" (a relationship I still haven't figured out). They learned the family legends from their grandparents, whom they saw regularly.

That's why this book, *When Families Made Memories Together,* seems so important to me. There's still a chance to learn from those days. And we should, because they very clearly define that elusive term, "family values".

Let's hope these stories remind us of what we once had, and desperately need to find again.

ON A SUMMER SUNDAY in 1934, the Oscar Strock family posed for this picture. Little Mary, 6, sat on her mother's knee, while big brother Clancy, 10, smiled from behind.

"It was at a family reunion in my Grandpa Strock's backyard," Clancy recalls. "He, my father and uncle were neighbors, so I was fortunate to grow up with family all around me."

As Contributing Editor of this book, Clancy shares vivid memories of the days when families were far more closely knit.

Parents, grandparents, aunts, uncles and cousins lived nearby. They worked together, played together, and if adversity struck, were always there for each other …because that's what family was for.

TODAY, Clancy is a Contributing Editor of *Reminisce* Magazine. He is a former professor of journalism at the University of Nebraska.

Chapter One

Dad Was Our Hero

Dad Was Our Hero

ON FATHER'S DAY in 1957, Jack Boyce may have wanted to relax and read the Sunday paper in peace. But his five children had other plans and decided to show Dad how much they love him. Clockwise from left are Wendy, Ricky, Susan, Mary Lynn and Lynda.

I feel sorry for kids who grow up without a dad in the house. Growing up is a puzzling, frustrating, disorganized business and you need all the help you can get. It's a lot easier with both a mom and dad around.

Looking back, I realize that mostly my dad tried to teach me about right and wrong.

Some was straightforward teacher-pupil stuff: "This is how you do it." Dad was not an especially patient teacher, more likely to finish a job himself than wait for me to bumble through it. But I did learn that there is only one way to do anything, and that's the right way.

When I didn't do something right the first time, then I'd surely get to do it again until, by golly, it was done right.

Dad Kept His Promises

Dad never made threats. He made promises, as in: "If your teacher gives you a licking at school, I promise you another one when you get home."

Some things were non-negotiable. My mother's decisions were final, and going to Dad for a second opinion was not a good idea.

I learned that my mother always was to be respected, and a smart mouth brought swift and terrible retribution.

A lot of the really important stuff I learned from Dad was absorbed just by hanging around, watching and listening. Dad taught by example and showed a lot of wisdom in the way he lived.

I learned that you can't do anything about things you can't do anything about, so never let them keep you awake at night.

I learned that most of the bad things you worry about never happen anyway. Don't borrow ahead on trouble.

I learned that most of the bad things that *do* happen are things you can survive, even though it may not be very pleasant.

Smiles Solve Problems

Dad was living proof that a smile solves problems better than a clenched fist.

I learned that being able to help people who need a hand is not an obligation, it's a privilege.

I learned that complaining doesn't make anything better, and people don't want to hear about your troubles anyhow.

I learned that there's no shame in saying "I don't know". Only a fool pretends wisdom he doesn't have.

I learned that you live up to your promises, and a handshake is a bond.

I learned that you should never volunteer advice. Alas, I have a tendency to forget about that. Dad never, ever told me how to live my life. But I knew he'd give me his best counsel if I asked for it.

I learned a lot from Dad. And I'm sure that if you asked my sister, Mary, she'd share the same memories and have some special ones of her own. It's no big news that fathers and daughters have a much different relationship than fathers and sons.

To a daughter, Dad is a shoulder to cry on, a place where she can safely share things that "Mother would never understand", a calm eye in the midst of life's hurricane.

Too many kids are growing up without a dad these days. On the following pages you'll see how much they are missing...and perhaps recall with fondness how very much your dad gave you.

—*Clancy Strock*

Milkman Did Simple Job with Dignity

By Virginia Wallerius, Haledon, New Jersey

THERE WAS A TIME when even the most humble occupations were performed with excellence and pride. That certainly was the case with my dad, who was a milkman for nearly 45 years.

Dad left in the middle of the night, 7 days a week, to make deliveries. When I woke to the early-morning sound of clinking glass, that meant Dad was home to reload the truck. If I hurried, dressed and ate a quick breakfast, I could go with him on the rest of his route. I loved those days!

Dad collected payments three afternoons a week, but he had a big heart. When customers were out of work, he let them run up a bill rather than deprive their children of milk. He always knew about his customers' problems, because they told him whatever was in their hearts—and he sympathized.

Watching Dad taught me how to be reliable. When snowstorms came, he battled the drifts to serve his customers. Just like the mailman, he couldn't be stopped by a little bad weather!

He taught me friendliness, too. He said a smile didn't cost a cent and it made others happy. He was so determined to see the bright side of life that Mom called him "Pollyanna"!

Best of all were the times Dad and I took off on father-daughter outings. Between stops, we'd sing the songs he taught me at the top of our lungs.

Dad eventually sold his route, when the convenience stores began selling milk. He lived to see his 88th birthday.

Recently, I heard the song *'Til We Meet Again*. Tears welled in my eyes because it was one of the songs we used to sing. If I could have just one wish, it would be to ride around town with Dad in his old milk truck once more. We'd sing as loud as we could, and I'd savor the moment just one more time.

DAIRY BEST. Milkmen like this one made sure customers had their milk at the crack of dawn. Virginia Wallerius often rode along with her dad on his route.

"Dad Made It Easy to See God as a Loving Father"

AS A RESEARCH chemist, my dad helped develop new products and improve those already on the market. He introduced one of the first diet-shake powders and experimented with one of the earliest ice cream powder mixes. I still remember sitting with my sisters and playmates on our back steps, acting as his tasting judges!

Later, when Dad expanded perfume bases at a lab in New Jersey, we girls and our friends received vials of his latest essences. Somehow perfumes didn't impress me the way ice cream had, but I was still proud of my dad. To this day, I feel pride whenever I buy a bar of Dial soap—his most prestigious accomplishment.

I have always admired Dad. He knew how to interest me, whether he was taking me to a Shirley Temple movie or gazing at the stars and discussing astronomy. When I first learned about God, it wasn't hard to accept Him as a loving Father. My dad had already given me a glimpse of Him.
—*Betty Hargis, Lillian, Alabama*

DADDY'S GIRL. This picture of Betty Hargis and her father, Arthur Cade, is her favorite. She was 1 year old when photo was taken in 1922.

Cop's Shut-Eye Left Hotel Manager, Guests Teary-Eyed

OUR SMALL TOWN in Maine had only one police officer, and my dad was it. He walked his beat all night long.

One cold winter night he got tired, sat down in the lobby of our small hotel and fell asleep. The mail train woke him and he hurried out, leaving his nightstick behind.

Early the next morning, the hotel manager found the nightstick. As he examined it, he tripped a button that quickly filled his eyes—and the whole hotel—with tear gas!

All 10 of the guests, clad in long johns, nightgowns and sleeping caps, were evacuated. The doors and windows had to be kept open all day.

It was quite some time before Dad was welcome in that hotel again—and then only *without* his nightstick! —*Muriel Le Duc Longmeadow, Massachusetts*

HOOD-McPHERSON'S "PLOW PUSHERS"

He Got Through Depression with a Song in His Heart

By Kathryn McWhorter
Panama City Beach, Florida

BY TRADE, my father was a union steam fitter, and proud of it. But when the Depression came, no work was available. He had a wife and baby daughter to provide for, so he turned to his first love—the guitar.

He got several other unemployed musicians together and formed a band, "Uncle Bud and His Boll Weevils". They got their own radio program and became a popular attraction at rural barn dances throughout Alabama, Mississippi and Georgia. They also performed at schools, churches and movie theaters—anywhere they could make a little money.

Sometimes when Dad performed, Mother and I would go along. I always looked forward to that, because I usually got to sing with Dad! He'd stand me on a chair in front of the big round microphone, prop one foot on the chair to steady it, then put his head close to mine while we belted one out.

I had a repertoire of about four songs; my favorite was *Dark Town*

Strutter's Ball. If the crowd wanted an encore, it was usually *It's a Sin to Tell a Lie*. Shirley Temple was at her peak of popularity then, and Mom made sure I looked as much like the child star as possible!

I have so many memories of those days. I can still see Daddy typing his

---

"Dad put a tiny harmonica in his mouth and played songs—with no hands!"

---

program and taping it to the top of his jumbo Gibson guitar. I remember watching the musicians put their instruments in the special wood trunk Daddy built and mounted on the back of the used Buick they traveled in.

One of the most fascinating things, for a little girl, was watching Daddy put a tiny, 1-1/2-inch harmonica in his mouth and play songs on it—with no hands!

We moved to Memphis, Tennessee a short time later, and soon ventured to Nashville to see the Grand Ol' Opry. I

remember it as though we were there last week. Little Jimmy Dickens was performing, and I got to meet him backstage. (Getting backstage was easy. With that big guitar case in Dad's hand, no one questioned whether or not he was with the show!)

Although I didn't know it then, that was the beginning of the end of Dad's musical career. We'd moved to Memphis because he'd found a construction job. I'm sure he was torn between staying in the band and making a "regular" living. He loved music so much that he must have viewed the transition with mixed emotions.

I'm glad I didn't realize then that Dad's show-biz days were coming to an end. It would've been too sad. But I'll always have the memories—and Daddy's tiny harmonica.

"UNCLE BUD and his Boll Weevils" began playing on radio and at barn dances after the members lost their regular jobs in the Great Depression. The group's leader, guitarist Lewis Marston, is at far right in the photo above shared by his daughter, Kathryn McWhorter.

Compassionate Lawyer Shared His Zest for Living

By Lucy Meyer, Midlothian, Virginia

WHEN I WAS growing up, I longed for my father to be like the dignified dad on *Father Knows Best*. On weekends, while my friends' fathers were dozing, mine was out dancing.

A lawyer during the day, he often spent Saturday nights leading a conga line or doing the Mexican hat dance in the local dance hall.

He took up golf in his 50s, and took to the links in crimson slacks and bright yellow shirt. That made him easy to spot as he was hacking his way out of the rough. Friends delighted in telling us, "I saw your father battling the wild raspberry bushes on the golf course—the bushes were winning."

As we kids in the family matured, we hoped Father would, too. Instead, he painted the top of our car a blinding red to make it easier to spot in parking lots. And I'll never forget the weekend I came home from college and found him digging a hole in the backyard for a pile of his clothes after he'd tried to bring home a baby skunk for a pet!

Dad's youth had been hard, but he embraced life joyously. His mother died when he was a baby, and he was sent to live with relatives on a farm. Money was almost nonexistent, yet he became the first in his family to attend college, working his way through undergraduate and law school.

That gave Dad compassion for his poor clients, whom he often represented for free or for a reduced fee. He even loaned them money until their cases were settled. (That was legal then.)

We complained that he was too trusting. He replied, "Instead of spending my life being suspicious of everybody, I'd rather be cheated a few times." He also pointed out that the Bible provided the best rules for living ever devised.

Dad was good to his courtroom adversaries, too. I remember a telegram another lawyer sent when he was unable to attend an occasion honoring my father: "I greatly value his sincere and fatherly advice, profound judgment, twinkle in his eye and kindness of heart. He even offered to loan me money to pay my alimony."

My father's philosophy was simple. He once wrote: "There is no such thing as finding true happiness by searching for it directly. It must come, if it comes at all, indirectly, by the service, the love and the happiness we give to others."

In his late 70s, he took a challenging, controversial case and worked on it for 2 years without charging a fee. His client was a black man, and times being what they were then, no other white lawyer in the area would represent the man.

My elderly father battled for this young man's future—and won. As a result, he received an award for courageous advocacy from the American College of Trial Lawyers.

When he died at 87, those who came to pay their respects included the man who cleaned his office, two former governors and a U.S. Supreme Court justice.

But long before that, after becoming a parent myself, I appreciated his zest for living and his endless compassion. I realized he was special, even though he was nothing like Robert Young. I wish I had told him so. ✦

YOUNG AT HEART. Lucy Meyer's father, George Edward Allen, believed in living life to the fullest. She shares photos above of him as a young man and at his 50th wedding anniversary celebration (seated in center).

Rugged Cowboy Took Tough Work in Stride

By Vala Ruth Benzinger, Colton, Oregon

DAD WAS BORN and raised on a ranch along the Cimarron River in southwest Kansas. He went to school only through third grade; then he was needed at home.

When he grew up, he became a cowboy, but not the fancy-dressed kind with shiny boots, a big hat and Western shirt and pants. He wore Levi's, a faded blue shirt, a slouch hat and well-worn boots. He chewed Bull Durham tobacco when he couldn't afford Prince Albert, which was most of the time.

For $25 a month, plus a house and use of a milk cow, Dad did all the work there is to do on a ranch. He fixed fences and stocked hay. He rounded up, branded, dehorned, cut and doctored cattle.

Knew All His Cattle

He knew those animals the way most of us know people. I could never figure out how he did it, but he could ride up to a herd, give it a quick look, then turn to Mom and say, "Girlie, that old mottled-faced one's not here."

The way I remember Dad is always working and never really resting. He worked from daylight until dark 7 days a week and never had a vacation in his life. He only took off for funerals.

Dad never missed a day's work because of the weather, either. It was never too hot or too cold. I often saw him

put on a couple of shirts and his Levi's jacket (the only coat he had), tie a scarf across his hat and ears, wrap gunnysacks around his boots and go out in a blizzard to feed the cows, which meant moving several full hayracks to the range. He'd come in at noon, eat, drink a pot of coffee and go right back out until dark.

Only Sick Once

I only remember one time when he was so sick he didn't keep working. He was delirious, and even then he kept trying to get up to go feed. It made quite an impression on us five kids.

We'd never seen Dad in bed in the daytime. We all thought nothing could happen to our daddy, because he was the best, strongest bronc rider in the country.

Later, Dad broke and trained horses. He taught them to roll over, sit up,

"The way I remember Dad is always working and never resting..."

shake hands and tell how old they were. He also trained them to lie down next to him. Then Dad would crawl onto the horse's back, and the horse would carry him to the barn.

BUCKIN' BRONCS were a welcome challenge to Vala Ruth Benzinger's cowboy father. During World War II, his riding skills drew crowds every Sunday from an air base near the family's Kansas home.

When the war broke out, an air base opened nearby. Before long, word got around about Dad's riding, and the soldiers started coming out on Sundays to watch.

Mom would make dinner, usually fried chicken, for as many as 15 to 30 boys. My folks did their best to give them a little taste of home before they were shipped overseas.

An illness took Daddy from us at a young age—46. But he kept working as long as he could ride. A couple of years ago, I went back to Kansas and retrieved his old bronc saddle. Now the little ones can sit in it and pretend they're cowboys...just like Great-Grandpa.

A MAN AND HIS HORSE. Vala Ruth Benzinger's cowboy father had a special kinship with horses. He stopped riding only when his health began to fail.

Dentist Dad "Did It All" in Small Nebraska Town

MY DAD received his dentist's degree in June 1919, then worked as a farmhand to earn enough money to start a dental office in Table Rock, Nebraska. He wasn't just the dentist, but the lab technician, bookkeeper, receptionist and janitor—and he made false teeth, too!

Dad also was our local hospital's anesthesiologist, and gave free dental clinics at the school for children whose parents couldn't afford treatment. He served on the town board, and was school board secretary for nearly 20 years. He was instrumental in seeing that the town had a library and that the school got a new gym.

Even with all this, Dad still found time for me and my siblings. We went swimming together in summer and ice-skating in winter, and we often played cards in the evening. He was a great example to all of us, and proof that "where there's a will, there's a way". He was a wonderful dad!

—Mae Finkner, Pawnee City, Nebraska

Small-Town Editor Touched Many Lives

By Nina Bunyea, Penryn, California

MY FATHER was editor of our Oklahoma town's weekly newspaper, and I spent much of my time at his office. When I was small, my "toys" there were the large type fonts used for headlines. They made great building blocks, but my jumbled piles of type didn't thrill the printer.

So, in keeping with Dad's idea that every activity should be educational, he required that I learn to replace the type properly. By the time I started school, I could print and read well—upside down and backward!

Early on, I learned how to proofread the paper and insert corrections. How thrilled I was when I found a grammatical error in Dad's copy—although I knew full well I'd have to be able to cite the rule and reason for the correction. When I developed the maturity to write articles for the paper, he was even more thrilled than I was.

Religious faith was very simple for my dad: Follow the Golden Rule, and recognize that much religious doctrine is man-made, for man's purposes. He moderated many of our religion arguments by saying, "If Jesus walked in, what would *He* say and do?"

All this makes Dad seem stiff and preachy. Quite the contrary. He was fun to be with, playing countless games and allowing forbidden privileges (like popcorn) when Mother wasn't home.

We listened to the radio for hours

FATHERLY TYPE. Photo reminds Nina Bunyea of the times she spent with her father at the newspaper. Through that experience, she learned to read even before she started school!

on end as we did crosswords, my homework or cryptograms. He told stories by the hour, always requiring me to participate as well—sometimes by providing the ending.

Cared for Others

My dad created long-lasting memories in the community, too. We had no idea of his largess until after his death. A steady stream of visitors came to our door bearing hams, cakes, pies and stories that began: "It was a cold winter. I had no coat. He took me to the store, picked out the warmest one they had and gave it to me with the warning I was to tell no one…"

Others told similar stories involving shoes or dental work or medicine. Big, burly men cried as they told me of the very practical ways Dad had not only helped them, but showed them that somebody cared.

His funeral was just like him—full of jokes and personal memories, told by a minister through his tears. We were celebrating a life that had been far more influential than we realized, and a spirit far too large to be curtailed by death.

When I go to my hometown, I am recognized as being my father's daughter. Family and contemporaries tell me I sound like him. It's just about the nicest compliment I can think of.

HEADS OF THE FAMILY. Renee Kerns shared this 1918 photo of her husband's family, including cousins, aunts and uncles. As in most families back then, the father's word was always final.

Dandy Dad Cut a Dashing Figure

By Sara Riola, Lakewood, New Jersey

AFTER MY FATHER died in 1988 at age 95, we discovered he'd been something of a "dandy" during his single days in New York City! His private papers included these recollections from 1915:

"On a Sunday afternoon, young blades (dandies) paraded on Upper Broadway, some sporting fancy canes and vests. Others escorted young ladies along Riverside Drive to Grant's Tomb and beyond.

"Occasionally they passed a tallyho—with coachman, footman and four horses—bearing well-dressed ladies and sporty gentlemen to the races at Belmont Park or some other destination.

"Nice girls did not drink liquor or smoke cigarettes, although a few of the more daring had tried a puff, strictly in the privacy of their own homes.

"A young man might smoke, but it was not favored. His drinking habits were just as limited. Young people spent their evenings at home, in the parlor or on the porch; or they might go to the neighborhood ice cream parlor for a soda."

Later that year, Father met his future wife at Plymouth Church in Brooklyn Heights, where they later married. Their first home was at 10 Pineapple Street, in the shadow of the Brooklyn Bridge.

He walked the bridge every day to his job on Wall Street, along with hundreds of other "commuters".

By the time I was born in 1916, my parents had moved to Flatbush, and Father's days of "dandying" were forever behind him.

IN STYLE. Sara Riola's father, Ralston Hewitt, dressed in the latest fashions for this formal 1913 portrait.

'Blushing Bride' Brought Down the House

WHEN MY FATHER was about 40, he signed up to appear in a variety show at our town hall. Although he came home from rehearsals in high spirits, he never told us what role he was playing. Little did we know the impact his performance would have on our household!

The night of the show, the crowd was so large that extra folding chairs were jammed against the walls, and latecomers had to stand in back. Mother hadn't wanted to come—she hated large gatherings. But she felt duty-bound to attend Dad's theatrical debut.

Where Was Dad?

The show was a series of small skits featuring local talent. Two sisters in cowgirl outfits played guitars and sang. A man stood on his head and drank a glass of water. But where was Dad?

At last, he made his grand entrance as part of the finale. From the back of the hall, a bridal couple began their procession to the stage. Strains of *Here Comes the Bride* filled the hall...and so did my 300-pound father.

Behind the ring bearer, flower girls and wedding attendants, the bride and groom marched in solemnity and splendor. The tiny, timid village cobbler was the groom, and there, towering 6 inches over him, was my father—the bride!

A blond wig covered Dad's black pompadour, and his big round face was heavily made up with lipstick, mascara, paint and powder. A small girl trailed behind him, toting his train and filmy veil.

Mother Was Not Pleased

Mother was horrified. "Oh my goodness!" she gasped. "What possessed him to disgrace us so?"

The audience was in hysterics, and every time Dad opened his mouth to say something, the rafters shook with laughter.

Mother sputtered and seethed as we walked home in silence. I was confused—*I* thought my father's name belonged in lights! The audience thought he was *so funny*—why didn't Mother?

Many days passed before things returned to normal at our house. A long silent period spelled death for any theatrical aspirations my father might have had. Despite his rare talents, he decided to forgo a stage career and returned to selling Chevrolets. —*Catherine Bauer*
Morrison, Colorado

RIDING THE RAILS. Clyde Dailey (right), with brother-in-law Daniel Chapman, spent more than 3 decades running streetcars in central Indiana. He first ran the interurban line's tiny "dinkey" and later became a dispatcher, motorman and conductor, says daughter Margaret Scott of Indianapolis. The photo was taken in 1914 in Cambridge City, Indiana.

Tunnel Escapade Backfired on Dad

OUR ROUTE to Grandma's house took us through a dimly lit railroad tunnel, an ominous and exciting place to my little brother and me.

Dad made it even more exciting by stopping our Model A roadster halfway through and turning off the ignition. After a moment, he'd restart the engine. The resulting backfire would echo off the tunnel walls, making us kids yell with glee!

The longer the engine was off, the louder the "pop". In an attempt to get the loudest "pop" possible, Dad paused a little too long one night and the muffler blew off the car! That was the last of the "pops", but it was great fun while it lasted!
—*John Elliott*
Mustang, Oklahoma

Desire for Cigars Went Up in Smoke

MY DAD TAUGHT us a lot—often just by doing "little things" he knew we'd remember.

He had a small cigar-making shop, and my two cousins and I often stopped there on the way home from school.

One day when we were about 10 years old, Dad made a little cigar for each of us and sent us on our way.

I'm sure he knew we were going to light up on the way home, and we did.

By the time we arrived, though, none of us felt too good, and I'm sure we looked a little green!

As we grew older, the thought of smoking only made us feel sick. None of us ever started smoking, and we're all in our 70s now. I'm sure Dad had our welfare in mind, and I'm forever grateful for his wisdom. —*Vincent Straub*
Erie, Pennsylvania

New Citizen Served His Country Proudly

ONE DAY my father reminded me to go to the post office—a task I should have done the day before. Then he took off for a morning of fishing to provide food for supper that night.

When I brought the mail home, there was a letter telling Dad to report for jury duty—that morning! Luckily my brother-in-law was there, and he went out to find him.

Before long, Dad came tearing up the road, turning into the driveway so fast he ran right over a lilac bush! He didn't even stop to check the damage. He just raced into the house to change and take off for the courthouse.

He wouldn't have missed jury duty for anything—he had just received his citizenship papers, and he was proud and honored to serve his new country.
—*Helen Marzullo, Seattle, Washington*

DAD WAS A GREAT "POP". John Elliott remembers how, on the way to Grandma's house, his dad would purposely make the car backfire in a tunnel much like this one in the Great Smoky Mountains.

"I Thought God and Daddy Must Be Very Good Friends..."

THERE IS SO MUCH I love and remember about Dad—little things like the way he threw up his right hand to say good-bye as he went off to work... the way tears came to his eyes when hugged by one of us kids...the way he commanded the mules in the field with a "gee, haw, giddyap".

But I remember him most at suppertime, when the whole family was present, heads bowed, and he asked God's blessing.

When I was very young and Daddy prayed to God, I always thought they must be good friends for Daddy to talk to him every day, and wished I could be God's friend, too. —Leathel Lloyd
The Dalles, Oregon

Even Joe Louis Couldn't Compete with Her Dad

NO ONE could top my dad—not even the great Joe Louis!

In the early 1950s, the famous boxer came to our town of West Point, Nebraska for an exhibition match. My dad, Garland Phillippe, had been a professional boxer himself and was going to be the referee.

Before the match began, I got to meet Joe Louis. "Who did you come to see tonight, little yellow-haired girl?" he asked.

I planted my hands on my hips and shot back, "Garland Phillippe!" Joe smiled and shook his head.

"My daddy used to be a motorcycle cop, and he was a professional boxer in California and he could whip you, Joe," I told him.

But Joe didn't seem to mind. He just smiled, patted my head and said, "I hope that my kids are as proud of me as you are of your dad." —Nancy Wit
Fremont, Nebraska

Hats Off to Dad for Special Easter Outfit

MONEY WAS SCARCE on our Wisconsin farm in 1934, but I desperately

PROUD SHARECROPPER Sherman Hobson posed with his young wife, Ruth Belle, in 1920. Daughter Leathel Lloyd, one of their six children, recalls, "Their life was not an easy one, but I believe they were happy. I know they were strong."

wanted a new Easter outfit. My 2-week school break was coming up, so I asked Dad if I could do something to earn $10—the price of a beautiful Easter outfit I'd seen in town.

"If you want to clear a few acres for

sheep pasture, you've got a deal," Dad responded.

After 2 weeks of chopping, sawing, raking and burning, Dad told me I'd done a good job and gave me the money. But when he dropped me off at the store, I was $1.98 short. The $10 was enough for everything but the hat. What's an Easter outfit without a bonnet?

I grabbed the rest of my purchases and ran to find Dad. When we returned to the store, it was closed for the weekend. I should've been happy with what I had, but I really pined for that hat. Dad dropped me off at the library and said he'd be back in half an hour.

When we got back to the farm, I tried on my new clothes for all to see. Just then, Dad walked over with a big grin, hands behind his back, and plopped that gorgeous bonnet on my head. He'd gone to the store owner's house and talked him into opening up just so he could buy me that hat! —Irene Mooney, Calimesa, California

DAILY GRIND for Clarence Althauser of Westerville, Ohio meant making "house calls" to local farms with his portable feed grinder. "He had long routes, 6 days a week, from early morning until late evening, but he liked what he was doing and never complained," recalls his daughter, Betty Robbins of Columbus, Ohio. The service, in business from 1935 until 1943, spared farmers a trip to the mill to have their feed ground.

ON THE HOMEFRONT. Like these men, Charles Meade's father served his country as an air raid warden.

This 4-F 'Recruit' Was an A-1 Patriot

By Charles Meade Jr.
Hauppauge, New York

I'LL NEVER FORGET the day Japan attacked Pearl Harbor. As soon as we heard the news on the radio, Dad was determined to do something to help the war effort.

First he went to the recruiting office to enlist, even though he was a married man with four children. He was told he couldn't serve; he was classified 4-F. But that didn't stop Dad. Couldn't he enlist anyway, even if only to answer telephones? He couldn't, but he kept pushing for reclassification. (He later was reclassified to 4-C, but the military never took him.)

Dad's next move was to sign up as an air raid warden. Then he enrolled in a Red Cross first aid course. He took his new duties very seriously, but still thought he could do more. He volunteered to man a reporting center at the courthouse from midnight to 4 a.m.

The first night of his watch, there was a terrible storm. His partner, Andrew Brehenny, assumed that Dad wouldn't want to venture out on such a night, so he went to the courthouse alone and settled down to what he thought would be a lonely 4-hour vigil. But he didn't know my dad.

At 12:05, Dad walked in. Mr. Brehenny was so astonished he couldn't speak. Finally he asked, "How did you ever get down here alone?"

Dad just said, "Oh, I found it all right." He had never been to the courthouse before, and he walked the six or seven blocks in a downpour...and he was blind.

"It was nothing," Dad said.

The Air Raid Warden Service didn't think so. Its weekly publication ran a story commending him for his efforts.

"Don't we wish more of us had his spirit," the story said. "We take off our hats to this great patriot."

Dad's life was tragically cut short; he was only 42 when he died. But in the short time he was here to guide me, he deeply influenced the rest of my life. I love him just as much today as when he passed away 45 years ago.

OUT STANDING in his field in 1959 was Noble Miller. Son Lowell, of English, Indiana, said his dad loved the country.

Race Driver Triumphed Over Grueling Conditions

By Jack Scott, Raytown, Missouri

MY DAD, Burt Scott, was employed by Henry Ford in 1903 and did many things for the famous automaker. He drove for him on lumber-buying trips to northern Michigan, put together and tested the first Ford tractor and did lots of troubleshooting.

But by far, the most important and noteworthy task he did was driving the winning car, a Model T, in the first transcontinental auto race in 1909. The contest started in New York City on June 1 and ended in Seattle on June 22.

Considering the terrible road conditions, uncharted mountain paths and continuous maintenance problems faced by Dad and C.J. Smith, his mechanic and backup driver, this was undoubtedly the most grueling race of all time.

Roads Disappeared

Their car sank in mud up to its hubcaps in Missouri, plunged 14 feet into one Kansas stream and "floated" across another, and got mired in quicksand in Colorado.

In some areas, the roads were so bad that they drove through cornfields instead. As they entered the Badlands of Wyoming, the roads disappeared entirely; they bumped over steep wagon trails that were so narrow they could barely accommodate a horse.

At Fort Steele, Wyoming, the wagon bridge over the Medicine River was washed out. Dad had to either make a 300-mile detour or drive across a half-mile railroad trestle that rose 150 feet above the river. He chose the latter option—and then had to talk an irate train conductor out of arresting him!

To me, what Dad accomplished seems downright impossible. He had the toughest task ever, yet he did it with style and humility.

"T" PARTY. Celebrants met Jack Scott's father, Burt, at the finish line when he drove the winning Model T in the first transcontinental auto race (above). Among the well-wishers was Henry Ford (at far right wearing the bowler). Top photos show Burt and backup driver C.J. Smith during the race (they're in the car on the left).

Border Cop Didn't Need Height to Walk Tall

FROM 1920 until his death in 1962, my father worked in law enforcement. My earliest memories of him are as sheriff of a small North Dakota town. In 1929, he was hired by the U.S. Border Patrol.

We lived on the St. Clair River in Michigan, a mile from the Canadian border. Many times the river froze in winter, stopping all traffic—except for the "rum runners" who used sleds to pull contraband in from Canada.

One night Dad and his partner split up while patrolling for rum runners. It was pitch dark, but Dad could hear a sled coming across the ice. He couldn't alert his partner, so he did some convincing playacting. Dad was only 5-foot-7 and 150 pounds, but he made up for his size with a courageous spirit and an air of authority.

When the men pulled their sled to shore, Dad shone a light in their faces and gave "instructions" to his partner, who, of course, was nowhere in sight. Then he anchored his light in a solid position, stepped out and handcuffed the men.

When his partner returned a few minutes later and the smugglers realized Dad had arrested them single-handedly, they were disgusted to say the least!

—Mrs. Don Baldwin, Lamoni, Iowa

"Dad Was Always There Whenever I Needed Him"

MY FATHER was not just my best friend, he was my best *everything*! I was an only child and could do no wrong, at least in his eyes, and he was always there whenever I needed him.

When he built a hospital, he trusted me enough to let me help lay beams and flooring. When the Baltimore Orioles were in town, we'd go to the games together.

When I was in first grade, he was hospitalized. I missed him so much that I sometimes left school to visit him, running as fast as my legs would carry me. The teacher begged me to stay, but I wanted my father—nothing else mattered!

In high school, he taught me how to drive. This was in the 1930s, and I was the only girl with a car to use. When I came home late from school activities, he was always waiting for me at the end of our mile-long lane. Sometimes he was asleep, but he was always there!

I loved my dad more than anyone in the world, and he's my guardian angel today.
—*Evelyn Poteet*
Hancock, Maryland

Father and Daughter Were an Inseparable Team

MY DADDY WAS very special to me, and we went everywhere together—usually because I couldn't bear to be away from him. Whenever he went somewhere, I'd cry and beg until he let me come along.

Family always came first for Daddy. I remember the summer he was plowing behind two horses, his feet wrapped in rags because he had no socks. I remember the winter he worked outside in the freezing cold with no gloves. Yet I had socks, and I had gloves. Daddy never complained about times being hard, although they surely were.

Daddy showed us how to be honest, truthful and caring. He was a deacon and Sunday school teacher all his life, and taught us about God and the right way to live. He often said we had a good mother (he was right), and that God had sent her to him.

He always faced his responsibilities, never spoke an ugly word and never lied to anyone. When he died at 74, he'd never paid a single bill late.

To me, Daddy was the greatest man who ever lived, and I miss him now just as much as when I was a child and he went somewhere without me.
—*Martha Ford, Truman, Arkansas*

RIDE 'EM, COWBOY! As a Pennsylvania farm boy, Ernest Williams (at left and above left) dreamed of being a cowboy. When he was old enough to leave home, he hopped a train to North Dakota and made his dream come true. After a stint with the Army in World War I, he returned to farming, but never lost his love for horses and riding. "He had a good sense of humor, and more patience than I would have had," says one of his 11 children, Ada Beegle of Easton, Pennsylvania. "We were all glad he was our dad."

Pop Took Long Hours, Hard Work in Stride

IN THE 1920s, my pop owned our small Washington town's mercantile store, selling groceries, clothing and shoes. He worked 7 days a week, leaving at 6 a.m. to build the fire and staying until 6 p.m.

Sometimes he even went back after supper. But I never heard him complain about having too much work.

On Sundays, Pop would take us kids to the store with him, letting us run loose and "play store" while he did the bookkeeping. We had the most fun pushing each other on the floor-to-ceiling shoe ladders that ran on a track the length of the store. Pop let us have our choice of cookies from the glass-fronted bins, and we each got a candy bar.

Whenever we got too rambunctious, Pop would yell, "You scalawags, quiet down"—and we did. I now marvel at his powers of concentration, with all the confusion we must have been creating!

During the Depression, my soft-hearted pop gave out too much credit, and it cost him his beloved store. I was always proud of him—and I still am.
—*Mrs. James Roherty*
Columbia, South Carolina

Cider Business Brought Family The Sweet Taste Of Success

By Betty Hespell
Souderton, Pennsylvania

MY PARENTS had five children under the age of 9 when the Great Depression began. My dad, Maurice Zeigler, had a job at Ford Motor Company, but work soon became scarce and there wasn't enough money to make ends meet. For a while Dad picked flowers and bittersweet to sell door-to-door.

Then Dad decided to try something else to feed and clothe his family—the cider business! He somehow acquired a small press and converted our little one-car garage to a cider mill.

I have many memories of him using a car jack to pump a stack of crushed, cloth-wrapped apples separated by square slats.

Advertised with Poems

Each year, Dad wrote a poem to advertise his cider, and we kids delivered them to all the neighbors. We helped fill the jugs and load up the trailer he used for deliveries, and sometimes our friends pitched in, too. They knew Dad would reward all of us later with a picnic!

As the years passed, the business grew, and now Zeigler's Cider is sold all along the East Coast. Dad never became wealthy, but he left us a heritage

SWEET BEGINNINGS. Maurice Zeigler gave his family a new start during the Depression by turning their garage (above) in Lansdale, Pennsylvania into a cider mill. It later became a successful business. Like the man at right, he hand-fed apples by the bushel.

that is priceless. Even after he retired and turned over the business to his sons and son-in-law, he still spent much of his time at the plant.

He would stand by as the apples were being washed and pick out the best ones to take to the widows and the poor. That's what he was doing just days before he died at age 76.

Trouble Was Afoot When He Stashed Cash in Shoes!

MONEY WAS TIGHT during the 1930s, especially for my dad, a farmer with a wife and three daughters to support. One year after finishing his own harvest, he hitchhiked 500 miles to the South Plains of Texas to help my grandfather and his neighbors harvest cotton.

It was very hard work. Dad could pull 1,000 to 1,500 pounds of cotton a day. He earned several hundred dollars for his labor, which was a lot of money back then. He hitchhiked home with the money "safely" stashed in his shoes.

To our despair, when he got home and pulled off his shoes, some of that hard-earned cash was beyond redemption—the walking had destroyed it. That was the last time Dad hitchhiked with money in his shoes!

That was also the last year Dad went to South Plains alone. After that, we all drove down with him to help with the harvest, and in 1939 we moved there for good.

Dad raised crops and worked for other farmers, and when he wasn't in the fields, he drove a school bus, roofed houses and did carpentry. I'll never forget how hard he worked to support his family. —*Agnes Lewis*
Earth, Texas

BEING THE FIRST rural route mail carrier west of the Mississippi, Robyn Torbert's father used a horse (much like this man did) to carry his load.

Rural Mail Carrier Always Delivered—on Horseback!

By Robyn Torbert
Bella Vista, Arkansas

I HAVE great respect for the job my dad did. He was the first rural route mail carrier west of the Mississippi River!

Dad's route in northern Missouri covered 27-1/2 miles of dirt roads, some of them just a single lane. He usually worked his route on horseback, but sometimes used a small cart in summer or a sleigh in winter.

At Christmas, he often needed two extra horses just to carry all the packages. I remember seeing little red wagons and sleds tied onto the horses, and larger packages strapped atop their backs.

Dad took his job quite seriously, delivering not only in sleet and snow, but through rain, high water and mud. He knew how important mail was to rural people. Many supplies were bought through the Sears catalog, and folks relied on Dad to deliver them.

Dad delivered other things, too. Many times the phone rang before he left the house, with someone asking if he could pick up medicine from the doctor's office or a package from the variety store. I don't know if Uncle Sam would have thought this "cricket", but Dad's philosophy was, "I always want to help people when I can." And that he did.

Mom made special clothes and a woolen mask to keep him warm in winter, but she worried about the long hours he spent in the bitter cold. If he wasn't home by 8 p.m., she'd start making calls to check on him. The party line was great for this, because several people could chime in with their reports.

Mom usually heard something like, "Oh, he's okay. He stopped here a short while ago to get warm and we gave him a hot bowl of soup. He's back on the road again."

On those nights, we children were allowed to stay up, lessons finished and nightclothes on, until he came home. How great it was to see him come through the door!

In spite of all the hardships, I can't recall Dad ever staying home because of illness or bad weather. He was loyal to his people. Fortunately, in later years, he was able to buy a Model T, and that made his job much easier.

MINERAL POINT'S MAILMAN. Donald Condon shares a 1930s photo of his father, who was the mailman in rural Mineral Point, Wisconsin.

Persistent Pooch Dogged Mailman's Steps

FOR 30 YEARS, Dad worked as a mail carrier. He had one particular route for 20 years, so he got to know everyone very well and took an interest in their lives. It made him so happy during the war years to be able to deliver a letter from a loved one far away from home.

But the most memorable aspect of that route involved a German shepherd puppy who sat on his owners' porch, waiting for Dad to come by each day. The dog's name was "Wren", and he soon started following Dad along his route.

Wren became Dad's companion and protector, walking the route with him for many years. Sometimes when Dad arrived at the postal station in the morning, he found Wren waiting for him at the door! The local newspaper even wrote a story about them.

Miles Didn't Matter

After several years, Wren's family moved to another town 15 miles away. Dad missed his old pal so much—and apparently Wren missed him, too.

One cold day Dad arrived at the station, and there was Wren. He was ragged, dirty and tired, but waiting for his buddy, just like always! Wren apparently had run away from his new home and found his way back across the 15 miles separating him and his pal. Dad returned Wren to his family that evening.

Many years later, the family called to say that Wren, now 19 years old, was very ill. When my kindhearted Dad went to see him for the last time, Wren still remembered his old friend. And Dad shed some tears.

—*Charlotte Augustin*
Oceanside, California

Preacher's Influence Shaped Her Life

By Jane Davis, Banning, California

DADDY was a preacher in small Oklahoma towns during the 1920s and '30s, and his sense of humor was a valuable asset in those rough economic times.

Being a country preacher in those days often meant working without a salary. We were paid in eggs, potatoes and other food, and Dad worked part-time jobs or did manual labor to help us get by. He loved us greatly, and did whatever was necessary to keep us as comfortable as possible.

We moved often, partly because pastorate terms in our church lasted only 2 years, but also because whenever Dad built the congregation to a certain level, he wanted to move on. We'd go to camp meetings, and he'd ask the conference board to send him to a church that was hurting in some way.

Daddy was a strong force in our lives. He was a great musician who taught us to sing beautifully, and he encouraged us to expand our vocabularies. He loved using "$10 words" and would make a game out of trying to find as many ways to use them as possible. When I heard a new word, I'd discuss its meaning with Dad before getting up the courage to try it in conversation.

When we moved from Oklahoma to California during World War II, the other kids made fun of our "Okie" accents, but we knew the English language. A brother and I were allowed to skip a whole grade because we tested above the state requirements! All five of us were good students who were on the principal's list throughout our school years.

Dad gave up preaching to contribute to the war effort, but he didn't stop min-

IN GOD'S SERVICE. Jane Davis' father, Floyd Lee, ministered to homesick servicemen during World War II. That's Jane and her brother Sammy with their dad.

"He couldn't rest thinking about the boys waiting to be shipped to war..."

---

istering to others. He couldn't rest on Saturday nights, thinking about all the young homesick men milling around the San Francisco harbor, waiting to be shipped off to war. He'd walk around the piers, talking with them, until he felt God had led him to a particular one. Then he'd ask that young man to come spend the evening at home with us.

These lonely boys enjoyed Mom's excellent cooking, our lively conversations, the songs and laughter. Dad addressed each of them as "son", and closed every evening with a prayer of safety for our guest and his family.

I saw many of those boys hug Dad hard, their eyes shining with tears, when we took them back to the ship the next morning. Dad believed if he treated other young men as he'd want his sons to be treated, maybe someone would return the favor. He had two sons at war, too.

My father helped shape my life, and I miss him greatly. His influence gave me self-confidence, a sense of humor and a love for others. He was the most unforgettable character in my life.

Dad's Adventurous Spirit Kept Clan on Its Toes

IMPROMPTU PICNICS. This photo reminds Dee Cherry of the times her father would pick a picnic site simply by driving a certain number of miles and stopping. And they always had a bushel of fun!

By Dee Cherry, Bedford, Texas

WHEN I WAS little, I thought roller-skating was the only way to travel. One day in 1939, Dad came outside and asked me to take off my skates. He sat down on the stoop, lengthened the skates, put them on and wobbled all over our brick-paved street. I was giggling like crazy, and all the neighbors came out to watch. What a sight!

Dad also had a unique method of determining where we'd have picnics. After Mom filled a basket with fried chicken, potato salad, fruit and iced tea, Dad would pick a number at random and announce, "We'll drive __ miles and picnic." When the odometer hit the exact number he'd mentioned, we'd stop—no matter where we were!

Once we ended up on a backroad near an abandoned farmhouse with apples ready for picking. We took home a bushel basket full, and Mom canned them for the winter.

HOME-TESTED TILE. When Clyde Dailey of Milton, Indiana sold these tiles to area farmers, he could boast they were home-tested—he tried out each batch in his wife's oven! Daughter Margaret Scott of Indianapolis shared the 1955 photo.

Baker Cooked Up Sweet Memories for Daughters

MY DAD owned a bakery in Maquoketa, Iowa, and rose in the wee hours to turn out scrumptious bread, rolls, pies, cookies and cakes.

When I was in first grade, we read a story about a gingerbread man. Was I ever proud when my dad baked and decorated a big gingerbread man for every child in my class!

When my older sister was that age, Dad would bake Christmas fruitcakes for her schoolteacher, piano instructor and Sunday school teacher. He'd pull her in a wagon or sled, depending on the weather, to deliver them.

Dad has been gone quite a while now, but I have fond memories of him, those gingerbread men and all the fun we had.

—Bette Drake, Janesville, Wisconsin

Depression-Era "Payment" Became Prized Possession

MY SISTER was born at home in 1934, deep in the Depression. My dad, a cabinetmaker, didn't have enough money to pay the doctor.

The doctor looked around our living room and spotted an octagonal lamp table Dad had made for Mom. He said that if Dad could make one just like it for him, the bill would be paid in full. He got his table a few months afterward.

Years later, when I was expecting my first child, I made an appointment with the same doctor, whose office now was in a prestigious building in the heart of the city.

When I entered his waiting room, the first thing I saw was the table Dad had made! The doctor told me several people had tried to buy it, but that he'd never part with it. It was one of his most cherished possessions. I had never been prouder of my dad than I was on that day.

—Jane Barnard
Tazewell, Tennessee

Summer Job Gave Him New Appreciation for Dad

I NEVER REALIZED how hard my Dad worked until the summer of 1940. I was 15 years old, and I was hired as his helper at the Union Ice Company in Berkeley, California. The pay was $5 for a 10-hour day, and on a busy Saturday we sometimes handled 4 to 5 tons of ice.

One day we had lunch at a diner adjoining a pool hall. I thought I was a hotshot pool player, so I challenged Dad to a game of straight pool. To my surprise, he cleaned the table twice before I even got a shot!

He then confided that in winter, when business was slower, he sometimes had time to play snooker for 25¢ a game.

That summer I really learned to appreciate my dad. I not only learned how hard he worked, but that he could be a fun guy.

—Dale Hall
Martinez, California

DOWN TO BUSINESS. Like this boy, Dale Hall spent summers working with his dad.

Wise Father Helped Son Feel Like a Man

By Virgil Axtman
Hartford, Wisconsin

THERE WEREN'T many times Pa showed his tender side, but I'll never forget one time that he did. He was plowing with six horses, and I took him his lunch in the field. When he finished, he asked if I wanted to help him plow. I was overjoyed!

The plow had a small single seat, so Pa swung me up and sat me on his lap. He gave me two reins and said, "When you want the horses to go to the right, pull the right rein. When you want to go left, pull the left. If you want them to stop, pull back on both and holler 'whoo'!"

Plowed Fields

I slapped the reins, hollered "giddyap", and six mountains of muscle sprang into action. Having all that power in my hands was like driving a bulldozer. I felt like a million bucks!

Pa let me stay with him until sundown, when we drove the team back to the barn. Ma was angry—she'd been worried about me. "We men were plowing the fields, Ma," I said proudly.

Horses Did the Work

After that, I watched the horses the milkman and iceman used to pull their wagons. The horses went to customers' houses all by themselves, while the driver was in the back of the wagon preparing the next order. There was no communication between horse and driver; the horses

MILLION-DOLLAR MOMENT. Virgil Axtman's father made him feel like a million bucks when he let Virgil help plow the fields. Only later did Virgil realize that with one swat of the reins, the horses pretty much did the job themselves!

did the whole route themselves.

Then it dawned on me. *I* didn't plow that field—the horses did it themselves! When I asked Pa about it, he just smiled and said that was true. One swat with the reins and the horses knew the rest.

"I just wanted you to feel good and have a great experience," Pa said. What a sly old fox he was!

Hard Work Suited Wichita Lineman

DAD GREW UP on a farm near Wichita, Kansas, so he was used to working hard. When he graduated from high school, he became a lineman for the local power company.

I remember the ice and wind storms that broke the wires—always at night, it seemed. The telephone would ring, and off he'd go—sometimes for a day or two. In summer, lightning and wind would knock out power lines and transformers. When one particularly awful thunderstorm flooded Wichita, Dad and the line crew were out for nearly 3 days and nights before they came home.

Although the work was hard, it must have been good for him—he just celebrated his 89th birthday!   —*Lloyd Creed, Wichita, Kansas*

ALL GEARED UP. Lloyd Creed's father, also named Lloyd, wore all his pole-climbing gear for this portrait with a fellow power company lineman. Lloyd is on the left.

Father's Gift Taught Kids The Meaning of Sharing

IN THE LATE 1930s, my dad drove a school bus when farm work was slow. The bus had no heaters, so he'd heat bricks for us to put our feet on.

One day the snow was pretty deep, and he stopped to pick up a young boy who'd walked about 2-1/2 miles in his bare feet. The boy had no shoes, but he loved school and didn't want to miss a day. Dad opened the door, laughed and said, "Hello, barefoot boy." Then he stopped to warm the boy's feet and wrap them in his coat.

We didn't think much more about it until that afternoon, when the boy got off the bus wearing a new pair of boots. We were all so happy for him—and he marched through the snow with such pride! When I looked at my dad, he grinned and winked, and I knew where those boots had come from.

The six children in our family all had shoes with worn-through soles that were patched with inner tubes, but we never resented what Dad had done.

I know he must have had a hard time paying for those boots, because money was so short. But what a lesson he taught us about love and sharing! We learned so much just from watching his example.
—*Nell Simmons*
Henrietta, Texas

SPECIAL DELIVERY. **Marjorie Sedlacek sometimes gave her dad a helping hand on his long, steep mail route in Ashland, Oregon. On "catalog days", they'd load the "wish books" into their Buick, and Marjorie would hop out at each house to deliver them. At Christmastime, her dad worked well into the wee hours. "Mom and the other wives would take snacks to the men at midnight on Christmas Eve," says Marjorie, who now lives in Portland, Oregon. "They even delivered the mail on Christmas Day!"**

Dad's Lesson in Water Safety Made a Big Splash

ONE SUMMER my dad borrowed a canoe for my sisters and me to use. As he hoisted it over his shoulder for the walk to the lake, I thought he had to be the strongest man alive.

After putting the canoe in the water and securing the bow line, Dad lowered himself into the boat and began explaining the importance of water safety. Canoes were more unstable than the boats we were used to, he said. We'd have to keep our center of gravity low to prevent the craft from tipping over.

To emphasize his point, Dad carefully stood and began rocking the canoe from side to side. Just then, the waves from a passing speedboat made Dad lose his balance. He fell into the water and was out of sight for what seemed an eternity. My sisters and I froze with fear until he surfaced and said sternly, "The first one to laugh is the next to get wet."

Then, of course, *he* burst out laughing!
—*Carol Berner*
Lake Geneva, Wisconsin

Trolley Motorman's Job Fulfilled Boyhood Dream

MY FATHER'S DREAM, as a young boy, was to be a motorman on a trolley car. His dream came true in 1915, when he was 18 years old. The pay was 20¢ an hour, and he worked 10 hours a day, 7 days a week.

In those days, motormen wore uniforms, which were inspected regularly for neatness. Shoes had to be polished, trousers neatly pressed, and blue shirts topped with uniform jackets. I could spot Dad walking home from a block away, and I was so proud of him!

I remember him coming home the day before Easter with chocolate Easter baskets for my two brothers and me, and a special egg filled with candy and jelly beans for my mother. He was happy at his job, even if he had to work holidays.
—*Josephine Reinike*
New Hyde Park, New York

A STREETCAR DESIRE. **Since he was a young boy, Josephine Reinike's father had always wanted to become a motorman on a trolley car like these in Atlanta in 1917. His dream came true in 1915, when he was just 18.**

BOWLED OVER. **When Jewell Bown and her nine siblings needed haircuts, they didn't go to the barbershop—their dad was their barber! "The 'bowl haircut' was in fashion then," recalls Jewell, of Onida, South Dakota. "Daddy just put a bowl over our heads and cut around it. I remember crying over several of those haircuts, but when I see some of the hairstyles nowadays, I don't think we looked too bad!"**

Dad Steered Sledders To Four Blocks of Thrills

WHENEVER SNOW began to fall and it looked like good sledding weather, we knew there'd be a knock at our door. My dad was a town councilman, so he could be counted on to block off the best sledding street with sawhorses.

Even better, he'd take everyone for a ride on our *big* sled—a Flexible Flyer that could hold up to 15 kids! We'd all pile on, then Dad would tie a rope around us and steer from the back as we sailed down four city blocks. What memories!
—*Nancy Otto*
Irwin, Pennsylvania

Compassion for One Child Led Him to Help Many More

ONE DAY my dad was driving by a school when a young boy dashed past the crossing guard and into the street. My dad's car hit the boy, breaking his leg. A policeman who saw the accident said it clearly wasn't Dad's fault, but Dad couldn't leave it at that. He visited the boy in the hospital every day and brought him little gifts.

During his visits, Dad noticed some of the other children suffered from infantile paralysis and couldn't lift their arms. He went home and built an arm-and-pulley apparatus with weights for the children's beds. When attached

to a child's wrist, the weights balanced the arm so the child could draw, write or put a puzzle together.

The doctors were so pleased with Dad's invention that he made more for them, and even sent some to another hospital—all at no cost. —*Ray Davis*
Palm Harbor, Florida

His Generosity Touched Child's Heart Forever

MY DAD was only 5-foot-9, but he was the biggest, most generous man I'll ever know. Times were hard in the 1930s, but he always managed to take good care of us.

Most of the kids in our neighborhood had bicycles. My sisters and I wanted one badly, but we knew it was hopeless. Just getting food on the table was a tremendous task.

On Christmas morning 1938, we awoke to find three brand-new bicycles next to the tree. Tears just rolled down my cheeks. Years later, I found out Dad had lost the sight in one eye in a work accident, and had taken his insurance money to buy those bicycles. That Christmas will live in my memory forever—just as I know it did in Dad's.
—*Virginia Jackman, Phelan, California*

Jack-of-All-Trades' Creations Were Envy of Neighborhood

DAD NEVER MADE a lot of money when we were growing up, but he made sure we had nice things to play with. He was a jack-of-all-trades and could make or build anything we wanted.

PULL, DAD! **Jean Munn of Rockford, Illinois loved it when Dad pulled brothers Billy and Bobby (from left) and herself down snowy winter streets.**

Dad made each of us a bike from old parts, and built stilts for us to walk on. Best of all, he built us a backyard playground, complete with swing set, merry-go-round and playhouse—all from scraps!

Our playground was the envy of the neighborhood. Dad and Mom never had to go looking for us, because all the kids were playing in *our* yard! The other kids' dads didn't take the time to make such great things for them. Many of my friends said they wished they had a dad like mine. I'm glad that I did!
—*Dlores DeWitt*
Colorado Springs, Colorado

GOING TO GREAT HEIGHTS. Arla Crossier and her brother Gary try out the stilts their dad made for them in 1945.

Father's Labors Saw Them Through Lean Years

By Charles Martin
Bartlesville, Oklahoma

DURING THE 1920s and again during the Great Depression, my father worked at a local vegetable grower's truck garden. Our home was several miles away, so he walked to work each morning at dawn and walked back home at dusk.

The work was backbreaking, with hours of stooping, bending and kneeling to hoe, weed and pick row upon row of vegetables. All morning long, he looked forward to his lunch break. It was difficult to carry a meal and keep it fresh in hot weather, so my mother prepared his lunch mid-morning and I delivered it.

I often stopped at a local grocery store about halfway to the truck garden to buy a pint of cold milk for him—a real treat after a morning of working in the hot sun. My timing had to be just right, though, so the milk didn't sour.

I'm sure those days were a struggle for my parents. Dad's wages were small for such hard work. But many families existed on whatever they had, and we all survived.

Today, the truck garden has been replaced by banks, shopping centers, restaurants and housing developments. Hundreds of people pass this site every day, never dreaming that many people once worked here, earning a meager living on a few acres of land.

FIELD OF DREAMS. Like these men, Charles Martin's father provided for his family by working long hours at a local vegetable grower's truck garden.

This Cafe Owner Went the Extra Mile

By Lucille West, Barryton, Michigan

I STILL CAN picture my dad's tiny restaurant, the New Park Cafe in Kalamazoo, Michigan. I loved going there when I was growing up during the '40s and sitting at the counter to watch Dad cook in his chef's hat.

He always had a smile and a friendly greeting for everyone, and his food smelled and tasted so delicious that he was always busy. During the war years, Dad went the extra mile for customers, making his own recipes for things that were rationed and unavailable.

Dad and his restaurant are both gone now, but the precious memories will be with me forever.

Gift Still Reminds Her Of Dad's Thoughtfulness

WHEN I WAS 14 or 15 years old, I saw a cedar hope chest in the Sears catalog and knew that's what I wanted for Christmas. But we didn't have much money that year, and Dad was working at odd jobs just to feed us all. I put the hope chest out of my mind.

When Dad finished doing some work for a neighbor, she offered him an old clothes closet she no longer needed. Dad remembered my wish, took that closet apart and made a cedar chest for me for Christmas! He also used the wood to make a jewelry box for my sister.

That chest is still my prized piece—a reminder of a young girl's wish, and all her dad did to make it come true.

—*Tammy Peterson, Omaha, Nebraska*

MADE HOPE A REALITY. This man reminds Tammy Peterson of the hours her father spent making her a cedar hope chest.

His Hobby Filled Their Lives with Music

By Carolyn Watkins, McKinney, Texas

SOME YEARS it was a struggle for my parents just to put food on the table for their family of 10, but our house was always filled with music. Whenever Daddy had the blues, he'd get out his fiddle and play.

Daddy's love of the fiddle started when he was just a boy. He never had any lessons—he just picked it up from watching and listening to others play, which he did whenever possible.

Every year when he took us to the county fair, we always headed straight for the fiddlers' contest at the bandstand. All of us children would sit with Mother on an old quilt while Daddy got as close to the bandstand as he could.

On weekends, Mother and Daddy would load all us kids into our black '46 Ford, and we'd go to a neighbor's house, where Daddy and other musicians would play 'til midnight.

We kids would play and dance until we were exhausted, then collapse on the neighbors' beds, falling asleep to the delightful sounds of Daddy's fiddle.

When Daddy retired, he started building fiddles in a little shed in his backyard. I think he was happiest when he was creating one of his masterpieces. He made about 17 in all, and each one was cut, hand-rubbed and stained with love.

Before he died, he made sure each of us kids had one. Those fiddles now are proudly displayed in our homes.

I have so many special memories of Daddy and his music. Some might have considered him poor, but to us he was a humble man, rich in love for his family and for the fiddle.

A FATHER'S LEGACY. A portrait of Carolyn Watkins' father, Eddie Walters, hangs alongside the fiddle he made for her just before his death. "Whenever he played the fiddle, no matter where it was, crowds would gather around him," Carolyn recalls. "He brought so much joy to people's lives."

Pharmacist Always Had Helping Hand for Others

By Mary Jo Griffin
Sun Valley, California

WHAT A WONDERFUL human being my father, John McDevitt, was. He was a pharmacist, the best father in the world and a friend to everyone.

Many people came to his drugstore in Oelwein, Iowa just to visit and socialize. One of the "regulars" was a doctor who would cut paper dolls out of the newspaper for my sisters and me.

When the Depression hit, many men who were out of work traveled around looking for jobs. They always seemed to stop at the store for help, and Dad would send them to the cafe across the street for a meal.

He could never refuse anyone who needed medicine, either, even though he knew they couldn't pay for it. He eventually lost the store because of the many unpaid accounts on the books. After that, he worked at any job he could find, and we never heard him complain.

I thank God every day for my parents and the example they set for me.

FRIENDLY PHARMACIST. Like Mary Jo Griffin's father, Casey Chaplin (far right) ran a neighborhood drugstore. Casey operated his pharmacy for years in Hartford, Wisconsin.

Kids Flipped Head Over Heels for Dad's Contests

MY DAD LOVED competition, so there were contests continually going on in our house. The first one I remember was the standing-on-your-head contest. Each of us would pick a spot in the house and then try to stand on our heads, like Dad did. The one who stood the longest won.

We had doughnut-eating contests and banana-eating contests. When we traveled, we had contests in which we earned points for spotting specific things—but Dad's version of this game was unlike any other.

Instead of looking for something like a certain type of car, we'd be hunting for, say, "a man riding some kind of Irish toy". The things he dreamed up were unbelievable!

Dad taught us how to slide down the banister on our stomachs, walk on stilts, hop on pogo sticks and ride bicycles—all with contests.

He was quite a guy, and our lives certainly were never dull. Even when he got older, he continued his antics with the grandchildren, and they absolutely loved it. Today, they still talk about "Pop-Pop" and his wonderful games!
—*Mary Lew Renninger*
Macungie, Pennsylvania

No Lie: Dad Taught Her Importance of Honesty

"TELL THE TRUTH" was Dad's motto. He was born on Washington's birthday, and said the only difference between them was that "George Washington couldn't tell a lie. I can, but I won't".

He brought that lesson home to me when I was in second grade and wanted a bottle of ink and a pen. I said I needed them for school, thinking that'd improve my chances.

Dad kept asking if I was sure I needed the pen and ink for school. I insisted I did—until he said, "I'll ask your teacher at church Sunday. If you're telling the truth, I'll buy them, but if you're telling a lie, you'll get a spanking."

I knew I was doomed, so I told the truth. A few days later, Dad came home with the pen and ink, saying he'd bought them because I had told the truth! —*Carolyn Self*
Kansas City, Kansas

Chief's Cool Deal Lit Fire Under Youngsters

AS FIRE CHIEF of a small Illinois village in the 1930s and '40s, my dad made a deal with us kids. If we would weed the town's empty lots in summer, he'd have the fire department flood them for us in winter—so we always had our own "ice-skating rink" nearby!
—*Marilyn Huntsman*
Salem, Oklahoma

STEERED CLEAR. This farmer reminds Dorothy Sayen of the time she and her father were haying and disturbed a hornets' nest. See her story below.

Stirring Up Hornets' Nest Was a Cracker Jack Idea

MY FATHER was a wonderful individual.

He was a former Baltimore Orioles baseball player, and he had some colorful expressions. I never once heard him swear, but whenever sufficiently provoked he'd cry, "Red roaring Moses!" When he greeted someone or saw an old acquaintance, he'd yell out, "You old sardine, you!"

Whenever he and I went to the ballpark as spectators, Dad would belt out these colorful exclamations, to the amusement of those around us.

I'll never forget one incident from the summer of 1914, when I was 8 years old. Dad and I were haying on the farm that he'd homesteaded. Suddenly his pitchfork pierced a hornets' nest in a haycock on the wagon.

Dad was deathly afraid of hornets, and he waved them away from his face with his hat, until his hat flew out of his hand and landed right on top of the nest!

Dad cautioned me to stay clear, and left his hat where it was until we were done haying. Later, he told me, "If you'll get my hat, I'll buy you a box of Cracker Jack every week for the rest of the year." I got his hat, and he kept his promise. As long as I live, I will never feel richer than I did that year!

— *Dorothy Sayen, Hancock, Michigan*

Picnics, Camping Made Time Together Precious

DADDY WAS full of fun, but he worked so long and hard to make ends meet that our times together were very precious. I especially liked it when he took my friends and me on picnics in our old Model A, or to the medicine shows and carnivals that came to town.

Sometimes we'd camp in the woods. Daddy would hunt squirrels for stew, which he cooked over an open fire. Then we'd pile up beds of leaves and spread quilts on top of them to sleep. I felt so safe next to him when a hoot owl cried or the leaves rustled!

When he came home at the end of the day, I'd run and hide, and he and Mama would pretend they thought I'd run off. Sometimes I'd wait for him to look for me, but usually I couldn't stand it—I had to run out and let him scoop me up in a big hug. I always felt safe in his arms.

— *Mary Jane Lowry*
Blossom, Texas

His Help Led Team to Championship Season

DAD WALKED to work every day, and his route home took him past the field where my sixth-grade softball team practiced. So I'd holler over and ask him to "ump" for us.

Even after a hard day's work, he always put down his lunch pail to umpire and give us batting and catching tips. I was so proud—this was *my dad*, and he was taking the time to help our team!

Thanks to his help, we made it to the championship that year.

— *Lois Tamel, Oak Creek, Wisconsin*

QUALITY TIME. Mary Jane Lowry (above left with brother Dick DeBerry in 1926 and above right in 1938) recalls how her father always made time for family despite the many hours he worked to make ends meet.

Farmer's Hard Work Paid Off

By Bernadine Wells, Bethany, Oklahoma

MY DAD had one of the toughest jobs ever—struggling to earn a meager living for a family of five on a small western-Oklahoma farm during the "Dirty '30s".

During wheat harvest, we only caught brief glimpses of him as he went to and from the fields. After harvest, he'd plow the fields with a variety of plows and cultivators pulled by a four-horse team.

The days were long—he was out of bed before sunup, took a quick break for lunch and didn't return until after sundown.

After a long, dusty day in the field, he was hot, tired and dirty. On the way back up to the house, he'd plunge himself into our horse tank to remove some of the grime. That water was so cold, we

could hear him howl all the way to the house—that's how we knew he was on his way home!

After the busy season had passed, Dad took time to help my two sisters and me with our homework, played cards during the long winter evenings and enjoyed programs on our battery-operated radio.

I know he was exhausted at times on the farm, but he always drove us to school functions—and to school if we happened to miss the bus.

He had a tough job most of his life, but his hard work paid off. In his later years, he and my mother were able to relax and enjoy their retirement years, mortgage-free, on their farm.

FARMING FATHER. Like this man, Bernadine Wells' father spent many long hours on his farm.

Coal Miner's Gritty Job Was Filled with Hazards

By Paul Marshall, Alta, Iowa

OUR SMALL FARM in south-central Iowa had once been part of a company coal-mining town. The company had moved on long ago, but there was still a mine on my uncle's farm next door.

That's where my father and other local farmers worked in winter.

Dad would leave very early in the morning to walk to work. He returned after dark, so covered with black coal dust that we kids didn't dare touch him until he'd had a bath.

After supper, we'd sometimes sit on his lap while he read us the funnies. Like most miners, he had very well-developed wrists and forearms from all the pick and shovel work. We kids decided Popeye must have been a miner before he became a sailor!

Cave-ins Were Feared

Dad worked in the main tunnel in rooms only 2 to 4 feet tall, so conditions were very cramped. And the miners faced several hazards. Twice-daily explosions to shake loose the tightly packed coal filled the mine with fire, smoke and dust. Cave-ins were greatly feared, and a deadly odorless gas that formed in mines could render a man unconscious without warning.

Now and then, Dad hauled coal in our Model T truck to those who couldn't haul it themselves. Father didn't like trucking coal in spring, because if the truck ever slid into a mudhole with a load on, it took two teams to pull it out.

Once in a while, Dad hauled explosives for the mine. Today, OSHA might frown on carrying blasting powder in the back of a Model T on bumpy dirt roads. Dad didn't have a choice.

By today's standards, my dad's life may sound a little harsh, but I never heard him complain about it.

WORKING IN A COAL MINE. This group of miners in Pennsylvania remind Paul Marshall of his father, who worked as a coal miner in winter. The hours were long and the conditions were bad, but his father never complained.

Whistle Told Her Daddy Was Almost Home

A MAN WITH wavy hair and very long legs—that's how I drew my daddy on my Big Chief tablet when I was small. In the evening, I listened for the special three-note whistle that meant he'd walked onto our block. I was allowed to run as far as the first streetlight, where I waited for him to catch me in his arms, admire my "picture" and carry me home.

Daddy made a pretty backyard for us. In addition to a swing and sandbox for my sister and me, we had pink roses climbing trellises, a yellow clay birdbath with cutout wooden figures, a heart-shaped fish pond with weeping willow trees on either side, and a barbecue with an "oven" on top. I can still taste the juicy spare ribs Daddy cooked there!

—Mary Krewson
Hazelwood, Missouri

FIRED UP. Ernest Maile starts up the grill on his homemade barbecue, which featured a curved "oven" on top. Daughter Mary Krewson says photo was taken around 1935 near St. Louis, Missouri.

GARDEN OF DELIGHTS. Mary (foreground) and sister Carol loved the cheery backyard their dad created for them. Mary's sitting on the edge of a heart-shaped fish pond he built around 1935.

Dad's Sacrifice Was Greatest Gift of All

By Albert McGraw
Anderson, Alabama

AT THE HEIGHT of the Great Depression in 1931, Christmas was only 2 days away and not a single toy had been purchased for my two siblings and me. Dad had all but worried himself sick pondering how he might buy at least one toy for each of us, but he was batting zero.

We owned a hog that could be sold for $4, maybe $5. Dad had planned to slaughter it later in the winter; if he sold it now, that meant taking meat off the table.

The corncrib contained 12 to 15 bushels of corn. Shelled corn was selling for 35¢ a pound. But selling it would take cornmeal from our table, and winter feed from our mules. Besides, Dad needed to save some for seed for next year's planting.

Mom had already sold most of the chickens, and had only six hens and one rooster left. There was no way she could spare any more. The entire lot wouldn't

MEMORY LANE. Like this boy and his father, Albert McGraw has fond memories of his dad, like the Christmas he sacrificed for his children.

bring enough to buy even one meager toy for each of us anyway.

Finally, in desperation, Dad decided to sell all 400 pounds of cotton seed he'd saved from that year's crop. He took the $2.20 he received and bought a spinning top for my little brother, a giant sack of beautifully colored marbles for me, and a big doll and half a yard of

beautiful dress goods for a Sunday frock for my little sister. In addition, each of us found a big juicy apple, an orange, candy and nuts in our stockings on Christmas morning!

That was one of the best Christmases of my life, for I realized even then that I had the best dad anyone could ever wish for.

Show-and-Tell Let Her Share Pride in Dad's Skill

TO THIS DAY, I still marvel at all the things my dad could do. I was especially proud of his work as a blacksmith, and when my second-grade class had show-and-tell, I took my classmates to his shop.

Dad's quick smile and kind way made all the children feel right at home. He went to great lengths to explain why the fire had to get so hot, how the bellows worked and how he hammered the fired metal into different shapes.

It was such a joy just to listen to Dad give the name of each tool and explain what it was for. I could name each of those tools, too, but hearing my dad do it made me feel so proud!

—*Iris Robertson, Lakeland, Florida*

NO HORSING AROUND. This man reminds Iris Robertson of her blacksmith father. She still marvels at how he could put shoes on huge horses and not hurt them because he knew exactly where to place the nail.

His Horse Sense May Have Saved Children's Lives

By Emily McNeel, Gold Beach, Oregon

MELTING SNOW and spring rains often turned the small stream near our farm into a raging river, swamping a low-lying road and drainage culvert. Papa knew he could drive his horses and wagon through water as deep as 2 feet, so he placed wooden stakes with painted measurements along the road to guide him.

One morning in 1920, we were on the wagon with Papa and saw the water had risen overnight. What we didn't know was that the current had *moved* one of the stakes! By the time Papa realized how deep the water might be, we couldn't turn back. We had no choice but to try to make it to the other side.

Papa climbed onto the wagon tongue to loosen the reins in case the horses needed to swim. He kept up a reassuring patter, talking to them as if they understood what was happening. Few people were Papa's equal with horses, and the animals would work their hearts out to obey him.

As Papa climbed back into the wagon, his face was ashen and his eyes full of fear. If the water had swept away the planks atop the culvert, we would plunge into a 6-foot hole.

"If the wagon goes down, try to swim to the surface, grab anything that floats and hang on," he said. "I'll try to swim to shore for help."

We were too scared to cry, so we just sat, paralyzed with fear as we watched the swirling current. The horses began swimming, and Papa talked to them in reassuring tones, guiding them as best he could with the lines.

At last, we felt the wagon wheels touch the culvert's smooth planks. The horses soon were back on solid ground, and we made it to the other side, soaking wet, cold and lucky to be alive.

When I finally found my voice, I turned to my father and said, "We're sure lucky you were such a good driver and knew the road so well."

I'll never forget his answer. "Just be thankful we had a good God to guide us," he said.

Dad Kept Wall of Silence Around Youthful Mistake

MY DAD WAS a plasterer, and during summers and on Saturdays he'd let me tag along and scrape plaster off the sub-floors so new flooring could be laid.

One day when I was 10 or 11 years old, I accidentally bumped a wall Dad had just finished. But I'd watched him so often that I was sure I could fix the damage myself.

I put plaster on the wall with a trowel and scraped it off, just as I'd seen Dad do many times, then added more and scraped again. When I stood back and surveyed my work, I was convinced Dad would never know.

Many years later, I told him about that day. He just looked at me and smiled. "Do you remember that I sent you to the truck for something?" I couldn't remember, but he said he fixed the wall while I was outside. And all those years I thought he never knew!

—*Mary Huddleson*
South Lebanon, Ohio

Chapter Two

We Worked
As a Team

We Worked as a Team

I count myself lucky. I'm fortunate because I grew up in a time when families worked together. Not that we had a whole lot of choice in the matter—back then hard work didn't just make your life better, it was survival.

I remember a mom-and-pop grocery store in the little town where I grew up. The family lived upstairs over the store. Mom and Dad tended the store, stocked shelves, waited on customers and kept the books. The kids helped out, too, including grocery delivery right to your back door.

The whole family worked as a team, and they never did get rich. But they survived the tough times and shared the joy and pride in having made it on their own, *together*.

As William Wislen notes in his story on page 52, "Those were the days when kids were expected to grow up fast and do whatever their families needed."

I recall the year I "grew up fast". It was a winter of record snows during the '30s. We lived in the country, and our road to town was blocked by drifts much too high for the horse-drawn snowplows to tackle.

The Men Dug in

The county offered a dollar a day to anyone who would help shovel out the road. I was probably 12 years old and big enough, Dad decided, to wield a scoop shovel. I worked side by side with him and several other men, opening up the road.

There never was any question about one thing: My wages went into the family kitty. It was a proud time for two reasons. Being asked to help shovel meant Dad must have decided I was approaching manhood. And I was helping out with the family grocery bill.

Another family on our road lived just on the edge of town and had a sizable commercial produce operation. We called them "truck farms" in those days. They had an enormous brood of children, all of whom shared in the backbreaking labor of starting plants in the greenhouse, transplanting them to the field, hoeing weeds and harvesting the crop.

I suppose some today would say those kids "missed their childhood". Maybe that's how they remember it, but I doubt that. I'll bet what they remember far more is the closeness they felt in working together as a family...and a sense of pride in making it through the Depression.

The money you made from your paper route, or working as a Western Union messenger, or clerking at Woolworth's or mowing the lawns of the well-to-do...most or all of it was handed over to Mom. It helped out with the rent and the groceries. Or Mom hid it away so you could buy your own school clothes in September.

One thing was understood: It wasn't *your* money—it was *family* money. And that never was a problem. We shared in the work and we shared in the fun. That's what a family was all about.

No, none of us want to bring back those desperate days when money was so scarce. Nevertheless, there's a lot to be said for the old-fashioned sense of family solidarity that comes from working together, with each member chipping in as best they can.

It's something you can take pride in for the rest of your life.

—*Clancy Strock*

ALL FOR ONE. Parents like Mr. and Mrs. Max Dockendorf relied on their children (left to right, Mary Margaret, Lyle, Karen and Janice) to help plant the large garden on their farm in Danville, Iowa. For their hard work, the entire family was rewarded with delicious homegrown fruits and vegetables throughout the year.

Gardening with Dad Was Tough, Necessary Work

By Michael Lacivita, Youngstown, Ohio

AS A YOUNGSTER growing up in the Great Depression, I was the only son in our family and considered myself my Italian immigrant father's sidekick.

We often worked side by side, and I especially looked forward to spring, when I could help him prepare our "hotbed" for seedling plants. This was an important job, because we survived on produce from our garden during those tough years.

We grew mostly plum tomatoes for canning and sweet Italian "goat horn" peppers, using seeds that Dad carefully saved and sun-dried from the previous year's harvest.

Our diligent preparation of the seed bed was an annual ritual. First Dad would shovel the soil into an old copper washtub and set it on top of some paving bricks. Next, he'd start a wood fire beneath the tub to sterilize the soil, killing any "bugs" in it. Our plants were too precious to take chances with.

Plant and Transplant

Before he replaced the soil, Dad put a layer of fresh manure in the bottom of the bed. Then, when the phase of the moon was just right, we'd plant the seeds and cover the bed with an old

PRIZED PEPPERS. Michael Lacivita's father, John, shows off two of the meaty "goat horn" peppers he grew in his garden for over 60 years.

window frame, to act as a makeshift greenhouse. At night we covered the frame with a worn-out rug to keep the cold away, and removed it again each morning before the sun came up.

When the seedlings sprouted, we'd transplant them to be "hardened". They went into our large garden, which took up half the vacant lot next door (our neighbors used the other half). Dad and I worked for hours in that garden—and it was backbreaking work.

Battered Worms

I helped dig, plant, weed and water, carrying pailful after pailful during dry spells. We didn't use chemical fertilizers, but on rare occasions we could afford a load of "organic gold"—our term for horse manure.

We didn't use pesticides, either, so we fought a continual battle with the tomato worms and pepper slugs. It always seemed they chose the biggest and best of the lot to feast on!

Despite Dad's ability to throw a few choice "Italian epithets" at these opportunists, he always said you should plant extra vegetables for the bugs, birds, rabbits and squirrels. And we did.

Gardening with Dad was hard but necessary work. He planted his garden the same way for 60 years. His last "garden", planted just months before he died at age 88, was a flower box filled with his beloved goat horn peppers.

Today, I've added other varieties of tomatoes in my own garden, but I still plant Dad's peppers. I prefer a meal of those sweet fried peppers to the best steak anytime! ◄

HAY THERE! This farming family knew all about teamwork when it came to haying season! Adeline Wiklund of Shelley, Idaho says she and husband Elmer pitched the hay while son Jimmie "loaded and tromped it". Daughter Dorothie expertly handled the team of horses, and youngest son Dale rode behind in his wagon. Photo was taken in the early 1940s.

Washday Required 11-Person Assembly Line!

WASHDAY at our house was really 2 days. That's how long it took to do the laundry for our family of 12 back in the 1920s. And *everyone* in the household had to pitch in to get that big job done.

Our work began on Monday, when we formed an 11-person assembly line to collect water from the spring.

The oldest children dipped it out with gallon syrup buckets, and the middle ones passed it up to Papa, who stood in the wagon and poured it into two big barrels. The youngest children passed the buckets back down the line to be refilled.

We hauled the water up the hill to the "washhouse", a building that had originally housed our kitchen. The huge fireplace still had hooks hanging in it for iron cooking pots. It was the perfect size to hang two black wash pots. We used one to heat water for the washing machine; the other was used to boil clothes.

Next morning, Papa would start a fire under the pots and heat the water. Then he'd pour hot water into the big wooden washing machine. The machine stood on four legs and was made of staves, just like a barrel. It was half as deep.

Kids Were Agitators

Attached to its lid was the agitator, which dropped into the tub when we put the lid on the machine. There was a wheel on top that we children had to turn by hand to work the agitator.

We'd *turn and turn and turn* until we thought our arms would break. Then another would take over, then another.

Next, we'd screw a wringer onto the side of the tub, and we had to take turns turning *another* handle to wring out the clothes.

We put the clothes in bags and dropped them into the boiling wash pots for a lye bath. After that, the clothes went back in the washing machine to be rinsed, *twice*, and were run through the ringer, *twice*.

It's a good thing there were so many of us, because that took an awful lot of turning!

When the clothes were finally ready to hang on the line, you can bet we were all ready for dinner!

—*Edith Finch*
Hamilton, North Carolina

Baker Boys Raised Dough as Parents Vacationed

By Louise Pranzini, Cherry, Illinois

AS I think about this story, it seems as if it occurred in another lifetime. Years ago, kids took on grown-up responsibilities *so early* in life.

My family owned a small-town bakery in Cherry, Illinois. In 1928, my parents took a 3-month trip to Italy to visit my father's relatives. They left me, age 10, and my brothers Peter, 13, and Domenic, 15, in the care of Mother's parents.

A cousin took charge of the little store at the front of our bakery, and Peter and Domenic ran the bakery itself.

Having two teenagers run a business enterprise for 3 months may seem unbelievable today, but Peter and Domenic had grown up in the bakery and knew what to do.

Needed Supplies

They'd mixed bread dough manually and cut out the 1-pound loaves by hand ever since they were 5, when they had to stand on benches to reach the counter.

One day after Mom and Dad had left, Domenic noticed the flour supply was running low. He contacted the flour company and ordered more…a whole carload! *And the salesman obliged*!

Through the years I've often wondered if the man had reservations about taking an order that size…after all, he was dealing with a 15-year-old!

The flour soon arrived by train, and the boys contracted with a trucker to deliver the flour to the bakery. When our flour shanty out back was crammed full, Domenic and Peter found themselves in a predicament. What would they do with all that flour remaining in the truck?

The boys walked from house to house taking orders—and they sold it all!

When my parents returned from their trip, they found a shanty full of flour, a bill marked "paid in full" and an extra $300 in their savings account!

SALES "FLOUR"ISHED. Louise Pranzini recalls that her parents trusted her brothers Domenic (pictured at right) and Peter Marchiando to run the family bakery. The boys displayed keen business sense and made some extra dough!

Young Farmers Earned Their Wages

By Nellie Jones, Memphis, Tennessee

MY PARENTS raised four children on their 15-acre truck farm in northern Missouri. Our acreage stretched out behind the back door in checkerboard patches of strawberries, watermelons, tomatoes and beans.

Daddy taught us how to work the crops at an early age. We didn't get paid for planting, weeding or routine chores, but at harvesttime he paid us at the same rate as his hired help.

I first earned wages at age 7, for picking strawberries. The 70¢ Daddy counted into my palm was enough to buy pink cotton material for a new dress, plus a little extra for a soda pop and candy bar. I was *so proud* of that dress because I had earned the money to buy it. I wore it as my "Sunday best" all summer.

Part of Life

I might have preferred to spend my free time playing instead of working, but we kids accepted work as a normal part of life. Then again, Daddy wasn't too hard on us. We were allowed to take breaks in the shade with a

HARDWORKING COUPLE. Janie and Henry Harmon of Roosterville, Missouri taught their four children the value of hard work. Daughter Nellie Jones says it's a lesson she still appreciates.

cool drink. And on the hottest days, we took a longer rest at the house after our noon meal.

I remember Daddy's philosophy was, "Do your work first; you'll enjoy your play more." And play we did, as a family!

Fun and Games

On long winter evenings we sat around the kitchen table playing dominoes, checkers and card games while Mama popped corn or made a rare batch of fudge.

In summer, we played croquet, sat on the porch to watch the lightning bugs and stars, or went to town for the band concert on the courthouse square. Afterward, Daddy would treat us to double-dip ice cream cones.

Today's children might not consider such a childhood exciting or thrilling enough, but I always felt secure and loved.

I'm glad my parents taught my siblings and me to value hard work, to take pride in doing our work right and to enjoy one another when the work was finished.

Midnight Visit Eased Father's Loneliness

By Lloyd Raymond
Upland, California

IT WAS MIDNIGHT in our little town of Middleboro, Massachusetts, and all was quiet.

Nearly every house in town had been dark for an hour or more. A very proper aunt of mine once remarked, "Decent people just don't stay up after 10!" And in our town, that was just about everybody.

Ordinarily, we would've been asleep along with the rest of the townsfolk. But this night we weren't home. Mother, Dad and I were sitting in the huge, dark boiler room of a factory on the north end of town.

A week or two earlier, there had been another layoff at the shoe factory

where Dad worked. He came home that night looking tired and worried. "Been laid off again," he told Mother as he took off his jacket.

Soon Dad found a temporary job as a night watchman at another factory. His shift began at 8 p.m., so he had his

> *"We walked 3 miles to the factory north of town where Dad worked..."*

"lunch" at midnight. Poor Dad, eating all alone in that hot, grimy room with fires roaring beneath the boilers! But for one night, at least, he wouldn't have to be alone.

After supper, Mother had busied

herself in the kitchen, preparing Dad's lunch and a thermos of hot coffee. It was a cold night, and we had a long walk ahead of us—at least 3 miles. Only a few people in town had cars, and we weren't among them.

A little before 11 p.m., we bundled up in warm coats, hats, scarves and gloves, lit a lantern, picked up Dad's lunch pail and began the long trek through the dark.

To me as an 8-year-old, the walk seemed to take forever, but finally we spotted the factory in the distance.

"We're almost there," Mother said. We quickened our steps.

Just as we arrived at the factory, the big town clock struck midnight. Dad got his lunch on time—and had us for company to boot!

She Learned Soda Shop Business From the Ground Up

By Cookie Curci-Wright
San Jose, California

ONE OF THE most memorable periods of my childhood was working with my dad at his popular soda shop in the mid-1950s. It was called Rocci's Pronto Pup Creamery, and it was one of the most popular spots at the time in Willow Glen, California.

I'd just turned 13 when Dad asked me if I'd like to work in the shop and start learning the business. Just knowing Dad considered me responsible enough to work alongside him filled me with pride and a sense of maturity.

Eager to Serve Sodas

Now he'd teach me all the nuances of operating his beloved soda fountain and lunch counter, just as he'd taught my mother and brother!

I began to imagine how great it would be working behind the counter, creating one soda fountain masterpiece after another, looking efficient, grown-up and pretty in my pink pin-striped uniform.

Dad brought me back to reality on my first day of work. He handed me an apron and showed me to a sinkful of dirty dishes and glasses that had to be washed, dried and put back on the shelves before rush hour.

It was obvious I'd have to start at the bottom of the ladder and work my way up!

As the weeks progressed, Dad taught me all there was to know about his business, from kitchen cleanup to hot fudge sundaes. He also taught me that every job, no matter how small, was worth doing well, and he demonstrated that every day.

Whistled While He Worked

Dad worked hard and cheerfully, even when doing tedious tasks like cleaning, polishing and filling the ornate row of stainless-steel cola and syrup dispensers. He did it the same way every night, whistling a happy tune the whole time.

I'm glad I had a chance to share Dad's joy in working hard at a job he loved. Thanks to him, I also learned a trade that provided me with a good living for years to come.

TALLYING THE TILL. Cookie Curci-Wright's dad, Rocci Curci, totals the day's receipts at his soda shop while waitress Juanita Brown stands by (above). "During the 1950s and '60s, Dad had the town's most popular burger shop—long before Big Macs and Whoppers," Cookie recalls.

FEELING HUNGRY? Rocci Curci cooked up everything from ice cream sundaes to three-course T-bone dinners in his soda shop. The shop's loyal customers helped keep the business going for over 30 years.

WE WORKED AS A TEAM   43

Everyone Helped on 'Apple Butter Day'!

By Alice Goodwin, Marysville, Ohio

OUR FAMILY'S yearly apple butter-making ritual would start on a November Friday after school. Mom made an early supper while Dad sharpened the paring knives on the whetstone and the boys cleaned the 20-gallon copper kettle.

Meanwhile, my sister and I washed the apples we'd picked at the orchard the week before. When Dad bolted the hand-crank peeler to the kitchen table, we were ready!

Dad put the first McIntosh in the prongs of the old peeler and cranked. As the sharp blade circled the apple, strands of thin red peel fell to the floor.

The rest of us were seated around the big dining room table, each with a pan and knife. The crisp sounds of cutting began as apples were cored and sliced. The pieces were dumped onto large pans in the center of the table, then stored in the cold basement until morning.

At first, the slices were good to eat and even fun to core, but as the evening wore on, fingers began to hurt, eyelids drooped and our bellies were full to the

BEST APPLE BUTTER. Each year, families prepared bushels of apples for making sweet apple butter. The time-consuming process was well worth it!

brim! At last, when 5 bushels were cored and the peelings gathered and taken to the hogs, everyone headed off to bed.

On Saturday morning, a call from Mom brought us kids scurrying down the stairs. Breakfast was quick—cold cereal, toast and hot chocolate, which hit the spot on a cold morning.

The boys carried pans of apple slices out to the open fireplace for Dad to pour into the kettle...the red-hot embers beneath it were just right.

Around mid-morning, Mom took down a special jar from the china cupboard. Grandma and Grandpa had given each of us kids a shiny silver dollar. Mom washed them, and Dad dropped

> *"Crisp sounds of cutting began as all of us cored and sliced apples..."*

them into the kettle of steaming applesauce to help prevent sticking.

By noon, the sauce turned dark and thick as Dad and the boys slowly raked the kettle with the wooden stirrer, and from the house drifted the aroma of hot buckwheat pancakes that we'd enjoy for lunch.

At mid-afternoon, sugar and cinnamon oil were added. The glass jars were filled with dark red apple butter, sealed tight, then carried to the cellar.

Our shiny coins recovered, we kids took turns swiping a slice of Mom's fresh bread across the bottom of the kettle. Then we washed the kettle and put it back in the basement.

With supper over and the evening chores finished, we took our turns at a bath before collapsing into bed. We were glad the busy day was over—but proud of another winter's supply of apple butter safely stored away.

Work Was Fun with an Appreciative Audience

MY MOM could raise the foam on a milk pail faster than anyone I ever knew, and she taught my sisters and me how to milk our gentle Jerseys before we were 10.

We three girls were fortunate to have a schoolteacher who could play piano. She taught us to sing in harmony, and so, when we did the milking every morning and evening, we'd sing to our cows.

In warm weather, we milked the cows out in the lot and people sometimes stopped and listened to us sing. My father thought we were pretty good, so one summer when a talent show came through Iowa, he entered us in their contest.

Our voices weren't strong, but people seemed to like our childish harmony and we won third place. Personally, I think we did our best singing to our favorite audience...those beautiful Jersey cows.
—*Wilma Davis*
Indianola, Iowa

Family Needed a Miracle to Survive

By Mary Trimble
Berryville, Arkansas

IN THE EARLY 1930s, my family was renting a small farm on the outskirts of Marshfield, Wisconsin. We had little money and few possessions, but my five siblings and I were raised with more valuable assets—faith, hope and love.

In addition to farming, Dad worked as a salesman for the Jewel Tea Company, selling spices, kitchenware and cleaning products to businesses and housewives in the surrounding towns.

One windy, snowy evening, he returned from a long haul over icy roads and wearily eased himself out of his Model T delivery truck. Then he absent-mindedly pulled something from his pocket, not realizing he'd also dropped a small roll of bills—the cash receipts from his sales.

The amount, $64, wasn't large by today's standards, but that was quite a bit during the Depression!

Blizzard Was Raging

I can imagine the shock and panic Dad must have felt when he put his hand in his pocket later and realized it was empty. That money represented nothing less than our family's survival. Without it, Dad would have to forfeit his meager pay for quite some time to reimburse the company. There would be no money for food or rent.

By the time Dad told us about his loss, darkness had fallen and a blizzard was raging. I was 4 years old then, with three older brothers and two older sisters. Each of us immediately bundled up to go outside and search.

Armed only with faith and a few candles stuck in fruit jars, we left the house and started hunting around the yard.

The wind had blown the snow into drifts. Finding $64 in loose bills now would take a miracle.

We searched in ever-widening circles until finally my sister Katy shouted, "I found some money!" We eventually found $62, all of it stuck to bits of hay protruding through the snow.

How did we find all but $2 of that money in the dark, during a blizzard? There was no doubt in our minds. Our family's faith in a higher power had combined with enough hope and love to make a miracle.

DEVOTED DAD George Walter Hoag farmed and worked as a salesman to support his family of eight during the Depression. "He was quiet and shy—a real homebody," recalls his youngest daughter, Mary Trimble. "I'm sure the sales job was hard for him."

Mom Taught Young Worker to Keep Her Promises

ON SATURDAY MORNINGS, it was my job to load the wagon with vegetables and fruit from my family's garden and berry patch to sell in the neighborhood. I'd start off selling two cucumbers for a nickel, but if I still had some left by late afternoon, I'd get rid of them by selling three for a nickel.

One day I heard about a farmer named Mr. Arkell who was looking for people to pick strawberries. I went there the following Monday and was hired on the spot. My pay was 2¢ per basket. I couldn't wait to get home with the good news—I had a summer job!

I worked for almost 10 days, then heard of another farmer farther down the road who was paying 3¢ per basket. When I told my mother I was going to apply there, she said, "Oh no, you won't! You gave your word to Mr. Arkell, and you'll pick for 2¢."

When you gave your word then, it was law!

—*Barb Fairbrother, Stittsville, Ontario*

Building New House Was a Labor of Love

MY GRANDPARENTS' home had been a haven to several generations of family, and by the early 1950s it was badly need of repair. So their sons and son-in-law decided to undertake the enormous chore of building them a new cinder block house.

I was about 3 then, but I remember all the commotion and noise. The family spent each weekend and every minute of spare time trying to complete the two-story house before cold weather set in.

The men did all the construction while the women cooked and tried to keep the children out of the way.

We children had been warned to keep away from the men, but my curiosity got the better of me. While Mom was busy, I sneaked over to watch my father work on the roof. He spotted me on the ground and was afraid I'd be hit by falling debris. So he took me up the ladder and set me down beside him.

THE HOUSE THAT LOVE BUILT. The men in Donna Tanner's family joined forces to build a new home for her grandparents near Ansted, West Virginia. The house is in the background. Donna's father, Basil McGuire, is second from right in the back row.

I felt like I was on top of the world—until Mom came looking for me. She didn't see me 'til I waved and yelled, "Hi, Mommy!" The stern look on her face told me, and Dad, that I'd best come down.

It took many hours of labor and a lot of sweat, but my grandparents finally moved into their new home. A tree swing and seesaw were built in the backyard for the grandchildren, the doors were always unlocked and the whole family gathered every week, making memories in the house that love built.

—Donna Tanner, Ocala, Florida

Young Cotton Chopper Brought Home 65¢ a Day

WHEN I GREW UP in north Alabama, every family member was expected to work at any farm job available to help eke out a living. Even then, we often came up lacking.

I began chopping cotton at age 9. We started at dawn and stayed with it until well past sundown. By the time we got home, I was so tired that I sometimes fell asleep at the supper table!

I was paid 65¢ a day rather than the going rate of $1 because I couldn't keep up with the older folks. I thinned out the cotton stalks and moved along as fast as I could, but my mom would inevitably have to leave her row to help me catch up.

When I turned 12 and "graduated" to adult status—and pay of $1 a day—I felt as though I'd found a gold mine!
—Albert McGraw, Anderson, Alabama

Family Pitched in to Clean Chicken House

ON OUR FARM in north-central Kansas, crowing roosters provided our daily wake-up calls. In those days, many rural families kept small flocks of chickens for eggs and meat, and ours was no different.

In early spring, usually on a Saturday, we'd help our parents with the annual cleaning of the brooder house. After scooping out all the debris, we would thoroughly scrub the chicken coop from top to bottom.

The warm late-March sunshine filtered through the windows and streamed in the open doorways, quickly drying the concrete floor.

One of my brothers would haul a bale of straw from the barn while the other two fetched pitchforks from the hayloft. While they were busy spreading the fresh straw across the floor, my sister and I washed the feeders and waterers.

Grandpa added the finishing touch, mounting large, bright-colored posters of the latest automobiles on the chicken house walls. He'd raised many flocks of his own in this same pen, and every spring, he dutifully decorated their drab brown walls.

—Karen Ann Bland, Gove, Kansas

Toddler Had a Bead on Helping with Piecework

I WAS ABOUT 3 when my parents started earning extra money for us by doing piecework at home. Their job was stringing glass beads onto wires attached to threads. The threads were sold to the garment industry to trim dresses, shoes, buckles, purses, headbands, lamps and drapes.

My job was to pick up beads that rolled off the oilcloth-covered kitchen table into the crevices of the wooden floor. The tiny colorful beads fascinated me, and I felt privileged to handle them and help my parents in the serious work of earning a living.

My parents were happy, too, because this task kept me occupied and out of mischief. That enabled them to work more, which was important because they were paid very little.

We worked by the light of a wire-caged bare bulb that protruded from one wall. The scene was a study in silence, poverty and industry, yet the warmth and love in the room were tangible. I knew it then; I know it now.

My parents' struggle to support us did not diminish their love for each other, even though they were doing a simple, repetitive task for which the only known machine was human hands.

—Helene Kolodny
Cardiff By The Sea, California

Spring Spruce-Up Left House Sparkling

By Angie Monnens
Richmond, Minnesota

AS SOON AS the last remaining snow-banks melted, Mama began planning for spring cleaning. Every family member would have a job to do.

We four girls were assigned to clean the bedrooms, sorting through the closets and storing winter clothing in boxes and trunks. Each item was carefully folded and packed, with exactly six mothballs (no more, no less) in each container.

We enjoyed this task, because it gave us a chance to peek at the handful of dog-eared movie and romance magazines we'd hidden on a closet shelf that winter. Mama disapproved of glamour magazines, so our friends loaned us theirs. Each of us would take turns reading aloud while the others cleaned.

Beat the Rugs

When the bedrooms were finished, we washed windows until they sparkled. Then we carried all the heavy quilts, blankets and rag rugs outdoors and hung them on the clotheslines. The boys took out the mattresses and laid them across planks nailed to sawhorses.

Using an old wire rug beater, we'd beat the rugs and mattresses with all the force we could muster until they were dust-free. This was great fun—and good therapy for whatever ailed us! We especially liked getting outdoors and breathing in the cool, fresh air, too, because at this time of year the whole house smelled of paint, furniture polish, ammonia or Fels-Naptha soap.

The Floors Shined

Most homes didn't have carpeting then, so our oak floors were freshly varnished every spring. Wooden chairs got a thin coat of shellac after Mama made sure all the scratches had been removed.

The next day, the floors were covered with the huge oval rugs Mama crocheted each winter from strips of old clothes that we had torn up and rolled into balls. She crafted rugs of various sizes and shapes, taking great care to make colorful combinations that matched each room's decor.

The last room to clean was the kitchen, where we scrubbed the cupboards, pantries, drawers and shelves with stiff-bristled brushes. Then we'd wash all the "good dishes", even though they were stored in a hutch and didn't get dirty. Heaven forbid anyone should see a speck of dust in Mama's house or on her dishes!

Surprise Awaited

After weeks of cleaning, the entire house sparkled. One year, on the Saturday night before Easter, our parents said they had a surprise for us because we'd done such a good job.

We squealed with joy when Mama handed each of us a store-bought coat with tam to match—the first Easter coats we'd ever had that weren't hand-me-downs.

How proud we felt wearing them to church and hearing our friends' compliments the next morning! Our hard work had all been worthwhile.

MOTHER'S HELPER. The entire family played an important role in annual spring cleaning activities...no matter how small the task (or the person!).

Clan's Still Cooking Together After 50 Years

EVERYBODY had a job to do in our big Italian family, and keeping the family fed was priority number one.

We lived in town but had a garden over an acre in size. We planted and picked strawberries, rhubarb, tomatoes, cucumbers, squash, peppers, watermelon and more produce of all types.

The whole family went on berry-picking expeditions, seeking highbush blueberries at a neighbor's farm and red and black raspberries along the roadside. On those days, I usually picked myself a case of poison ivy!

Mama and her work force of five daughters canned hundreds of jars of tomatoes, pickles, relish, jam and jelly. After-ward, our jar-lined cellar shelves shone like colored gems.

With so much food being put up, all seven of us cooked— even Papa. When it was his turn, the rest of us would just get out of his way, because he would dirty every dish, pan and utensil in the kitchen to make his special tomato sauce!

Mama made her own spaghetti, and we all helped to make a special type of tiny macaroni. Mama's 97 now and still organizing us in these pasta-making gatherings. We make a big batch, eat some right away and freeze the rest. Fifty years later, we're still cooking together!

—Jo Pizzonia, Meriden, Connecticut

Seamstresses Shared the Wealth with Neighbors

CASH WAS SCARCE on our farm during the Depression. Crops brought little in those days, so we had to look for other ways to make money.

We found one at a bedspread factory in Tullahoma, Tennessee, about 20 miles away. The company's muslin spreads were printed with designs, and everywhere a dot appeared, a seamstress took a stitch to make a tuft.

On our first visit, my mother, two sisters and I were allowed to take home only two bedspreads, because the manufacturer wanted to make sure our work passed a rigid inspection. It did.

The next time, we were allowed to take as many bedspreads as we could handle. The four of us could earn about $3 a week if we worked most afternoons.

Soon all of our neighbors and friends were sewing tufted bedspreads, too. My father would bring a truckload out to the country once a week, delivering them to any women who could sew them. A week later, he'd gather them up and take them back to the factory.

We often saw our neighbors walking to each other's houses in the afternoon, a bedspread tucked under one arm. Everyone would sit together on the porch and visit while they sewed.

The bedspreads were sold in department stores, craft shops, roadside stands and specialty shops all over the country. I still see similar ones today, but they're all machine-made. I wonder if anyone makes tufted bedspreads by hand anymore.
—*Annie Lucille Webster*
Adrian, Michigan

Chore Chart, Rewards Taught Responsibility

RIGHT AFTER the Depression, my father was offered a government job that took him away from home except on weekends and holidays.

Mother had arthritis, which limited the household tasks she could do, but Dad made sure she got the help she needed by making up work charts for all four children.

As each of us completed a specific chore, Mother would put a star on the chart. We lost a star for every squabble or argument, but could restore it by voluntarily doing a job not assigned to us.

At the end of the week, if 75% of the chart was filled with stars, we could break a silver seal at the bottom to reveal a special treat. It might be an extra dollar, or permission for a friend to spend the night. Dad always knew what our desires were, and rewarded us accordingly.

If only one of us had a perfect chart for the week, we got to break a gold seal, which concealed an even bigger surprise—a weekend trip, or a day at the fair with extra money to spend.

This arrangement was a big help to our mother, and saved her many arguments while Dad was away. It also taught us to take responsibility for working for what we wanted.
—*Patricia Collins, Bend, Oregon*

Berry-Picking Trips Were All-Day Outings

ONE OF MY fondest childhood memories is of going to the mountains to pick huckleberries with my aunt and uncles. We always took a picnic lunch and spent the whole day there.

When we'd filled three washtubs with berries, we'd bring them down the mountain, put them in a wagon and take them to the train station 3 miles away. They were shipped to a manufacturer who used them to make medicine. We worked together picking berries every summer.
—*Edith Henegar*
Wellington, Alabama

Daughters Revived Rug-Making Tradition in Tribute to Moms

BACK IN THE 1920s and '30s, my Ukrainian mother and her friends made rugs outdoors every summer. All the daughters would get up at 5:30 a.m. to help with this project, and each of us continued until we were old enough to work at our own jobs.

We prepared material for the rugs all winter long. Cloth that could no longer be worn or used was cut into 1-inch strips, then rolled into a ball. By summer, each household had several bushels of balls ready to recycle into those beautiful carpets that never seemed to wear out.

In 1974, six of us got together to make rugs again, just as our mothers had done. My husband set up in our yard the long "beater" on which the strips are woven, and we got to work.

It took us 6 hours to make 60 feet of carpet, but they were fun hours—and a tribute to our mothers. We spoke of them the whole time we worked.
—*Helen Timo*
Bentleyville, Pennsylvania

CUTTING A RUG. As children, these women helped their mothers weave rugs from cloth scraps every summer. In 1974, they gathered at the home of Helen Timo (far left) to make their own carpets one more time.

Son's Business Lessons Were Tailor-Made

By Irwin Valenta
Greensboro, North Carolina

DAD'S TAILOR SHOP in Berwyn, Illinois specialized in custom-made men's suits, topcoats and overcoats.

The business flourished because Dad was an expert at cutting the cloth and because of his charm in dealing with his customers' wives. They invariably accompanied their husbands, and I often heard them remark, "Get a suit like Mr. Valenta's—it's so handsome."

Dad was a real pro at making clothes for a body that needed a little help. If a customer's legs were bowed, he'd cut the pant legs so they hung straighter. Low shoulder? Prominent shoulder blades? Big tummy? Dad could handle it.

My parents rarely took a vacation because Dad felt he needed to be on hand for his customers at all times. But August was always slow, so one summer when I was home from college, I suggested they take some time off.

I knew how to measure for a suit and was sure I could handle the small amount of business we'd have. With some reluctance, my parents finally left for a 4-day trip to Michigan.

Under New Management

My first day in the shop was uneventful. One longtime customer came in looking for a pair of pants, but when he

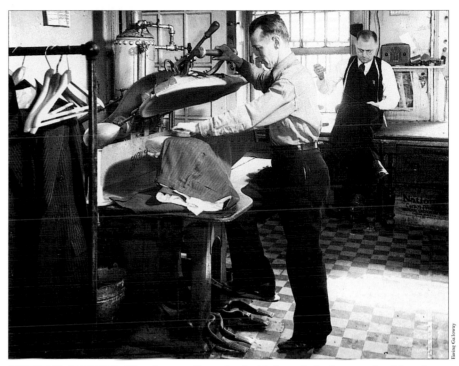

PRESSING MATTERS. Like these tailors, Irwin Valenta's father worked hard to satisfy his customers. He also taught his son the business.

heard Dad wasn't around, he promptly left. The next day, another pants customer came in. He liked the cloth and pattern I suggested, but thought our $8 price was too high.

On my third day, I had yet to make a sale. Shortly after lunch, a customer walked in, browsed among the bolts of fabric and finally said, "I'd like a pair of pants from this one. How much will they be?"

I wasn't about to bat zero my first time in charge—I wanted a sale! "Seven dollars," I said with authority. The man nodded. I took his measurements twice and reviewed the order several times, convinced I'd done a good job.

A couple of weeks after Dad returned, he asked if I remembered that sale. Of course I did.

"I had a little trouble with it," he said. "And I thought that you should know about it." My spirits sank immediately. I

had so wanted that order to go smoothly!

"I had to make the customer another pair of pants," Dad said. "He asked for a false waistband, which wasn't written on the order. In addition, Irv, the material he selected was from a bolt that had just enough yardage left to make a full suit. Taking a pair of pants out of that length limits the remaining cloth to only a pair of pants with the remainder going to waste.

"And one other small thing. The cloth was expensive, too—you should've charged him $8.50 for pants made from that material.

"But don't feel bad for a minute," Dad went on. "I'm telling you this to add to your feel for the business. I know there is a lot I haven't taught you.

"As for the pants with the regular waistband, here they are. They've been altered to fit you. It's nice material... shouldn't go to waste."

You can believe that *every time* I put on those pants, I remembered the many lessons that one sale taught me, and the father who helped me learn. It also made me, the college man, painfully aware one does not learn everything in books.

Perhaps Dad viewed it as a learning experience, too, because I can't recall my parents ever taking another vacation!

Family's Love of Outdoors Kept Food on the Table

I GREW UP in western Kentucky during the Great Depression, the youngest child of a sharecropper. We didn't have any luxuries, but we always had plenty to eat—in part because of our shared love for the outdoors.

We often took long walks in the woods near our home. In fall, we hunted hickory nuts while we learned the names of the trees. In spring, Mom picked wild greens—a welcome change from the dried beans, potatoes and canned foods that made up our winter diet.

Later in spring, we'd take our dinner and spend the day hunting ginseng. We didn't find a lot, but Papa dried the roots we did find and sold them.

We enjoyed looking at the trees, flowers and wildlife as a family—and those walks helped us keep food on the table, too.

—*Faye Edmunds, Hopkinsville, Kentucky*

This Family Got By on Ferns And a Prayer

By B.D. Kyle
Grand Junction, Colorado

IN THE SUMMER of 1938, my dad, mom, brother and I left Los Angeles to look for work in Oregon. We loaded our '29 Buick and headed north in hopes of harvesting hops.

On the way, we camped out each night, Mom cooking over an open fire and all of us sleeping under the stars. I was 7 years old, and this was some kind of adventure.

Eventually, we reached Salem and found work picking hops. After the harvest, Dad was still short of money, so he pointed the Buick toward the strawberry and bean fields farther north. That's when one of the car's ancient tires blew.

We had no spare and there was nowhere to buy another inner tube even if we'd had enough cash. So Dad got out his tools, removed the old tire and stuffed it tight with some big leafy ferns growing alongside the road!

Needed Some Help

We got to our next stop, a strawberry farm, without incident—but how much longer could we drive on a tire crammed with ferns?

After the strawberry harvest, we still needed money, so Dad persuaded a rancher to let us hoe around his fruit trees.

HEAVEN'S HARVEST. Strawberry picking reminds B.D. Kyle of a time the family's prayers were answered while helping a rancher at harvesttime.

We stayed in one of the labor camp shacks while Mother prayed fervently for help from above.

Several days later, my brother raced in from the grove, waving a wallet he'd found while hoeing. Buried a good half foot under the surface, it was wet and dirty, but perfectly folded.

We all gathered 'round as Dad slowly opened it—and found 12 soggy dollar bills! There was nothing else inside; the rancher said it wasn't his and told us to keep the cash. Mom, her prayers answered, laid the money out to dry on her Bible.

When our work was done, we happily piled into the car with the fern-packed tire and drove to town to buy a new tube. Hard work, and Mom's prayers, could solve most any problem.

Autumn Stirs Golden Memories of Togetherness

By M.G. Langoni
Williamston, Michigan

CRISP FALL DAYS bring back golden memories of my six brothers and sisters, Indian summers in northern Michigan and canning in my mother's kitchen. She usually had at least three pairs of hands assisting in her assembly line.

The smell of peaches will always remind me of Mother, in her juice-stained apron, lifting the lid from the steaming kettle and spooning the scalded peaches onto the drain board.

It was my job to take off the hot skin, so there was lots of bouncing from one foot to the other as I peeled! We were so proud as we placed the peaches in the big mason jars and watched Mother set them into boiling water to seal them.

When we reached the point where we could all take a break, we'd head for the garden to gather a colander of peas for supper. We shelled them as we sat in the shade of the large maple tree, talking about all the things so important to young girls.

Hats Off to Dad

Saturday brought special chores not normally tended to during the week. When I wanted a cowgirl hat in the worst way, Dad put us to work pulling mustard weeds out of the hay field so we could all earn hats.

My fingernails smelled like mustard for days, but it didn't matter. I now had the best cowgirl hat in the neighborhood, and it gave me and my baled-straw "horse" many hours of adventure.

At the end of the day, we'd lie in the cool dusk as the stars began to send their light our way. We'd inevitably grow restless, but Dad came up with clever ways to keep us quiet—like telling us that if we were very still, we could hear the corn grow.

Today, when our grandson comes to visit, we still enjoy the sounds of the evening. And through the ears of a precious 4-year-old, I can still hear the corn grow.

Love, Laughter Sweetened Apple-Drying Time

By Rosa Lee Self
Kannapolis, North Carolina

OUR PARENTS were strong-limbed and strong-willed—traits they needed to raise 13 children. They surrounded us with trust and faith, and our lives seemed as endless as the summer days.

I was born in 1904, and as the years passed, I was given my share of chores and responsibilities on our farm. At age 4, I had to mind my infant brother when Mom was gathering straw to make brooms.

Later, I helped with another autumn project—drying apples. Much of the laughter and love of my childhood is wrapped in my memories of those days. How well I remember the thick, sweet aroma of fruit baking in the sun, and the

---

"The best part was that we dried the apples on the barn's tin roof!"

---

rich taste of cooked apples in the half-moon pies Mommy fried in her heavy iron skillet.

Friends and strangers alike came from miles around at harvesttime, for our orchard provided more fruit than we could possibly use. It was a neighborly time, with everyone working together to pick, peel and core the apples while enjoying a long visit.

At the end of the day, everyone would carry their apples home in a clean sheet or flour sack. Then we'd spread the fruit in the sun to dry until it could be stored without spoiling.

The best part was that we dried our apples on the tin roof of the barn! We children were assigned the chore of carefully spreading the apples there on a clean old sheet.

We took a new batch of apples up each morning, turned them several times during the day, then brought them down at night. This kept us busy climbing up and down from the roof, and we loved it!

The roof slanted just enough to add an element of danger. What adventures we imagined as we climbed the ladder, crawled over the eaves and clambered onto the warming tin.

We laughed as we stirred and turned

the crescents of fruit, moving carefully so we didn't lose our balance and tumble into the cow lot below. Sometimes we tasted a small slice, smelling the rich aroma as the sun's heat turned the juices to sugar.

And we smiled, our eyes sparkling with anticipation of the hot fried pies we'd have on cold winter evenings, prepared with a mother's love. It was a treat that warmed our hearts as well as our stomachs.

Today, I have a shelf lined with photographs of those I love. Each smile, each laugh, each dear memory forms an endless succession of heartbeats, a strength that stretches across the years. Just as they are in my heart, I know I am in theirs. This cannot die. Like love, it continues endlessly—a family then, a family now, a family always.

Day of Work Came Before Day of Rest

IT TOOK a lot of work to get ready for the day of rest when we were kids!

All 10 of us had our Saturday chores, such as scrubbing the wood floors (no linoleum in those days), blackening the range and polishing 10 pairs of shoes. The washtub was brought in so everyone could bathe, and Mama put up the girls' long hair in rags for curls.

Come Sunday, we all watched Papa shave with his straight razor, waiting eagerly for the funny face he made so he could shave around his mouth. Then Mama squeezed into her corset, the girls donned their white dresses and we proceeded to church in our Sunday best.

After church, we changed into what Mama called our "second best" and sat down at the kitchen table for a delicious meal and whatever surprise Mama had made for dessert. When mealtime was over, Papa would tell us a story (he always made them up as he went along), puffing on one of the fat cigars he smoked only on Sundays.

The afternoons were spent playing croquet and making molasses candy and popcorn balls. In the evening, we played card games like "old maid" or checkers and dominoes. I always felt sad when Sunday was over.

—Alma Hofmann, Indianapolis, Indiana

I Went Swimmin' in the Old Skimmin' Hole

By Ethel Coyle, Richmond, Indiana

EACH AUTUMN when the nights get cool and the leaves begin to turn, I think back to an incident that took place in 1919. I was 5 years old then, growing up on a farm in central Kentucky.

Dad made sorghum molasses every year, and as the pale green juice from the sugarcane boiled down into syrup, it would begin to foam. Dad always skimmed this off into buckets, then emptied the buckets into a deep hole he'd dug nearby.

One year, Dad, Mom and our relatives were cooking the last batch of the day and it was getting dark. Lanterns had been hung to light the area, and my cousins and I were laughing and chasing each other around the pasture.

I was running through the dark when suddenly I found myself waist-deep in that "skimmin' hole" of warm, foamy molasses!

MAKING MOLASSES. The picture of this man making sorghum molasses in 1936 brings back sweet (and sticky!) memories for Ethel Coyle, whose father made the delicious syrup each fall.

After all these years, I *still* haven't found a way to describe the feeling of standing in that sticky syrup!

Tired as Mom was, and with plenty of work still to be done, she didn't need this aggravation. She sent me to the house with my 10-year-old sister who was to soak my clothes, bathe me and put me to bed.

If you think plunging into warm molasses felt awful, imagine my long walk back to the house as that sticky liquid began to cool! I'll never forget how strange it felt as my sister pulled off my long, gooey cotton stockings.

Of course, the family forever enjoyed telling of this episode, even long after Dad quit his annual ritual of making sorghum syrup.

Years later when we were visiting my mother-in-law, she fixed batter cakes with sorghum for my 5-year-old daughter, who looked up with a grin and said, "Gramma, I think this is the *goodest* thing!" I'm sorry to say I still have a little trouble enjoying sorghum syrup. ✦

Emergency Taught This Teen to Grow Up Fast

By William Wislen
Snohomish, Washington

THE SUMMER of 1925 was a good season for blueberries, so we leaped at the chance when one of our neighbors, Jim, offered to take several of us picking in his truck. Mom rounded up our buckets and promised Jim a blueberry pie for his trouble.

About a dozen of us went along, including a pretty girl who lived in the other half of the duplex we rented. She was about my age, but I hadn't gotten up the nerve to talk to her yet. If I picked fast and filled my buckets by lunchtime, maybe I could help her in the afternoon!

When we broke at noon, my parents and I were the only ones whose buckets were full. It looked like I would get my chance!

But while I was thinking "girl", Dad was thinking "berries". He found a clean, empty cardboard box and poured all our berries into it. Now our buckets were empty again! I'd do no picking for anyone else, no matter how pretty she was.

On the ride home, Mom seemed to be in pain. Dad had to help her out of the truck when we reached our house, and soon left to call the doctor. When the doctor came, he announced he was taking Mom to the hospital. Her appendix was ready to burst.

A Big Job

As Mom quickly packed a small suitcase, she said to me, "Looks like you'll have to take care of the berries. I know you can do it." I'd watched Mom can since I was big enough to climb on a chair, but this was a big job!

The next morning, after Dad left for work, I cleared off the table, took out the big canning kettle and got busy. I washed the berries and put them in the big kettle with some water. Then I added about as much sugar as I thought Mom would have done.

As I cooked the berries, I scalded the mason jars, then began dipping the berries into the jars and sealing them. It was a long, hot, sticky job, but by the time Dad came home, there were 40 jars on the table. I was exhausted.

Dad never said a word, but after supper we walked the 2 miles to the hospital and he told Mom all about it. She looked tired, but perked right up when she heard about the 40 jars.

When I apologized for not making Jim a pie, she said soothingly, "That's fine, William. I'm proud of you. Next winter we'll give him a couple jars of berries—he'll like that just as well."

I was 14 then; Dad had told me I was "almost a man" years before. Those were the days when kids were expected to grow up fast and do whatever their families needed. ✦

Chapter Three

Our Grandparents Were Wise and Wonderful

THE WISDOM of our grandparents came from years of experience, and they shared this hard-earned gift with us unselfishly. The lessons they taught carried us through the years, until we, too, became parents or grandparents.

Many of my very best memories involve my grandparents. Like most grandparents, they had been mellowed by the years. They'd survived being parents, which is no easy trick. They'd learned that kids generally turn out pretty well, despite being raised by inept amateurs. So they had a little calmer perspective on things.

During one visit I discovered a wooden box containing Grampa Stevens' treasured chessmen. He was not pleased to find me using them as toy soldiers. But instead of scolding me, he got out the chessboard and began teaching me to play the game. I was 8 at the time.

From then on, every time I visited he insisted we play a game or two. Near as I can recall, I was 14 before I won my first game. No, he wouldn't throw a game, even to a little kid. But he taught me a valuable lesson: You don't win unless you deserve to win.

Grampa often played pinochle at the Dixon, Illinois Odd Fellows Hall. If I was around he'd take me with him. On the way home we'd walk across the bridge over the Rock River and stop at Fulf's Drugstore.

Tough Choice Awaited

Inside, I'd agonize in front of the candy case before making a decision (almost inevitably I'd choose those hard, sugarcoated lemon drops), and Grampa would pull a nickel out of his little leather snap-top coin purse.

Then we'd walk back to the river, find a bench and he'd talk about his life. He'd tell me how he had played chess—sometimes five games at a time—via the telegraph when he worked for the railroad. Or how his father had known Blackhawk, the famous Indian chief. He'd talk about scoundrels and heroes, and quote long memorized passages from Dickens and Thackeray, his two favorite authors.

He recalled the day he was idly swinging on the front yard gate when a horseman thundered by, headed up the country road and yelled out the news that the Civil War was over. Grampa was 6 at the time.

He patiently listened to my childish problems. He took them seriously, and then offered his advice. Best of all, I knew what I told him would never get back to my parents. How many people get to have all their problems solved for them on the sunny banks of the Rock River?

"Three" Was a Crowd

When the Great Depression came, several of Gramma and Grampa Stevens' married children were forced to move back home as jobs and money petered out. There were times when three families plus an unmarried daughter all shared that modest little house.

Years later, when Gramma was 90 or thereabouts, I asked how she'd endured the strife and turmoil. "Oh," she smiled, "it taught me patience."

That was Gramma Stevens—this tiny woman was always an island of calm, the quiet eye of any hurricane that raged around her. Nothing escaped her, but she held her council and rarely indulged in being judgmental. She steadfastly loved her children and grandchildren, no matter what. They were hers, and that was enough.

I treasure every moment I had with my grandparents. As the stories on the following pages attest, many of us who were privileged to live near our grandparents grew up a lot better than we might have, thanks to them.

—*Clancy Strock*

A GOLDEN MOMENT. On their 50th wedding anniversary in 1911, Franklin and Mary Elizabeth Fitz Randolph of Salem, West Virginia relaxed and enjoyed the day. This touching photo was shared by their great-granddaughter, Patricia Smith, of New Smyrna Beach, Florida.

Grandpa Taught Boy the Value of Work

By Charles Pastana
Penryn, California

I'M NEARING retirement age, but I have no intention of retiring. I have my grandpa to thank for that.

It was June 9, 1955, the first day of summer vacation, and I was staying at Grandpa and Grandma's house for the week. I was 8 years old. I remember that morning as if it were yesterday.

Grandpa was up and ready, as usual, long before the old wind-up clock woke me with its clanging bell. He was sitting in the kitchen, a newspaper in one hand and a cup of hot coffee in the other.

I peered around the corner, wearing my best work clothes that Grandma had laid out for me. "Mornin', Grandpa," I said.

"Mornin', boy," Grandpa replied. "Come on in here and have some toast with me. (He called me boy as if it

> *"It was the hardest
> I'd ever worked..."*

were an honored title.) Today you're going to work with me. I'm going to teach you how to work."

Grandpa took me to the construction site where he was working and showed me how to pick up nails the workers had dropped. At the end of the day, the boss gave me a dollar for the boxful I'd collected. In 1955, that was a lot of money for an 8-year-old.

Over the next few years, I worked with Grandpa every summer. At first it was just for a week, but by the time I was 12, I was working the whole summer and doing more than just picking up nails. We worked on a lot of houses that year.

I rolled out black paper and nailed it onto the walls. I learned to put up line wire, then chicken wire for lath walls. It was the hardest I'd ever worked, and I loved every minute of it.

Grandpa taught me the value of hard work, the value of money and my own value. He taught me self-respect and a sense of pride. I'd learned how to get dirty and come up smiling.

Near the end of the summer, Grandpa bought himself a new lath ax. Then he called me into the garage, where we had all our important talks.

"Boy, this is for you," he said, handing me his old ax…the one he'd used for years to put food on the table…the one he'd used to earn the money for our fishing equipment and my first BB gun… the one he sharpened every night before carefully putting it back in his tool belt. That ax was his pride and joy. Now he was handing it to me.

"This is yours now, boy," Grandpa said. "You've earned it. Now that you know how to use it, you'll never have to worry about finding work or feeding your family when you grow up.

"Now," he continued, "I want you to put it away and learn some other way to make a living. If all else fails, remember that you know how to use this ax, and you know how to work."

I didn't know at the time how much Grandpa gave me when he handed me that ax. I know now.

HONED TO PERFECTION. Like the man pictured here, reader Charles Pastana's grandfather ended every day by sharpening his tools before putting them away. When Grandpa got a new lath ax, he gave his old one to Charles, along with the knowledge of how to use it.

Grandpa's Gift Changed 6-Year-Old's Life

By DeLila Chrisp, Worland, Wyoming

I WAS 6 years old when Grandpa Harley changed my life. But I didn't realize it until decades later.

For a lot of children, the first day of school is exciting. But it wasn't for me. I was very shy, and had dreaded this moment since I first heard about it. I *knew* I could be a great help on our Nebraska farm if only my parents would let me stay home. But that was out of the question.

During class, I spoke only when the teacher asked me a direct question. My size made me feel insecure, and my desk seemed to swallow me up. I was the only child whose feet didn't touch the floor.

Recess was even more traumatic—I especially hated it when we picked teams to play ball. Someone as small as me could neither run fast nor hit hard, and I always knew I'd be picked last. I soon began to feel very unimportant around my classmates.

My only friend in the whole world seemed to be "Old Barney", Dad's plow horse. He waited for me every afternoon when I walked down the lane from school.

There he'd be, leaning over the old board fence, and I'd feed him ears of corn and tell him all my secrets. Somehow Barney always seemed to understand as he rested his big warm nose on my shoulder and waited patiently for another ear of corn. Grandpa Harley would give me corn to feed Barney.

Reporter Visits

One day after school, I came into the kitchen and saw a stranger visiting with Dad and Mom. Beside him on the table was a huge black camera and a shiny silver flash. I'd never seen such a fancy camera before. What could this man want with us?

"DeLila, this is Mr. Tom Allen," my father said, "he writes human interest stories for the *Omaha World Herald*."

We got that paper every day! I often looked at the pictures of important people on the front page as I carried it in from the mailbox.

Mr. Allen turned to me and said, "Your Grandpa Harley has written to me, telling me about you and a horse named Barney." He'd driven all the way from Omaha, a big city I'd never even seen, to take my picture with Barney and write a story about us!

The story and picture ran a few weeks later, right on the front page! After that, my school days changed dramatically. You don't get your picture on the front page of a major newspaper without becoming a celebrity in the eyes of your 6-year-old classmates!

Decades later, when I reflected back on that year, I realized that Barney wasn't the only one who understood my problems. So did Grandpa Harley—a special grandfather with a gift to see inside his granddaughter's heart.

Grandma Made Everyone Feel Like Her Favorite

By Mary Toland
Citrus Heights, California

MY GRANDMOTHER lived across the street from us in our southern-Indiana town, and my three cousins lived two doors down. The whole family seemed to be together all the time—with a couple of exceptions.

In the summer of 1929, Grandma asked me to come over every morning and thread two or three dozen needles onto her spool. She supported herself by making beautiful quilts, and this saved her time when she was trying to meet a deadline.

I was just 7, and her request made me feel so important. I'd run over every day after breakfast, thread the needles and then go out and play.

But Fridays were another matter. On those days, Grandma and I had secret picnics on her back porch!

I'd creep to her backyard around noon. Grandma would lift me over the fence and send me to Mrs. Glavin's grocery store at the end of the alley to get two slices of

OUR LITTLE SECRET. Grandmothers were good at keeping secrets and always had time for grandchildren, making each feel special.

bologna and a small bottle of ginger ale.

I'd run back with the goodies and hand them over the back fence, then we'd sneak to the back porch together. Grandma always cautioned me to keep our little secret from my cousins and brother. This went on every Friday, until we moved to Ohio at the end of the summer.

I missed my grandmother, and although we exchanged letters weekly, I never got to see her again. During the Depression there just never was enough money for our family to travel.

Some years after we moved, we got word that Grandma had died. After her funeral, we all reminisced about our good times with her—and I finally told everyone about our secret Friday picnics.

That's when I found out my brother had secret picnics with Grandma every Monday, and our cousins Robert, Jimmy and Marvin had them Tuesday, Wednesday and Thursday. None of us had known about the others, and each of us had had the joy of being "Grandma's favorite".

Extended Families Were Common in Earlier Times

IN THE 1920s, there were no retirement or rest homes as we know them today. Most families, like mine, simply made room for older relatives to live in their home along with the rest of the clan.

My grandmother stayed with us until I was 9 years old. Some of my happiest memories are of the times I spent with her.

Grandma and I both slept later than the rest of the family, so we usually ate breakfast together.

Grandma Was Her Buddy

I ate everything she did—bread or crackers crumbled in milk, and Grape-Nuts softened with hot water

and covered with sugar and thick cream. I even drank the SSS tonic she drank to start her day.

My brother and sister were much older than me, so Grandma and I spent a lot of time together while they were attending school during the day.

Taught Her to Read

She was the one who had the time to play rook or dominoes and read to me.

When I started attending our one-room school, I was already able to read—thanks to Grandma—and the teacher placed me in the second grade!
— *Ruth Davis*
Higginsville, Mississippi

FARM FRIENDS. Ruth Davis raised pet hen "Snowball" on the family farm, where Grandma also lived.

We Cooked Up Memories in Grandma's Kitchen

By Katherine Shea, Gilbert, Arizona

IS THERE ANYTHING in the world more wonderful than Grandma's kitchen? No matter where I've gone, I've never found anything to top it! My Grandma Mac's kitchen was the hub of her house; everything special happened there.

When I was very young we lived far enough away from Grandma and Grandpa McConley's that my visits with them often lasted a few days. I loved those visits because Grandpa and Grandma Mac always let me do special things I couldn't do at home.

First thing in the morning I'd pad out to the kitchen in my jammies and Grandpa would "order me up a cup of coffee". Grandma served it in a special cup and saucer, with more sugar and milk than coffee. As Grandpa and I enjoyed our java, she'd make us old-fashioned oatmeal with a bit of cream and brown sugar, and a pat of butter on top. It was heavenly!

"Helped" Bake Bread

After breakfast, Grandpa would head to work and Grandma started baking. I loved to pitch in, so she saved me a bit of bread dough to work with. By the time I was done kneading, the dough was a sickly gray, but my little loaf went right into the oven alongside the rest—in a special pan, of course.

Grandma kept me occupied during baking time by letting me "shop" in her huge walk-in pantry. I'd browse through the shelves with a shopping basket, making purchases with pennies from a special purse, while Grandma bagged my "groceries". She must have spent an awful lot of time restocking her shelves after I emptied them!

If there was still time to kill before the bread was done, I'd drag Grandma's button box into the kitchen doorway and "sew" her beautiful buttons, stringing them together.

Grandpa Always Ate It

When the bread was finally done, Grandma removed my loaf from the oven with a flourish. It was hard, gray, wrinkled and dry, but she'd marvel that it was the most *beautiful* bread she had ever seen.

But the best time of all was at dinner. After Grandma loaded the table with mouth-watering pot roast, potatoes, green beans and applesauce, there'd be so much oohing and aahing as I presented Grandpa with my little loaf of bread.

He'd savor the aroma, carefully cut off a slice, slather it with butter and slowly bring it to his mouth. He'd roll his eyes, sigh with pleasure and announce that Grandma had just been surpassed as the world's greatest baker. Oh, how I'd puff with pride! I felt like the queen bee!

I'll never know how Grandpa made it through all those grimy gray loaves I made...and he'll never know what a special memory he gave me. I wish I could wrap my arms around him now and thank him.

Fortunately I still can, and do, thank my Grandma Mac for the wonderful memories she's made for me. And she continues making them today for my own children.

She Got Her Money's Worth—Even If It Caused a Scene!

SHORTLY AFTER my husband and I were married in 1931, my granny said she wanted to take us furniture shopping. That was music to our young ears, because we were making do with packing crates for end tables.

Granny took us to Joseph Horne's—*the* big department store in Pittsburgh at the time. First she bought us a lovely maple bedroom suite. But when we got to the mattress department, my husband and I wanted to run and hide!

Granny climbed onto a mattress and began bouncing on it determinedly, as if it were a trampoline. Next, she lay prone on it and began to prod and pummel it. We stood there utterly mortified, while other shoppers stopped to stare at this energetic little lady. She gave that mattress a real workover!

Finally Granny jumped up, brushed herself off, readjusted her perky straw hat and told the salesman, "This will do very well!"

Today, the maple bedroom suite is up in my guest room, but the mattress has long since been replaced. Whenever I see that furniture, I think of my funny, dear granny, so determined to help give me a good start in life...and to get her money's worth!

—*Mary Ellen Stelling*
Atlanta, Georgia

Spirited Grandma Had a Zest for Life

By Darnell White, Branson, Missouri

MY FUN-LOVING Irish grandmother had such a love for life—none of its gifts were wasted on her!

She always had cakes in the oven or in the works for drop-in visitors, neighbors…and the firemen. No matter what time of day or night she heard the sirens, she'd make a pot of coffee, pack some cake and fried pies and race off to serve the firemen as they fought the blaze.

Dallas, Texas wasn't a big city then, and all its fire fighters knew and loved "Miz Hays". So did the many downtown shopkeepers, who would call out and greet her by name as she passed.

Hoboes often came begging during the Depression. Word must have gotten around that Grandma would give them something to eat, and even clothes if they needed them.

Grandma cared little about what she wore or whether the various pieces matched. If she stayed tidy and clean, that was enough for her. Her daughters gave her money to buy new shoes, a new handbag or a dress, but Grandma just gave it to someone she felt needed it more, or used it to buy presents for others.

She loved holidays, and always made sure we had costumes for school plays

---

"All the fire fighters knew and loved 'Miz Hays'…"

---

and Halloween. In fact, Grandma never let a holiday go by without wearing a costume herself. She couldn't resist playing Santa at Christmas; her "ho-ho-ho's" were livelier than the department store St. Nick's!

Grandma adored the vaudeville shows that played at the three theaters in downtown Dallas, and often took my brother and me to the Majestic. We'd sit through the Paramount News and movies, then marvel as the organist and organ rose from the orchestra pit. The organist would play wonderful music on that marvelous instrument.

Then the curtain would rise and the vaudeville show would begin! Sometimes we'd watch the same movies again just to see the vaudeville performances

HOME COOKIN' was every Grandma's specialty, but Darnell White recalls a grandmother who shut down the stove to have fun with her little ones.

twice—and sometimes even a third time. It wasn't unusual for us to go to two or even all three theaters in the same day!

Grandma never turned down a chance to go somewhere, and she had plenty of invitations. If she had a cake or bread baking, she just turned off the oven. "To heck with that," she'd say. "I'll bake another when I get back."

Grandma loved to go fishing, and one time a nephew and his wife invited her along to White Rock Lake. Grandma took her favorite spot, and the couple went on down the bank. After a while, she saw the game warden approaching. He walked up to her and asked if she had a fishing license. Grandma just kept fishing and paid no attention.

"Ma'am," the warden repeated, raising his voice, "do you have your fishing license?" Still no response. The warden yelled the question a third time, but Grandma stared straight ahead.

Finally the frustrated warden walked down the bank toward Grandma's nephew and his wife. "That old woman up there sure must be hard of hearing," he muttered.

After he left, Grandma pulled out three wet but nice-sized fish from inside

her coat. There was no way she was going to give them up just because she didn't have a license!

Southern Lady Had Etiquette Rules For Radio and TV!

GRANDMA LOVED to listen to preaching on the radio and thought it was a sin to change the station if a preacher was on. One of my cousins had to be careful when he was trying to find a ball game on the radio if Grandma was listening nearby!

When we got our first television set, Grandma was visiting us. She was a very proper Southern lady, always making sure her skirt covered her knees—but she was especially careful about that when she watched TV.

She was convinced that if she could see the people on television, they could see her, too!

—*Joyce Clarida*
Ormond Beach, Florida

Ritual of Sharing Filled Boy's Saturday Afternoons

GRANDPA'S MUSTACHE was full, his voice rich and powerful. He'd emigrated from Italy a few years before, and to me, as a 6-year-old boy, Luigi Filandino seemed both strong and gentle.

I spent Saturday afternoons at his kitchen table, sharing a piece of fruit and a glass of watered-down wine with him. Grandpa worked hard on the railroad all summer long. In winter, he'd teach English to his fellow emigrants. Saturday afternoons he'd give to me.

He'd sit in his favorite chair, with me opposite him, waiting for the ritual to begin. He'd reach into his pocket for his special paring knife and ask me to pick out a piece of fruit from the bowl on the table. I'd hand him a pear or an apple, sometimes an orange. He'd hold it up, inspect it and ask me where he should start peeling.

I'd point, he'd make the incision and the magic would begin. I'd watch in fascination as the fruit turned round and round, and the peel, never breaking, curled about his wrist. When the peel finally fell to the white enameled tabletop, Grandpa would cut a slice of fruit for me to soak in my glass of "wine".

No food could be as delicious as what we shared during those moments. Those afternoons filled a 6-year-old boy with love that still generates a warm glow after all these years. It shaped that boy into the man he would become.

—*John Burns, Manassas, Virginia*

Fiddler's Tales Enhanced Grandson's Love of Music

*By Albert Bazzel
Turnersville, New Jersey*

AS A YOUTH, I spent many happy hours playing fiddle duets with my grandfather and hearing yarns about his days as a fiddler at square dances and husking bees in northern Ohio in the 1880s.

Grandpa traveled to and from fiddling engagements in a horse-drawn sleigh that sometimes carried as many as 20 people. That could be a rough way to travel in winter, with subzero temperatures and 4-foot snowdrifts, but most travelers were good-natured about it.

Grandpa often arrived at parties with his fiddle full of snow, and had to dry it out on the kitchen stove before he could tune it!

Grandpa would play and call out the square dance figures at parties that lasted until dawn. Sometimes, while everyone waited for the snow to let up, they told ghost stories to pass the time.

I had formal music training later, and through the years was blessed with talented instruction from many gifted musicians and academic professors. But it was Grandpa who put the fun in my music.

FIDDLIN' GRANDPA. William Pope played at square dances and husking bees in Ohio during the 1880s. His grandson Albert Bazzel played duets with him and still remembers the fun.

Granny's Daily Greeting Had Her Hurrying Home

AS A TEENAGER, I lived with my parents and grandmother on a farm in Tennessee. Every afternoon, Granny would sit in the porch swing and wait for the school bus to drop me off.

I would hurry up the path, singing and feeling the breeze blow through my hair, eager to see Granny's smile and hear her say, "I'm so glad you're home. I've missed you all day!"
—Elizabeth Parnell, Deltona, Florida

She Showered Loved Ones With Kindness and Wisdom

I LOVED MY GRANDMA, but not because she showered me with gifts—she had too many grandchildren and too little money for that. But she had a soft voice filled with kindness and wisdom, and a bear hug and kiss waiting for me each time I saw her.

During the Depression, when I was 11, my dad fell ill and was unable to work for weeks. Grandma kept our household in food until he got back on his feet. Every few days she'd appear unannounced at our door, laden with jars of home-canned fruits and vegetables.

When she left she'd always say, "When you need some more food, come to my house! Stop being so modest or you'll find yourself starving!"

Without her help, I don't know how we would have made it.

Many times since then, I've met people who were not only hungry, but ill-clothed. How good I felt after offering some assistance, just the way my grandma taught us.
—Albert McGraw Anderson, Alabama

Glimpsed a Tender Moment

ONE special afternoon, I walked into

BEAUTIFUL MUSIC from the old-fashioned phonograph put a little romance in Grandma and Grandpa's day— even if they did waltz in their everyday work clothes.

Grandma and Grandpa's house for a cookie and a glass of milk. I heard the Victrola playing softly in the dining room and rushed in to investigate.

Grandma and Grandpa were waltzing tenderly to a scratchy old recording of her favorite song, After the Ball.

She was dressed in a worn-out house dress and he in a pair of dusty old overalls, but they made an exquisite couple as they danced to the melody they'd courted to so many years before.
—Cookie Curci-Wright San Jose, California

High Heels Were Low In Grandpa's Opinion

WHEN MAMA was a young girl starting to date, Grandpa was very strict. He didn't approve of his daughters wearing "high heels"…which in those days were about 1-1/2 inches.

If Mama put on some new shoes for a date, Grandpa would make her take them off. "Actresses' heels," he'd mumble disapprovingly. Then he'd take the shoes to his workshop in the yard and chop the heels off!

Mama said she cried and cried. Every pair of shoes she and her sisters owned had toes that pointed up from Grandpa's chopping!

When I got older and wore high heels, Mama teased me about "actresses' heels" and we shared a good laugh. Grandpa was such a dear man, but so stern looking. I believe I'd have gladly given him my shoes to chop off at the heels.
—Jolen Smith Savannah, Georgia

LADY OF THE HOUSE. Margaret Putman loved visits to her grandparents' farm in Buhl, Idaho. In this '47 photo, she proudly poses before her very own "playhouse", a former chicken coop. "What glorious times I had on the farm," she recalls. "I got to feed the chickens, milk the cows, swim in the Snake River and pick wild raspberries to eat with fresh sweet cream for breakfast. I was my grandparents' only grandchild, so they showered me with so much adoring love."

False Choppers Fascinated This Youngster

WHENEVER Grandpa's false teeth refused to cooperate, he'd just take them out and eat without them. As a child, I was amazed that he could remove his teeth and touch his chin to his nose!

Try as I might, I could do neither. I'd pull on my own teeth with my fingers, but unlike Grandpa's, they just wouldn't budge. At one time I could hardly wait to have false teeth like Grandpa (although the passing years have sort of dimmed that ambition).

—*Walt Gearing*
Loma Linda, California

Baking Mud Pies Stirred Young Girl's Imagination

THE DEPRESSION was over when I was growing up in the 1940s, but times were still tough and hardly any children had toys.

My grandma had the gift of a creative imagination, and she could stir my interest in things through her creativity. Her enthusiasm added to the joy of living, and we didn't need toys to have fun together.

For instance, we loved to make mud pies. We'd scoop up a cup of soil, add water to make a smooth mixture, then pour the mud into a lid from a fruit jar. Now our pie was ready to bake in the sun and harden.

Grandma would take me by the hand and we'd walk together to the currant patch. We were looking for that one big special currant to decorate our pie. As we walked, we talked excitedly. I looked up to my grandma, and we had so much fun together!

Finally we reached the currant patch and started our search. Almost at the same time, we'd both spot a giant brilliant red berry that was just perfect. We'd pick it carefully and display it proudly atop our mud pie. Our pie was so beautiful I thought it was fit for a queen's dining table!

—*Juanita Soper, Thornton, Colorado*

Quiet Evenings on Porch Soothed Her Cares

WHEN I WAS a little girl, Grandma and I spent the summer evenings sitting on the porch and talking while she brushed my long hair. We planned to count 100 strokes, but as we talked we'd lose count

and have to start over. Sometimes we sat there all evening.

To this day I'm not sure which was more relaxing—having Grandma brush my hair, or talking out all the things on my mind.

It's been decades now, but whenever I spend a quiet evening on the porch, I realize that I still miss her.

—*Julia Morrill, St. Paul, Minnesota*

Visits to Idaho Farm Were Glorious Times

I LOVED visiting my grandparents' farm in Idaho. Visits there meant swimming in the icy-cold Snake River, picking wild raspberries to eat with sweet cream for breakfast, feeding the chickens and hogs, milking the cows and sliding on the hay in the barn. It's also where I learned to cook, embroider and ride a horse.

I had the most wonderful playhouse, too, made from an old chicken coop and "wallpapered" with magazine pictures. It was right next to an irrigation ditch, which I considered my own personal running stream. Those were glorious times.

—*Margaret Chesnut*
Fort Myers, Florida

GOING UP! Mr. and Mrs. J.W. Geissinger celebrated their 60th anniversary by taking their first airplane ride in 1921! In the cockpit is their nephew Flavius "Putch" Donaldson, an early airmail pilot. Putch landed at the couple's farm near Milford, Iowa to take them on their first airborne adventure. The Geissingers' great-grandson, Warren Ewen of Bettendorf, Iowa shared this photo.

Radish Sandwich Became Her Favorite Summer Treat

By Carol Weimer
Sun City West, Arizona

EACH SPRING I carefully look through the supermarket produce cases for the first white radishes of the season. They always bring back memories of my grandfather.

Grandpa farmed a few acres on the outskirts of our small Colorado town. He had a garden, a cow or two, and a few Rhode Island Reds to provide the eggs for Grandma's spice cake and ice cream, which we enjoyed every Sunday afternoon.

One summer morning, I walked the half-mile to Grandpa and Grandma's house and found him in the garden. "You're just in time, little missy," he told me. "The radishes are just big enough. We're going to have us a sandwich."

He twisted the tops from the radishes he held, wiped his fingers on his overalls and took my hand. At the outdoor pump, he washed the soil from the radishes until they glistened.

In the kitchen, he cut several slabs of homemade bread, spread it thickly with butter from the crock, sliced the crisp radishes into strips and layered them on the bread. "Bring the salt, missy," he said. "That takes the bite out of the radish." He filled two glasses with milk and we sat down.

I had been dubious. To me, "sandwich" meant peanut butter and jelly. But one bite won me over.

Every summer as I indulge in my favorite hot-weather treat—a radish sandwich with ice-cold milk—I seem to hear Grandpa say, "Now that, little missy, is food for the gods!"

Mary Ann Evans

"FOOD FOR THE GODS" is how Carol Weimer's grandpa described his favorite treat—a fresh radish sandwich! Carol and her granddad enjoyed radishes on thick slabs of homemade bread with glasses of cold milk.

Nothing Equaled a Night at Granny's

By Joanne Tepe, Waco, Texas

PLEASING CHILDREN came naturally to my granny. Even now I can see her hands stitching, stirring, mending, molding, creating and caressing—bringing happiness to the many little ones who passed her way.

I especially remember our Saturday outings during the 1940s. Granny worked in a factory all week, sewing uniforms for soldiers, but she somehow always managed to save just enough of her small salary to give me a special weekend treat.

First we'd go to the picture show, then to a cafe for the enchilada special. After our meal, we'd catch the crosstown bus back to Granny's tiny apartment.

Nothing equaled spending the night at Granny's! Sinking deep into her feather bed, we'd snuggle close while she read me "Tugboat Annie" from *The Saturday Evening Post.*

Sunday breakfast was my favorite homemade cinnamon buns with white tea. Then Granny freed my dark hair from the tight rag rollers she'd put in the night before, letting it fall into the Shirley Temple curls that I loved.

We'd put on our Sunday best—a gray flannel suit for her, and a red corduroy dress for me.

She would dust her regal face with Tussey powder (sometimes letting me

> *"She always saved enough of her small salary to give me a special treat…"*

dust my nose!) and set her three-cornered felt hat at a jaunty angle. Then she'd give me a freshly ironed handkerchief and I'd proudly knot my collection-plate nickel into one corner.

Off we'd march to church, Granny in her serviceable black oxfords, and me in my out-of-season sandals.

Today, whenever I smell dough rising, hear my own grandchild's laughter or sing *Amazing Grace* clear and loud, I think of Granny and all of the many pleasures she planted in my childhood garden. They bloom each and every day of my life.

SUNDAY BEST. Joanne Tepe (right) cherishes the memories of Saturday nights at her grandmother's and going to church together the next morning.

Feisty Grandpa Took in Toddler...at Age 81

By Lanya Bump, Greeley, Colorado

GRANDPA WAS a striking man... with his ramrod-straight bearing, shock of snow-white hair and full beard, he looked like a fierce old Viking. His eyes were a piercing blue, but they danced with merriment for me.

I was my mother's only child, and Grandpa's pride and joy. From the time I was only a few weeks old, he'd stop by in his buggy, collect some diapers and a bottle and take me with him wherever he went.

My mother died when I was 3, and Grandpa insisted that he and Grandma take me in. He was 81 and she was 79 at the time. They raised me for the next 7 years, until my father remarried and I went to live with him.

I became Grandpa's constant companion. When he drove his buggy to town to play checkers and talk politics at the feed store, I went along. He read

WHAT GENERATION GAP? Lanya Bump (center) was raised from age 3 to 10 by her grandparents, J.J. and Fanny Edwards. J.J. was in his 80s then, but he and Lanya shared a unique bond despite the wide age gap between them.

to me for hours; I could read before I started school.

He taught me to love nature, animals and life and answered all my questions truthfully without evasion or dissertations.

Grandpa spoiled me terribly. The only time he reprimanded me was when I was in first grade. At recess, I took some friends to the grocery store and treated them to candy, cookies and fruit.

"Just charge it to Grandpa," I told the grocer.

That evening when he picked me up at school, Grandpa sternly said, "Don't ever let me hear of you charging anything again. If you want money, ask for it." To this day, it irks me to use a charge account.

The fondest memories of my life are from the years I spent with my grandparents. Grandpa never treated me as a child, but as a companion. He was truly a grand old man, and I owe him a great debt of gratitude.

Wise Couple Shared Beauty of Life's Gifts

I ALWAYS THOUGHT the word "grandparents" could have been invented to describe mine. It seemed that everyone in town loved them, and they loved everyone in return.

In the gardens that separated our houses, Grandma grew row after row of beautiful flowers, and it looked like there was a butterfly for each flower.

She fixed bouquets for church, provided cut flowers for the ladies in town and made dried arrangements for winter. She said rainbows and butterflies were "God's surprise gifts of color". She helped me appreciate nature's beauty.

Grandpa cleaned the streets of our town with a push broom and cart for years, and knew every inch of the streets and alleys. He eventually lost his eyesight on the job, but no one ever heard him complain.

"God has other plans for me," he'd say. He taught us it wasn't an afflic-

tion that got you down, but how you handled it. He proved that every day.

He often said he was blind "only in his eyes". He loved for us to describe Grandma's flowers to him, and what ever butterflies were in the garden that day.

He knew every flower by name, of course, yet he insisted we describe the flowers in detail for him. He knew that we wouldn't really *see* them otherwise. What a wise man.

My grandparents were popular with everyone, including children. On Saturday, when Grandma baked, every child within a mile radius seemed to stop by her house to play croquet and eat her sugar cookies.

When Grandma introduced us to the other children as her "grandkiddies", we stood at least an inch taller and straightened our shoulders with pride.
—*Dora Mattox*
Middletown, Indiana

GRANDPA'S SIGHT might have been gone, but he taught his grandchildren to see life, says Dora Mattox.

Their House Was a Haven on Chilly Saturday Nights

I LOVED VISITING my grandparents on bitterly cold, snowy Saturday evenings.

We lived in Pilger, Nebraska, which had a population of about 600 when I grew up there in the 1950s. Grandma and Grandpa lived only four blocks away from us.

Mom was a waitress at a supper club, and she usually worked Saturday nights. But if a snowstorm came along, she'd get the night off, and we'd go visit Grandma and Grandpa!

Dad would drop off Mom, my two brothers and me, then go to the store to buy a few groceries and something to drink. We kids got thick malts in white waxed containers. What a treat it was to bite into the malt powder that clumped together at the bottom!

TUNING IN SOME FUN was easy back in the heyday of radio, as families spent cozy evenings together listening to their favorite programs.

Dad and Grandpa would sit at the table, trading stories about how they used to walk 5 miles through the snow to get to school. The rest of us played cards, usually slapjack or 500 rummy, while we munched on hot buttered popcorn.

When we grew tired of cards, my brothers and I would huddle under Grandma's quilt on the couch or on the floor in front of the oil stove. We watched, fascinated, as the flames rose and fell behind the two rounded glass doors, squinting until they looked like glowing red eyes.

The back of the stove held a small rectangular tray for water to keep the air from getting too dry. We kids always fought over who got to fill it. Grandma never had to worry about the tray being empty while we were around!

We didn't do much but talk, play cards and listen to the radio, but we sure had fun on those quiet, cozy evenings. While the wind howled outside, we had time to relax and enjoy our lives, and we did it as a family.
—*Jim Bahm*
Norfolk, Nebraska

Tales of Exotic Lands Sparked Appetite For Food and Travel

I HAD A POOR APPETITE as a child, but Grandmother took care of that. She bought a little table and matching chairs just for me and placed them under a huge rubber plant in the corner of her dining room.

One day as I ate lunch there, Grandmother explained that the tree was a eucalyptus and that we were in Australia with the koalas. The next day, the tree was an evergreen and we were up in Maine.

Then it became a palm tree and we were on Florida's Gulf Coast. Next we were under a cherry tree in full blossom in Japan, then under an orange tree in California.

Grandmother's interesting stories went on and on. Her tales not only helped me eat better, but developed in me a great desire to travel.

My parents were preoccupied with the hereafter, but Grandmother taught me to enjoy the here and now.
—*David Smith, Largo, Florida*

A HUCKSTER TRUCK like this visited Jo Carey's granddad's neighborhood, as recounted in story. This particular truck was driven in Laurys Station, Pennsylvania in the '40s, says Rayburn Krause, who shared photo of his dad's vehicle.

Say What? Practical Joke Had Ear-Splitting Outcome

THE STORY repeated most often in our family involves my Granddad Fraze, who had quite a reputation as a practical joker.

One day he was visiting a neighbor when the new huckster driver stopped by. Granddad told the salesman to be sure to stop next at the Frazes' (his own house) and to remember that Mrs. Fraze was extremely hard of hearing.

Then he hurried home and told Grandmother that he'd just met the new huckster driver and the poor sales man was almost totally deaf. Having set the trap, he went to the barn and stood just inside the door, where he doubled over in laughter listening to salesman and customer shout at each other!

You might wonder if Grandmother was angry when she discovered how she'd been tricked...again. But she just shook her head. She knew Granddad!
—*Jo Carey, Skwentna, Alaska*

A. M. Wettach

Chicken Was Crown Jewel
Of Sunday Dinner at Grandma's

By June West, San Carlos, California

CHICKEN FRICASSEE? No one today would classify this dish as gourmet cooking. But then, they never ate at my grandma's, and she knew how to make this dish a feast!

Grandma's Sunday menu never varied. It was always her special chicken fricassee, sometimes with mashed potatoes, other times with her light airy dumplings. The vegetable was either corn or peas (she didn't believe in salads), and for dessert we had vanilla ice cream with Oreo cookies.

Dinner was served at 4 p.m., but we'd arrive early, gathering in the kitchen to watch her cook. She'd cut up the chicken, dust each piece with flour and seasonings, then brown it in hot oil or butter.

Next she added the other ingredients—I wish I could remember what they were—and slowly simmered everything as mouth-watering aromas crept through her little house.

Grandma bustled about the kitchen chatting with all of us as she prepared the meal. She asked my brother and me about school and what we'd been doing. We felt so grown-up because she never talked down to us.

After a while, Mother and I would set the dining room table because Grandma believed that Sunday dinner should be "served special", and not just eaten in the kitchen.

When it was *finally* time to eat, Grandma's chicken was always the star of the meal. Not only was it tender, it had a special flavor I haven't tasted since those days. Just the memory of eating it can make my mouth water!

I have many recipes of Grandma's, but not her chicken fricassee. It wasn't written down because she used the "by guess and by golly" school of measuring.

I've scoured old cookbooks for her recipe, but I'd settle for one that just comes close…I know I'll never make anything that tastes as good as Grandma's dish does in my memories.

Mom Thwarted Plans of Do-It-Yourself Dentist

GRANDPA was born on the French-Italian border of well-to-do parents, and local custom dictated that he, as the eldest son, become a priest.

He was trained as a linguist and was fluent in seven languages. On the day before he was to be ordained, he decided that custom wasn't for him and signed on as a cook on a freighter bound for America.

He worked as a miner in Michigan, then moved to Wisconsin and worked as an interpreter in the courts. He married and had 12 children, and he was a most fascinating character to his grandchildren, as I well remember.

Grandpa was 90 and I was 7 when he came to live with us. One day he took me aside and asked if I knew how to take the streetcar to the dime store. When I said yes, he gave me 50¢ and told me to go there and buy him a nice new pair of pliers.

As I headed out the door, my mother stopped me. She'd overheard enough to be suspicious. When I told her what Grandpa had asked me to do, she took that half-dollar out of my hand and gave it back to him.

"If you have a toothache," she told him sternly, "go to the dentist. You're not pulling any of your teeth while you live in *my* house!"

—*Joy Mathews, Ocala, Florida*

Her "Joyful Noise" Often Drowned Out the Radio

GRANDMA LOVED to sing, both in church and at home. She often drowned out the voices on her favorite radio program, *The Mormon Tabernacle Choir*, broadcast from Salt Lake City, Utah.

She had misgivings about listening to a program produced by people of a religion different from hers. Still, she ignored the pangs of conscience long enough to joyfully join in singing those beautiful hymns at the top of her lungs!

—Joseph Schabell
Alexandria, Kentucky

MEMORABLE GRANDMA. Catherine "Kate" Schabell was about 70 when this photograph was taken around 1940. One of her 17 grandchildren, Joseph Schabell recalls her as a feisty and vigorous woman who lived to the age of 85. "We still think of her often," he says.

Even the Dogs Turned Tail And Ran from This Prank!

LIVING IN THE WOODS without electricity, Grandpa had to invent his own pastimes. He was a self-taught musician who could play accordion, banjo and violin. But his best skills were storytelling and playing practical jokes.

He often scared people with his "wildcat squall", using a mouth instrument that produced a blood-curdling noise not often heard in our part of the country.

One day during berry-picking season, Grandpa suggested we have some fun. He and I would hide in a brush pile and wait for some berry-pickers to come along, then Grandpa would give a call on his squaller.

It wasn't long until a neighbor couple, Marshall and Gladys, headed into the berry patch with their two dogs. As soon as they reached into the berry bushes, Grandpa blew on his squaller. We could see the hair stand straight up on the dogs' backs as they tucked in their tails and ran for home.

"It must be pretty big for those dogs to quit!" Marshall said worriedly.

"I think we'd better run, too!" said Gladys.

Grandpa and I fell onto our backs, laughing until tears rolled down our cheeks. Who needs TV for fun?

—Merle Thomas
Harrisburg, Pennsylvania

Juicy Fruit Ritual Made Overnight Visits Special

MY GRANDDADDY McKoy was about 6 feet 9 inches tall and skinny. He had black hair, was very darkly complected and drove a city bus in Wilmington, North Carolina.

My fondest memories of him are of the evenings he picked me up and took me home after he finished work. I was no more than 3 or 4, but I ran to his car as fast as I could. I knew I had something to look forward to when I spent the night at his house!

We stopped at a small gas station to buy a bottle of chocolate milk and a package of Juicy Fruit gum. Then we went home to sit at the table and wait for dinner. The big table had benches on each side, with throne-like chairs at the ends for Grandma and Granddaddy.

After dinner, I'd sit in one of the big chairs and color while Granddaddy sat at the other end, paying bills. After a while he'd look up at me and wink. I'd jump up and run to him, knowing he had a piece of Juicy Fruit with my name on it!

Granddaddy would pick me up, put me in his lap, then look in his pocket. Holding me there, he'd pull out the Juicy Fruit and give me a stick. That had to be the tastiest gum anyone ever enjoyed!

—Amanda McKoy
Wilmington, North Carolina

For the Record, She Thinks Her Grandpa Was Best Ever!

MY GRANDPARENTS lived next door to us, and I loved them both, but Grandpa was my hero.

He'd sit for hours telling us stories. If I had a button missing, he was the

TURN IT UP! Margaret Shiebel loved listening to her grandfather's phonograph with him. For this performance, she got as close as possible so she wouldn't miss a single note!

one who sewed it back on. We children weren't allowed to drink coffee, of course, but Grandpa would let me sit on his lap and sneak a sip from his saucer.

Best of all, he loved to play his phonograph records for us. We loved it, too, dancing around him while the music played.

I thank my grandpa for the sweet yesterdays and the special joy he brought to my life. He's been gone now for over 70 years, but I still love him.

—Margaret Shiebel, De Land, Florida

Hard Work and Iron Will Kept Spreads Snowy White

GRANDMA was a gentle, soft-spoken woman, but she had one rule no one dared disobey—do not sit on the beds! It took lots of hard work over laundry tubs and washboards to keep her snowwhite bedspreads fresh and clean, and she took great pride in them.

Whenever Grandma bustled past one of the four-posters, she'd invariably stop to smooth out a wrinkle no one else could see. And woe to all if the spread was marred by a smudgy fingerprint!

Even today, the sight of a bed made up in cool, airy white still reminds me of Grandma's counterpanes.

—Ruth Belangee, Alton, Illinois

Gratitude for Miracle Shaped Remarkable Life

By Muriel Ibarguen, Los Altos, California

MY GREAT-GRANDFATHER was a towering yet gentle man, and I first knew him when he was in his 80s. He'd once been a redhead, but now pure white hair bristled from his pink scalp like a halo gone astray.

His blue eyes twinkled, unfaded by the years, and his smile seemed to engulf the whole world. So did those big, gangly arms he held out in welcome to my brothers and me. We didn't walk into his embrace, we ran!

Born in a log cabin in Pennsylvania, Grandpa ran away at age 15 to join the Union army. During the second of his three enlistments, his father gave him a little gold compass "so he'd always be able to find his way home". He wore it on his watch chain for the rest of his life.

After the war was over, Grandpa went to work as a miner. At age 28, he was put in charge of an ore mine, and here he had an experience that set the course for the rest of his life.

One day Grandpa was climbing into a 100-foot well to replace a ladder when some scaffolding came loose and he fell. He dropped 40 feet and hit a landing, injuring a leg, fracturing his ribs and dislocating a shoulder.

Workers Rushed to Help

From there he plunged headfirst into several feet of water. It took the other workmen some time to scramble down the shaft and pull him out of the water, and they were surprised to find he hadn't drowned. Apparently the pain of his injuries induced him to hold his breath, preventing water from entering his lungs.

His survival was truly a miracle, and Grandpa never ceased giving thanks for it. He became a Presbyterian lay minister, a driving force in the YMCA and an inspiration to all who knew him.

TWINKLING EYES of her Great-Grandfather Russell are among the many happy memories Muriel Ibarguen enjoys.

For the last 10 years of his life, Grandpa cared for Grandma, who was bedridden. Except for some occasional preaching, he never left her bedside. He took care of all her needs, read to her from the Bible and showed his devotion to her in many little ways.

I loved visiting them. We'd sit in his big rocker beside Grandma's bed, always including her in the conversation. He'd tell stories of growing up in the log cabin, and of running away to join the army at midnight, with the neighborhood dogs yapping at his heels.

A Keepsake Compass

I was fascinated by all the charms on his watch chain, especially the gold compass. He promised that someday it would be mine. And it is.

When Grandma died, Grandpa said the only thing he wanted to do before joining her was to visit his grandchildren. He was doing just that when he suffered a heart attack and went home to her. We were saddened but not surprised. We never doubted for a minute that God would answer Grandpa's prayers.

Grandpa prepared his funeral text himself. It included the verse from Psalms upon which he had based his life: "He brought me out of a horrible pit, out of the miry clay, and set my feet upon a rock and established my goings." ᴥ

Simple Pleasures on the Farm Gave Him Memories to Treasure

EACH SUMMER I'd spend a couple of weeks at my grandparents' farm, but I'll always remember one particular day.

Grandpa's dog, "Ol' Jack", and I were playing in the creek while Grandpa plowed corn nearby. About mid-morning, Grandpa stopped work and asked me if I wanted to pick out a watermelon.

He led me to his "truck patch" and thumped several melons before deciding on a good one. We put it in a spring to cool, and it was my job to turn the melon for the rest of the morning so it would chill evenly. At noon, we topped off the lunch Grandma had packed with all the cold, vine-ripened watermelon we could eat.

That afternoon, Grandpa asked if I wanted to go fishing. He unhitched his plow horses, "Bill" and "Barney", and we both rode Bill while leading Barney back to the house. Grandpa picked up two fishing hooks with string tied to them, and we rode down to the river.

We dug worms, cut two poles and started fishing at one of Grandpa's favorite spots. It was a weekday, so we had the river all to ourselves, and before long we had a stringer full of fish. Grandma fried them for supper and added fresh garden lettuce, onions, peas and homemade bread. We had a feast!

That night, as I snuggled down in Grandma's comfy feather bed, I thought, "What a wonderful day". I knew it would live in my memory forever.

—*Leon Gullet*
St. Clair, Missouri

Grandma's Quiet Presence Anchored Child's Days

By Marilyn Christensen, Troutdale, Oregon

I CAN STILL HEAR the soft voice of my grandmother as she sat by a sunny window in her rocking chair, reading from her German Bible. She spoke little English when she came to live with us on our Minnesota farm, but I slowly came to understand her native language.

Ours was a typical farm family, so everyone else was very busy. But Grandma always had time for me. She often included me in her gardening chores, holding my hand as we walked through her tiny plot, picking a berry for me to sample or telling me how good the carrots would be next week.

She tended the delicate vegetable shoots with loving care. Her goal each spring was to harvest new potatoes and tender peas in time to serve them on the Fourth of July in a savory cream sauce. I don't recall a single year we were disappointed.

Her tiny garden always had room for a rainbow of petals nodding in the breeze, too. She liked to arrange sweet peas in a little white milk pitcher in the middle of the dining room table. Today I proudly display that pitcher in my home.

Her garden also included horse-radish for Dad. "Come, *kinchin*," she'd call, "we fix horseradish for your papa. Heinrich, he like it."

I'd watch as she dug the roots, peeled them and then cut them up. It was my

GARDEN OF LOVE. Grandma's plot produced a bounty of food, beauty and loving memories.

Lee Watson/Unicorn Stock Photos

job to turn the crank on the grinder as Grandma fed the strong-smelling chunks into it. No onion ever smelled as strong as that horseradish, and soon both of us would be crying and laughing at the same time. But my father loved horseradish, and Grandma loved to make it for him.

She showed her appreciation for him in another way, too. After the noon meal, Dad always took a short nap before returning to his labors in the fields.

After he stretched out on the couch, Grandma would move a chair next to him and patiently wave a flyswatter back and forth over him so he could nap undisturbed. She loved this strong, silent, hardworking man who had not only married her widowed daughter with two small children, but welcomed her into his home as well.

Winter's slower pace gave Grandma time to knit. Every Christmas, my sister and I received mittens, scarves and stocking caps. We were warm as toast as we walked down our long lane to wait for the school bus. We were wrapped in Grandma's love, and that shielded us against much more than just the Minnesota winters. ✦

Limburger Lover's Memories Are Nothing to Sniff at!

WHEN I WAS 9 years old, my grandparents lived at the top of a hill in a small town in northern New York. Every Saturday while Grandma took her afternoon nap, Grandpa and I would walk down the hill to a little store and buy some sour cream and Limburger cheese.

Grandpa and I sure loved that cheese, but Grandma hated the smell, so we had to go into the kitchen and shut the door to eat it.

First we'd cut two slices of Grandma's fresh bread for each of us. We'd top our first pieces of bread with some mustard and a good thick piece of that Limburger. It was *won-*

derful...but we weren't finished yet!

For "dessert", we'd spread our second slices of bread with sour cream and sprinkle on some sugar. After we finished our special snack, any leftover Limburger had to be stored in the "cheese dish" and taken out to the woodshed. That was Grandma's rule.

Then we had to get the pungent cheese smell out of the kitchen, so we'd open the windows and "shoo" it out. We *had to* do this even if it happened to be winter and 40° below zero!

Next, Grandpa would get out his big iron skillet and pop a batch of

corn on the old oil stove. This last effort really did the trick!

Finally we could open the door and go into the sitting room, where we'd find Grandma sewing in her rocking chair. Grandpa's rocker was opposite hers, and I sat on Grandma's footstool. We'd listen to *Amos 'n' Andy* on the radio while Grandpa quartered a big apple to share.

Though I was only a little girl at the time, I remember thinking, "This is probably the closest I'm ever going to get to Heaven here on this earth!" Looking back, that little girl was right!
—*Ellen Colloca*
Sarasota, Florida

Chapter Four

We Found Family Fun

We Found Family Fun

IN THE good old days, having fun was a family affair ...from piecing together a jigsaw puzzle, listening intently to Dad tell a story or singing along while Mom played the piano. Families used their imaginations—and whatever resources they had—to create endless hours of wholesome entertainment.

ALL IN THE FAMILY. In Washington, Iowa, the three Friese sisters (from left), Mary Catherine, Donna Mae and Joan, entertained the neighborhood with their accordion antics.

Just try to explain to your children or grandchildren how you had fun when you were a kid—way back in those prehistoric days before television, Nintendo, roller blades, Disney World, snowmobiles and in-ground swimming pools. Go ahead and try.

Truth to tell, we had *a lot* of fun. Maybe one reason was that houses were a lot smaller for most of us in those days, so families had to spend more time together by necessity. Many kids shared the same bedrooms, and they didn't even whine about not having enough closet space.

Those were the days before "family rooms", so we did family things in the living room, the kitchen or the dining room. In our home, the dining room table was always the place for family fun. It might as well have been, because we rarely ate there, anyhow.

The dining room table was the logical place to work on a new craze called jigsaw puzzles. The really tough ones often needed days to assemble. The best part about them was that everyone in the family could contribute—as long as you didn't sneeze.

Millionaire for a Night

For my money, the greatest single entertainment invention for the Depression era was the new game of Monopoly. Before the game started, you might have been worried about how you'd manage to buy a few groceries tomorrow. But once the dice started rolling, you forgot all that, because you were busily buying and selling property, collecting rent and building houses and hotels. You were rich! You were John D. Rockefeller. Monopoly was a magic carpet that *whooshed* you away into a world of affluence.

When we weren't playing around the dining table, our family often gathered around the piano. Mom played all the current hits—*The Isle of Capri, Red Sails in the Sunset, Deep Purple, Mexicali Rose, When I Grow Too Old to Dream* and whatever else was being featured on *Your Hit Parade*. By bedtime, we'd end up with *There's a Long, Long Trail A-winding* and *Good Night, Ladies*.

On Wednesday nights during our summers in Sterling, Illinois, there were municipal band concerts in Central Park. But first we stopped at the Carnegie Library, returning last week's books and checking out new ones.

Breakfast in the Park

Sunday mornings we'd pick up the *Chicago Tribune* at the tobacco store and then head for Sinnissippi Park and an outdoor breakfast overlooking the Rock River. What else can match the aroma of bacon frying in a cast-iron skillet and coffee perking over an outdoor fire?

During the winter in those Depression years, a local school had movies one night a week in the gymnasium. I think it cost 10¢ for the whole family.

Usually, there was a double feature—a cowboy picture or comedy for the kids and something a bit heavier for the grown-ups. All of them were silent movies, so we dutifully hissed the villain and cheered the hero. Who could complain? It was only a dime.

No wonder so many of us who lived through the '30s often say that "we didn't know we were poor". It didn't take money for the family to have fun together, as the following stories recall.
—*Clancy Strock*

Our Sunday Afternoon Ball Games Were Unforgettable

By Marcella Sedlak, Hennessey, Oklahoma

IN THE 1930s, a big part of our family fun was watching our small town's baseball team play each Sunday. And we didn't have to go far—my father had built the diamond on our farm!

Back then every little community had a diamond and team. The men played ball, the ladies visited or watched the game and the children ran around having fun together.

The players' uniforms were furnished by the town merchants. Bats, balls and other supplies were bought using the small admission fees paid by spectators. Adult admission for regular games was 10¢; 25¢ for all-day tournaments. Children were always admitted free. The whole family was welcome and enjoyed the day together.

At the tournaments, the ladies sold hamburgers like you never tasted before and all kinds of homemade pies, which sold out in a hurry. Soda pop was a nickel, but a few lucky ones got theirs at no charge if the bottle was wrapped with a paper label reading "free".

After all these years, the "old-timers" around here still recall those Sunday afternoons as some of the most enjoyable days of their lives.

BATTER UP! The Hennessey, Oklahoma Blue Jays had a good turnout, as usual, for this Sunday afternoon game in the 1930s. Marcella Sedlak's father, Joe Pacula, built the playing field on his farm and also managed the team. Below, the Blue Jays pose for a team photo with their manager (seated at center front).

Dad's Vaudeville Program Showcased Youths' Talents

By Marion Pasqua, Syracuse, New York

ORGAN MUSIC filled that warm summer night in 1933 as a magnificent Irish tenor sang *Danny Boy*. The audience was standing room only, with the overflow crowd hanging through the windows to catch a glimpse.

This show happened in our two-car garage, which was crammed with a stage, bleachers and an antique organ. It was the culmination of many weeks of work by my father, a young police lieutenant.

Dad believed it was a good idea to keep the young people in the neighborhood occupied during the summer, so he organized a vaudeville show to exhibit our talents—some of which we didn't even know we had!

We not only performed, but made costumes, worked as stagehands, paint-ed scenery—and loved every minute of it. My brother was the electrician, handling spotlights and footlights.

I performed a tango with a girlfriend, sang *Me and My Shadow* and also appeared with two other girls in a skit about a hobo.

There Was Drama, Too

My father wrote a dramatic story about a wounded American soldier being rescued during World War I. He ransacked the attic for clothing that relatives had worn during the war, then painted a realistic backdrop of "no-man's-land".

The authentic scene made a big impression on the audience—and on me. It seemed so real that I can still recall the emotions I felt that night.

The Irish tenor was a strapping police sergeant who offered to perform after hearing about Dad's project. The audience was rapt as his high, clear notes reverberated off the walls of the garage.

The crowd appreciated each act and seemed to enjoy watching the show as much as we enjoyed planning and performing it. The local newspapers ran several stories about the young policeman who worked—and played—so hard with the neighborhood children.

Barn Dances Brightened Summer for Whole Community

LIFE ON OUR northwest-Nebraska farm was mighty dull when my brother, George, and I came home from college for the summer in the 1920s. Determined to liven things up, we talked our folks into letting us organize a barn dance.

We got Mama's permission to use her piano, but she drew the line when we suggested lifting it into the hayloft on the sling we used for hay. Instead, with Papa's help, we moved the piano to the barn in a wagon, then rigged up two sets of ramps to get it onto the hayrack and up to the "dance floor".

Posted Deputy Outside

We hired a talented piano player, a friend of our mother's, and a four-piece orchestra made up of local farm boys and girls. This was during Prohibition, so we arranged for the sheriff to assign a deputy to make sure people weren't drinking outside.

After cleaning and sweeping to get the barn in shape and putting a few ads in local papers, we were ready!

There weren't any dances in our area, so we had people coming from all over. Many families brought their children, and before long all the beds in our house were full! Our younger siblings did a brisk business selling food from a stand on the side of the dance floor.

Nobody Wanted to Leave!

The only problem we had with that first big dance was getting people to go home! We hadn't set a time limit, and some of the revelers were still there at breakfast time the next morning!

The dance was such a success that we hosted five or six that summer. As a result, we made enough money for Papa to buy an electric generator. Thanks to our barn dances, we became the first farm in the neighborhood with yard lights and an electric-powered water pump!

—Marx Koehnke, Lincoln, Nebraska

City Kids Had Plenty of Fun In the Good Old Days

By Florence Archambault, Newport, Rhode Island

WE CITY KIDS might not have enjoyed the same fresh foods and outdoor pleasures that our country cousins did during the '30s, but we found plenty of ways to amuse ourselves!

I grew up in an industrial city just north of Boston. The more adventurous kids in our neighborhood (I being one of them) climbed the billboards that fronted our Main Street and took in thrilling bird's-eye views of the city below!

In the evenings when traffic was light, we took over a wide intersection for a roller-skating rink, going round and round with smiles on our faces and skate keys dangling from our necks.

In winter, our next-door neighbor flooded a vacant lot for a skating rink. I wonder if his landlord ever figured out why he had such a big water bill!

The Fourth of July was a treat in the city, celebrated with a parade and fireworks at our biggest park. On the morning of the Fourth, all of us kids would line up in front of our grammar schools where a policeman would hand out free "Hoodsie Cups".

These small cups of ice cream had lids with pictures of movie stars printed on the undersides. Today, these lids are worth money as collectibles. But we didn't save any…we were more interested in the ice cream!

Some games we loved were marbles, jacks and hopscotch, all played on city

---

"Growing up in an Italian neighborhood had advantages…"

---

sidewalks or playgrounds. Chalked-out squares for hopscotch were drawn all over our walks during summer.

Though we didn't get to enjoy the fresh milk, eggs and homemade ice cream that our country cousins loved, there were advantages to growing up in an Italian neighborhood.

Every evening at 6, we'd walk to the local bakery and buy a slice of pizza for a nickel. This was long before pizzerias, so those hot slices were a real treat, baked in a stone oven on a huge black sheet after the day's regular baking was done.

Vegetable peddlers and other vendors plied their wares up and down the streets, some of them with horse and wagon. The Swedish baker made a daily delivery to my grandmother's house right across the street from ours. I can still taste his fresh limpa bread!

We had no fireplace, but that didn't stop us from enjoying fresh popcorn. Dad simply went to the basement and stuck the wire popper into the open door of our big coal furnace!

Picnics Turned Auto into "Dining Car"!

THE MOST MEMORABLE PICNICS from my childhood took place in the backseat of our family car!

In summer, we often drove to Grandma's farm on Saturday mornings, a 4-hour trip through the Minnesota countryside. About 2 hours into the drive, one of us three little girls in back would complain, "I'm hungry! When can we eat?"

Mother would take that as a dinner-bell signal, reach for the paper sack near her feet and remove a paring knife, soda crackers and a ring of bologna. She'd hand back tiny sandwiches of quarter-inch slices of meat between two flaky crackers.

Instead of a red-checked tablecloth under a shade tree, we picnicked happily on the dusty maroon velour of our car's backseat. Treetops and telephone lines zipped by in a blur of blue skies and fluffy white clouds as we chewed contentedly.

When we'd complain of unquenchable thirst, Mother would produce a mason jar filled with pale lemonade that had grains of sugar and bits of lemon floating in it. The jar looked like a giant yellow jewel when the sunlight slipped through it and reflected back to us from the brass cap. Since I was the oldest, I got to take the first sip, then passed it on to my sisters.

None of the picnics I've attended or prepared since have tasted as good or satisfied my anticipation as well as those picnics in the car on the way to Grandma's.   —*Colleen Stuart, Clark Lake, Iowa*

Lakefront Summers at Grandma's Place Were Wonderful

OUR WIDOWED MOTHER worked hard to keep a roof over our heads during the late 1940s in northern New York. But she managed one luxury for us—keeping our small cottage on the eastern edge of Lake Ontario.

Although the tiny beach community was only a 30-mile drive from our house in town, it was like another world.

My sister, brother and I spent 9 months a year attending school, taking music lessons and working part-time. But in summer Mother wanted us to enjoy being kids, and all those things were forgotten when we went to the lake.

We had certain responsibilities—hauling water, doing dishes and laundry, starting supper and cleaning—but the rest of the time was ours. We took bike and boat rides, went fishing, built tree houses and rode inner tubes.

"Grandma", the lady who owned the beach, looked out for all the children and organized activities. Whenever we had some cold, rainy weather, she would open the hall above the bathhouse so

By Loretta Nixon, Bremen, New York

we could play bingo or listen to records.

She hired a small band for square dancing on Saturday nights and planned wiener roasts and "pie and cake nights" on the beach. There were baby showers and birthday parties, too, and a community potluck every Labor Day.

Whenever one of these events was about to begin, Grandma would give her schoolteacher's desk bell to one of us kids and let us walk all over the beach

> *"We took bike rides,
> boat rides, swam
> and went fishing..."*

ringing it. We had fun doing that—and we always had a group of kids following us, just like the Pied Piper!

There weren't a lot of amenities at the lake. We all shared an outside privy and had to stand in line, even if it rained. The

only phone was in Grandma's one-room store, where she sold milk, bread, ice cream and penny candy. The phone was to be used for emergencies only.

Just one family at the lake had a television, and we kids were intrigued by it. On nice nights they let us line up benches out on their porch and watch through the windows.

If we were too noisy, they'd shut the windows and our evening's entertainment would be over. We used to hate cold, windy nights because then they'd never open the windows at all!

Grandma is gone now; so are her bathhouse and store. Today, most of the cottages are year-round homes, with sewer hookups and cable TV. What a far cry from my rustic childhood! But some things never change. My mother still summers there, and I still think of it as my little piece of Heaven.

I only get back once a year now, but my heart still pounds and my eyes fill with tears the minute I make that turn in the road and see the lake.

Dad's Antics Made Birthday Parties Hilarious

MOTHER gave me birthday parties that were the talk of the neighborhood. After my guests and I played games like "Pin the Tail on the Donkey" and many more, it would be time for Dad's special game.

He'd ask for a volunteer who wanted to play, then ask that person to step out of the room for a moment.

He'd tell the rest of us to be quiet and not say a word when the game was being played. It went like this:

Two saucers were used, but one of them was smoked black on the bottom. When the other person returned to the room, Dad would tell him or her to do everything *exactly* as he did. First he'd rub his finger on the bottom of his saucer and then rub his nose. Then he'd rub his chin, cheek and forehead. Soon, the rest of us were laughing and giggling uncontrollably. It was all in good fun and the black marks washed right off.

Afterward, Mother would ask us to come to the table, where there'd be a beautiful birthday cake with my name on it and lit candles. Mom and Dad sure knew how to make a birthday fun!   —*Helene Smith, Ocean City, New Jersey*

Pianist Entertained Entire Neighborhood

WHENEVER I HEARD my mother start playing the piano on summer evenings, I knew it was time to come inside and take my post next to the phone, awaiting the calls.

Mother might start by playing tunes from *42nd Street*. Then came the inevitable ring of the phone. "Please ask your mother to play something from *Roberta*," the caller would say. The next might request a little Cab Calloway.

With supper finished and the dishes put away, all the neighbors sat on their front porches, reading the evening paper and rocking in time to Mother's music.

When I wasn't taking their requests, I pushed the porch glider back and forth with my foot, sniffing the lilacs, listening to the music and wishing those summer evenings would never end. —*Elizabeth Yudd Annapolis, Maryland*

Visit to "Baloney John's" Fun for Whole Family

IN THE LATE '30s, Dad would load Mama and us six kids into the old '31 Chevy and drive 30 miles to a family gathering place called "Baloney John's" on Long Island, New York. We loved it!

There was a petting zoo in front, with chickens, ducks, some rabbits and a goat or two. Inside, there was always a *huge* tray of cold cuts, plenty of dark German rye bread and a big knife so Dad could cut slices for us. There were beverages for everyone —and it was only a dollar for the whole works!

On the ride home, we'd all laugh and sing songs. Boy, that was fun. The car had no heater, but Mama dressed us warmly and body heat did the rest.

I'd swap all the TV's in the world to visit Baloney John's again and take another ride back to that dear time in my childhood. —*Bob Condra Madison Heights, Virginia*

Neighbors Took Turns Hosting Ice Cream Socials

ICE CREAM SOCIALS were held at different neighbors' homes every Saturday night when I was a child. Those with hand-cranked freezers brought the ice cream ingredients, and everyone else provided cakes and sandwiches.

While the women visited in the house, the men gathered outside to crush blocks of ice in gunnysacks. Then they packed ice and salt around the freezers and cranked until the ice cream was done. Usually there was a friendly competition to see who could crank the longest to make the firmest ice cream.

The children played outside, even if it

DYNAMITE DUO! According to Ruth Wark of Reno, Nevada, it was June of 1920 when she and her brother were loaded into these dynamite powder boxes (there were pillows in the bottoms) and tied on to this burro for the trek up to a family resort in southern California's San Gabriel Mountains.

was dark—but our parents never had to worry. Their only problem was keeping us from eating too much salted ice from around the freezers! —*Joyce Surface West Plains, Missouri*

Game in Hayloft Eggs-ploded into a Mess!

ONE THANKSGIVING, all my father's relatives met at his brother's large farm. The house was filled with laughter, crying babies, rattling dishes, delicious aromas…and a whole bunch of cousins just waiting to get into trouble. We didn't have to look far.

That afternoon, we decided to play "Feuding Hatfields and McCoys". We chose up sides, then climbed to the barn loft, hid behind hay bales and lobbed corncobs at each other. Anyone who got hit was eliminated.

We McCoys were bombarding the Hatfields pretty good, but our ammunition was dwindling, so I started scouting around for more corncobs. In a far corner, I spied a hen's nest with four eggs in it. I grinned, chuckling to myself, "*This* will end the war!"

I approached the nest and reached out for one of the eggs. At the slightest touch from my hand it exploded like a bomb, setting off the other three!

Phew! Rotten eggs! They had flown everywhere…and were all over me! I had them in my clothes, on my face, in my hair. It was worse than awful!

My teammates scattered as I crawled toward them. As the smell wafted to the Hatfield side, our opponents rose up as one, hollering, "We surrender!"

My mother sent me to the pond with a huge bar of Ivory soap and told me not to return until I smelled a lot better. It's a Thanksgiving I'll remember as long as I live! —*Vernice Garrett, Texas City, Texas*

Home Concerts Brightened Bleak Depression Days

I VIVIDLY REMEMBER the "concerts" my family had during the bleak days of the early 1930s. The band members were my schoolteacher-grandfather on violin, my mother on piano (I can still hear her banging out *Under the Double Eagle*), an uncle on trumpet and an aunt on cello.

Three of my grandfather's students, playing saxophone, clarinet and drums, were happy to come over to our house weekly and fill out the group.

Their talents weren't perfectly matched, and they were certainly no threat to the philharmonic, but they played with vigor and enjoyed their music and the camaraderie. In a time when any kind of enjoyment was difficult to find, they provided pleasure for all of us.

How I wish families could enjoy simple pleasures like that again! —*Phyllis Wilkinson Grants Pass, Oregon*

Family Sing-Alongs Wove a Magic Spell

WHEN SUPPER was over, Daddy usually settled down in his favorite chair near the table that held the Aladdin lamp. There he'd page through the latest copy of *The Progressive Farmer* until he dropped off to sleep.

But every once in a while, he'd rise from the supper table and casually ask, "Do you want me to sing you some songs?" The four of us kids would squeal with delight and run to take our places in the living room.

Seated in our places, we watched the door anxiously (no performer ever had a more worshipful audience). Soon, Daddy made his entrance. Standing straight and tall, he made a stiff bow as we clapped and laughed.

Though we knew all the words to the song Daddy was about to sing, we never tired of hearing it and watching his performance. When the clapping stopped, the show began. In a clear strong voice, Daddy began.

There once was an Indian maid, a shy little prairie maid, who sang all day a love song gay, as o'er the prairies she'd while away the day...

As Daddy sang, he *became* the fair maid, Red Wing. Again, we clapped and laughed at his antics. Then he plaintively sang the chorus, which ended with:

Her brave is sleeping, while Red Wing's weeping, her heart away.

Oh, how we loved that chorus! We knew all the words and said them under our breath as Daddy sang (we didn't dare say the words aloud, for that would break the magic spell). Each time Daddy paused to catch his breath before another verse, we'd shout, "Sing it all! Sing it all!"

And each time he sang the chorus, his gestures became more dramatic. Finally, it was time for the last verse. Daddy stood very still and lowered his voice to a whisper.

Then all the braves returned, and the heart of Red Wing yearned, for far, far away her warrior bold, fell brave among the foe.

We wiped away the tears from our eyes...for we had come to love Red Wing. Both the Indian maid and her warrior bold had become very real to four preschoolers who believed the beautiful stories their parents shared.

By Jackye Havenhill, Denton, Texas

We clapped our hands and begged for more, and Daddy began singing other songs. As he sang, he paraded around the room. And when each song ended, we yelled, "Do it again!"

While he was singing *Waltzing Matilda Home*, Mother walked into the room (Daddy's songs gave her a chance to clean the kitchen without interrup-

> *"We knew all the words but never tired of hearing it..."*

tion from us kids). He grabbed her around the waist and danced her across the floor as he sang. This brought gales of laughter.

Though it was getting late, no one seemed to want to break the magic spell. Mother went to the old piano and began playing hymns from a worn book. Soft music filled the room as we gathered around her to listen.

Then Mother looked up at Daddy and smiled, "Here's your favorite". When she began playing *When You and I Were Young, Maggie*, they sang the words together. We listened as their voices blended, enjoying the moment —but far too young to understand the deep love being expressed.

Our show time ended with a song we all knew, *Little Brown Church in the Vale*. We children couldn't read the words and didn't know all the verses, but we joined in on the words, "Come, come to the Church in the Wildwood".

Together, Mother and Daddy tucked their four sleepyheads into bed and blew out the lamp. There in the darkness, I felt safe and happy. I shut my eyes and pulled up the covers.

But, before dropping off to sleep, I prayed that somewhere there was a campfire bright and that Red Wing was lying there as happy as I was.

SING-ALONGS, like ones Jackye Havenhill's family had, provided a way for a family to have fun together, just with a piano and their own voices.

Parents Pulled Together To Make Sweet Memories

TAFFY PULLING was popular in the '30s, especially at our house, where candy was a rare treat. We children were only spectators, though; making taffy was considered a science to be handled only by adults.

Some households had steel taffy hooks, but my father pulled our taffy with his bare hands. He'd scrub up as carefully as a surgeon while Mother boiled the ingredients. When they reached the right consistency, she'd pour the mixture on top of our marble-topped buffet.

The recipe called for the taffy to cool, but Father never waited too long. He buttered his hands, then worked the mixture by throwing it up high in a twisting motion, looping and slapping it together. He pulled and worked that warm candy so hard, he later had blisters to show for it.

Fascinated, we watched as the taffy became firmer and whiter, until at last it was ready to be broken into bite-size pieces. What a thrill it was to roll those sweet luscious morsels around in our mouths!
—*Lee Romig*
Red River, New Mexico

Gifts from Aunts Dressed Up Playtime

MY SISTERS AND I played for hours under a chinaberry tree in the backyard. Our aunts gave us their old makeup jars, perfume bottles, powder boxes and pocketbooks to play with. To us, they were beautiful treasures!

These delightful castoffs included Pond's and Lady Esther cold cream jars, Avon containers of all kinds and Evening in Paris perfume bottles. The pocketbooks always contained little black change purses and mirrors.

Sometimes we were fortunate enough to receive a glorious black hat—and when we were *really* lucky, the hats had womanly veils with velvet dots. How dressed up we little girls felt wearing those beauties!
—*Catherine Piper*
Elberton, Georgia

Township Picnic Marked End of Planting Season

THE HIGHLIGHT of our summer was the township picnic, held early each July. It was held to celebrate the fact that the crops were all planted and growing. It was as good as a legal holiday in our farming community in Franklin County, Iowa, and all work came to a halt except for emergencies.

People started arriving at 9 a.m. by car, on horseback and on foot, carrying baskets filled with fried chicken, pies, cookies, pickles, bread and salads. Everything was delicious, and to this day I know of no other place where food was consumed as fast as it was at the Morgan Township picnic!

But my favorite events were the foot and sack races. The top three winners in each event received certificates worth up to 15¢ at the concession stand, and the runners-up received a stick of Juicy Fruit gum.

I was fleet of foot and won more than my share of the events, providing me with enough pop, candy and gum to last all day!
—*Robert Schwieger*
Fort Dodge, Iowa

Scary Halloween Prank Was a Blazing Success!

MY PARENTS always went all-out whenever my siblings or I had a party. Even my friends wanted to have their parties at our house, because they knew my folks would gladly welcome them. Mom would make great refreshments, and Dad would join in our games.

One Halloween, we were playing outdoors with the yard lights on, and Dad decided to play "ghost" and scare us a little. He covered himself with a sheet and was crawling up behind us when a pocketful of kitchen matches ignited in his pants.

He jumped up, whooping, hollering and dancing around...and he did scare us good. But the reason he did such a good job was because his pants were on fire!
—*Dlores DeWitt*
Colorado Springs, Colorado

Tom Swift Stories Launched Lifelong Love of Reading

THE WINTERS just before the beginning of World War I are still fresh in my memory.

In the evening, after the supper dishes were cleared away, we'd all gather around the kitchen stove. A coal oil lamp would be lit, with a reflector placed next to it to shed more light.

After doing our homework, we'd pop corn, make candy, play a game called "find the thimble" or listen to Dad read to us.

He read us *Uncle Tom's Cabin*, *Robinson Crusoe* and many others, but our favorites were the Tom Swift series about the adventures of a boy inventor.

Sometimes Dad would close the book at a crucial time or an interesting place, so we had to wait until the next session to learn how the story came out! We could hardly wait until the next time he opened the book.

I'm an avid reader today, and I feel I can thank my dad for that.
—*Lloyd Beckett*
West Jefferson, Ohio

SWIFT STORIES stirred young imaginations in the early 1900s. Edward Stratemeyer, who wrote the books under the pen name of Victor Appleton, penned over 400 books for young readers, including Rover Boys, Hardy Boys and Nancy Drew mysteries.

'Kamp Kar' Took Family of 10 Across the U.S.

By Charles Wagoner
Redding, California

BEFORE there were freeways, motels, fast-food restaurants and Winnebagos, there were people who liked to travel the United States. One of them was my father. A general science teacher and father of eight, Dad loved visiting our nation's beautiful, historic places.

To accommodate our large family, he turned an REO Speedwagon truck into something he called a "Kamp Kar". The children rode in a compartment behind the front seats—no padded, reclining or revolving seats here!

Over the rear-wheel housing was a built-in bed. Under the bed was a water storage tank and a luggage compartment that held our 10-by-10 umbrella tent, air mattresses, blanket rolls, gas stove, collapsible table and camp stools.

In June of 1927, after the whole family had helped take the city and school census in our town of Hastings, Nebras-

KROSS-KOUNTRY KAMPING. Charles Wagoner (at far left), along with his parents and seven siblings, saw many spectacular sights as they toured the country in the variety of "Kamp Kars" that his father designed and built.

ka, we loaded the Kamp Kar and left for points east. How far east depended on how long our census-taking money lasted, how that REO held up and how well we kids cooperated!

The roads were mostly gravel and Dad drove between 30 and 35 mph, so a good day's travel was 150 to 200 miles. Toward evening, we'd start looking for a place to camp. We might pull off at a grassy spot near the road, along a stream if possible or in a free campground with privies.

The older children would put up the tent and table and start the camp stove. While Mom made supper, all of us kids blew up the air mattresses.

One of us might be dispatched to a farmhouse to see if we could buy fresh milk. If not, we'd have diluted canned milk with our oatmeal in the morning.

After supper, we might sing, talk about what we'd seen during the day or listen to Dad's stories. When we turned in, Mom and Dad slept in the Kamp Kar with the youngest children, and the rest

> *"It was really something to travel through two or three states in a day!"*

of us slept in the tent. In bad rainstorms, we all jammed into the Kar.

The next morning, we packed everything away while Mom made breakfast, and usually got on the road by 8 a.m.

On this trip, we visited the St. Louis Zoo and historical sites in Kentucky, Tennessee, West Virginia and Virginia. We went to the Smithsonian, the Capitol and several monuments in Washington, D.C. and rode a boat around the Statue of Liberty in New York City.

In Maine, three of us spent a day fishing on a sailing sloop. We loved New England and thought it was really something to be able to travel through two or three states in 1 day!

In Canada, we took dips in Lakes Ontario and Erie and rode a cable car across the chasm below Niagara Falls. We headed home via Michigan, Illinois and Iowa, then returned to Nebraska on a small Missouri River ferry.

Though I was only 13 on that trip, I remember it vividly, as I do the many trips we took over the years in a variety of Kamp Kars built by Dad.

The summer trips he gave us were not only fun, they supplemented our education. I'll never forget the great times we had in Dad's Kamp Kars.

Car Race Game Still a Treasured Possession

IN THE LATE 1940s and early '50s, my parents sometimes let me stay overnight with my grandparents. My grandmother had the love and patience to spend endless hours

NEVER TIRED OF GAME. H. Lee Munson still holds dear his father's Auto Race board game that he played each time he visited his grandmother.

teaching and playing games with us.

Some games, like Scrabble, helped us with our spelling and increased our vocabulary. Others were played just for the fun of it. The one I liked best, originally bought for my father and his brother, was a board game pitting six race cars against each other.

The board has a horseshoe-shaped track with six lanes. The cars are Indy-style racers typical of the late teens and early '20s, with tall radiators, small running boards and long, high hoods.

A Buick, Ford, Paige, Maxwell, Dodge and Saxon race each other to the finish, trying to avoid accidents and blowouts.

I've spent my life working on cars, and today I count that game from my grandmother among my most treasured possessions.

—*H. Lee Munson*
Greenlawn, New York

Family Camped In a Canoe!

By Hortense Ralph
West Lafayette, Indiana

WHEN WE WENT CAMPING in the teens, our vehicle was a canvas canoe! My father was the captain of the "ship", and my grandmother, aunt and I made up the crew. We set off down the Tippecanoe River from Monticello, Indiana.

When we made camp, we laid a piece of canvas on the ground, then tipped the craft on its side on the canvas. One end of the canvas was pulled up and tied to two trees to make a "tent" over our heads. The remaining canvas on the ground gave us a dry spot to make our beds. We kept cooking equip-

CAMPING PIONEERS. Hortense Ralph (center) relaxes in "camp" with her aunt and grandmother during a canoe trip down the Tippecanoe River from Monticello, Indiana. The canoe behind them anchored a piece of canvas, which provided shelter and a ground covering.

ment and other valuable gear in the upturned canoe.

On one trip, our canoe scraped a sharp rock, slitting its canvas skin. We

made camp as soon as possible. After the canvas dried, my father poured melted butter on the slit. It held together long enough to carry us back home!

Trips to Drive-In Made Friday Nights Fun

ONE EVENING not too long ago, my husband and I were driving home after seeing our newest grandchild. Suddenly Paul said, "Hey, look at that old place! It's sure seen better days, hasn't it?"

I looked up just in time to see the remains of what once must have been a thriving drive-in theater. I visualized how it probably looked in the early 1950s, when Paul and I took our three children to the drive-in every Friday night.

We were a young working family and never had any money for luxuries. So when we received season passes to the drive-in theater, it seemed like a bonanza!

Off to the Show!

The films varied each week, but our routine never did. Paul came home from work a little early, and our three excited children were waiting for him at the door.

We'd have a quick easy supper of "Pineapple Spam", then Paul and our 6-year-old, Suzanne, would take over the kitchen for some serious snack preparation. The snacks they made were always the same—huge bags of popcorn and jugs of lemonade.

Meanwhile, I hurried toddlers David and Ginger through their baths and in-

By Elizabeth Hoch
Lilliwaup, Washington

to their pajamas. Finally, we were off!

It was still light out when we left, so we drove through the Oregon hills, admiring the neatly lined farms and orchards and singing the kids' favorite

---

"A crowing rooster signaled the start of the Pathe Newsreel..."

---

songs like *Row, Row, Row Your Boat* and *She'll Be Coming Round the Mountain.*

Gradually, the houses began to light up, the Klikitat Mountains turned a deeper shade of purple and we strained to see the evening star so we could make a wish.

Then we turned the car onto the noisy gravel lot of the theater, where the huge screen blinked its welcome against a darkening sky.

We hurried to secure our favorite spot, close to the rest room but far from the concession stand, with its bright lights and tantalizing temptations. Paul cleaned the windshield and adjusted the window speaker. We were ready!

At last, the speakers crackled, black letters and flashing symbols scrolled across the screen and a muffled cheer rose from the waiting audience in cars around the lot.

First came the familiar crowing rooster and the slightly scratchy music that signaled the beginning of the Pathe Newsreel. The kids always hated this part of the evening, but Paul and I thought it was a miracle to witness events from a world away, and only a few weeks ago!

The Looney Tunes were next, followed by an educational short and finally the feature film.

Siblings Snoozed

In the backseat, David and Ginger clutched their favorite blankets and toys as they dozed off. Suzanne sat between us in the front seat, proud to be with the grown-ups.

As the film progressed, Paul would reach behind her for my hand, and we'd sit in silent communication, cherishing the moment.

Now, 40 years later, no one in the family seems to remember what movies we saw, but it doesn't matter. What we remember most is the warm togetherness...in a magic place we could share with our children on warm summer evenings.

Chapter Five

Cherished Photos

Cherished Photos

BABY MADE THREE when the Dezso family sat for this portrait in Nelsonville, Ohio in 1912. Proud parents Michael and Mary got dressed in their Sunday best to show off baby Ella Jane, who is now Ella Jane Markhoff of Canal Winchester, Ohio... and who sent in this touching family photo.

When I was asked to furnish a photo of our family for this book, I suspected there might be a problem. Sure enough, there was. Among the thousands of prints and slides I have stored away, there's only one that shows Mom, Dad, sister Mary and me together.

Pondering this strange state of affairs, I came to realize that our family just wasn't very big on taking pictures. Our only camera was an ancient Kodak box camera that looked like a black shoe box with a lens on one end. For all its simplicity, it took decent enough pictures. But rarely was it loaded with film.

I guess the big reason we didn't take many family pictures is because get-togethers with Mom's or Dad's relatives were rather common occurrences. Everyone lived nearby and used any excuse—holidays, birthdays, anniversaries or whatever—to convene.

Each side of the family got together to gossip and eat. Mostly eat. The two tribes—the Strocks and Stevenses—didn't really intermingle. Mom's relatives were city folks and Dad's kin were farmers. City mice and country mice didn't seem to have much in common.

Reunions Are Rare

Nowadays it's not only a special event, it's practically a miracle to have all the brothers, sisters, nieces and nephews, grandparents and even great-grandparents together at one time. So naturally there's lots of picture-taking when they do all show up.

Not that it's easy, though. There are several things you can count on when you try to set up a family picture.

Uncle Walter and Uncle John will try to beg off because they're in the middle of a hot horseshoe game or don't want to tear themselves away from the football game on television.

The prettiest lady on hand will *always* say, "Oh, dear, you don't want me in the picture. I'll break the camera!"

The shortest people will insist on being in the back row, pleading that they aren't properly dressed or put on too much weight over the holidays.

Small boys will cross their eyes and stick out their tongues at the precise moment you snap the picture.

If there are 12 people in the picture, one will have his or her eyes closed and two will be looking at a bird flying overhead.

Someone will appear to have a telephone pole growing out of their head.

Back in the days before cameras were more common, most family pictures were taken by professional photographers. A decent exposure took a second or more, so you had to sit unblinking while the photographer counted "One…two…three". As a result, everyone in the picture appeared to have been stuffed by a taxidermist and put on display.

Family photos are precious records and irreplaceable history. Hearing about Great-Grampa Samuel is one thing. But *seeing* him brings the man to life.

Aunt Grace discovered a family photo taken when Mom was about 10 and sent me a copy. There are tiny Gramma and stern Grampa Stevens in their mid-30s, surrounded by their brood.

Suddenly I discovered an amazing thing. Mom at age 10 looked *exactly* like my granddaughter Dana at the same age. Put their pictures side by side and you've got identical twins. Yet the shots were taken 70 years apart!

Those two photos are a bridge across the generations that words could never provide. There's a lot more of that same kind of pictorial history on the pages that follow, shared by the readers of *Reminisce*. —*Clancy Strock*

1. That's Funny, Sis!

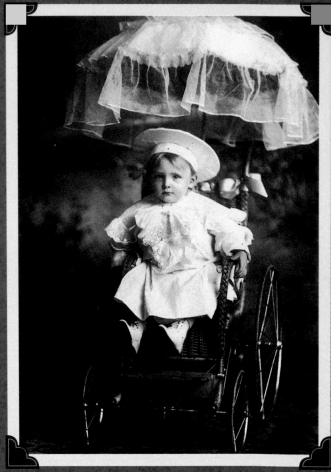

2. Precious Perambulator

1. *DRESSED-UP DUO.*
Brothers Stanley and Einar Bakke seemed not to mind wearing the rumpled raiments in which their four older sisters dressed them. Mrs. Einar Bakke of Kensington, Minnesota says the photo still makes her and her husband smile.

2. *THIS TOT* is ready to roll, with four wheels below and parasol on top. All he needs is someone to push! Grace Walter of Ingleside, Illinois sent this turn-of-the-century photo of Richard Meyer, an early-day acquaintance of her mother's.

3. *CYCLIN' SISTERS* Lillian Schwartz (at the helm) and Bertha Schaffner appeared eager to hit the open road in 1917 while Bertha's amused son, Melvin, looks on. This photo was taken behind the Schaffner home in Breese, Illinois. Melvin's daughter, Dorries Schaffner of Lyons, Colorado, shared the photo.

3. Rev 'Er Up, Ma!

4. *LITTLE SHAVER* David Johnson got his first real haircut at "Walt's Barbershop", recalls sister Nancy Krampert of Bayville, New Jersey. "He cried buckets," she says.

5. *BLOND KIDDIES* sat so nicely for Mom and Dad when their photo was taken in 1918. Aili Leppanen of Seal Beach, California is sitting on Dad's knee.

6. *A LITTLE LOCOMOTION* was all Alvin Lee was seeking in 1921. Alvin's brother C.C. of Teaneck, New Jersey recalls that he climbed a "pufferbolly" alongside the train his brother posed on.

7. *MAY BASKETS* were on the minds of her family members when they climbed this hawthorn in 1906, says Joyce Hayen of Chillicothe, Missouri.

5. Portrait of Togetherness

4. Real Clip Joint

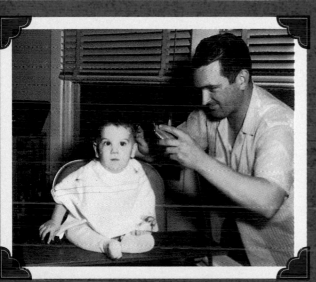

6. All Aboard!

7. Family Tree

8. Hello, Dollies!

9. Four of a Kind

8. *GRACIOUS GUESTS* of sisters Alice and Helen Kolden were just "dolls" about it all and never said a bad thing about the service at this tea party in 1909. Alice Stolee of Mesa, Arizona says the festive occasion was in Blackduck, Minnesota, but does not report who poured.

9. *THE FOUR SISTERS* of Elsie Sumerlin of Fort Worth, Texas posed in outfits made by their mother for this 1903 photo. Being 13 years younger and the baby of the family, Elsie wasn't around to have her photo taken this time.

10. *THREE FRIENDS,* one suitcase and a Model T were enough to make for adventure on a Sunday afternoon, says Elizabeth Leonardo of Flushing, New York. Her dad was taking the backseat on this trip, as the boys showed off the new car. The photo was taken just before her dad was drafted in 1917.

10. Three in a "T"

11. It's a Little Chilly!

12. Buckeye Backyard

11. *A THICK SWEATER,* bib overalls and hat are nice, but they can't help cold hands. Edwin Sloane, 3, posed for this photo in 1917, says son Mike of Greendale, Wisconsin.

12. *TRAVELING PHOTOGRAPHER* took picture in Chilo, Ohio in 1884 that included the great-grandmother (on the left) of Madge Mathews, Banning, California.

13. *THAT'S KNOT FAIR!* That rope's under the high chair because fidgety Uncle Adam didn't want to sit still for the photographer, says Doreen Tannehill of Jackson, Mississippi. He's tied to the chair with it!

14. *FASHIONABLE FROCKS* and high-topped shoes, both buttoned and laced, were worn by these ladies on photo day in the early 1920s. The picture was shared by Helen Wedeking of Clarksville, Iowa.

13. All Tied Up

14. Photo Fashions

15. Premiere Portrait

16. Now Steer Straight!

15. *LOVE, PRIDE* and strength of faith are what Marcia Johnson, Bothell, Washington, sees when she looks at first family photo of her mother and grandparents from 1915.

16. *START 'EM YOUNG* was Russell Engeldahl's philosophy, as he put his son Bob, 1, in the driver's seat in 1945. Bob's wife, Gail of Slinger, Wisconsin, shared the photo.

17. *BANDING TOGETHER.* The Brunkow family of Onaga, Kansas supplied music at the county fair in 1911. Della Jones of Palos Hills, Illinois sent the snapshot, which includes her mother, Goldie, on the left in the front row.

18. *JUST AN EXPRESSION.* Harry Mann (on left) looks reluctant to smile. His cousin Clarence Rennels isn't doing much better! Clarence, who lives in Brentwood, California, shared this photo.

17. Family at Play

18. Do We Hafta Smile?

19. Love That Hat!

20. Motoring Memories

19. *FASHION PLATES* Noble Gunning and his Aunt Alice posed for a photo in about 1918, says Noble's son, Lyle Gunning of Hudson, Ohio.

20. *RUNNING BOARDS* were good places to stand for little guys, as Ed Kappmeyer found out in 1914. Ed, who now lives in Oelwein, Iowa, sent this family outing photo.

21. *SUNNY SMILES* and spring flowers brightened the day in 1915 for Leon Steffens and his sisters Estelle and Marguerite, says Leon's daughter, Gail Engeldahl of Slinger, Wisconsin.

22. *PIONEER DAYS* were long gone by 1936, but not in Guymon, Oklahoma. That's where Neeta Musgrove and her parents dressed up for a Pioneer Day celebration. Today Neeta lives in Austin, Texas.

21. Smiling Siblings

22. Posed as Pioneers

23. Luck o' the Irish

24. Lesson in Sharing

25. My Only Sunshine

26. Out of a Rut

28. Twin Travelers

27. Apple Polisher

29. Scouting Outing

26. AFTER A PARADE in 1907, J. Earl Schoenberger of Shelton, Washington recalls his dad's car getting stuck in a streetcar track. Passersby lifted it out by hand!

27. AN APPLE A DAY, or at least on this day in 1912, was being held by Ruth Temming of Holly, Michigan. Eva All (right) was baby-sitting Holly and her siblings.

28. WICKER BUGGY for two was the talk of the town back in 1925, says Barbara Rinehart of West Hills, California. Barbara and her twin sister rode in woven splendor after Dad purchased this buggy.

29. GOOD DEEDS ABOUND when the Emerson family's around! From left, Jim, David, Dan, Lois and Doug were all in scouting back in 1946. Doug, of Bend, Oregon, sent in the photo.

30. One Goat Power

30. *DUAL HORNS* were a feature of the "Bakersfield Stage" that was ready to pull out with two passengers in 1928. Chuck Coleman of Camino, California sent the photo of himself at age 2 with 4-year-old sister Patricia.

31. *HIS BROTHER* was the firstborn in the family, so he got his photo taken with Mother in 1910, explains Paul Sogn of Medford, Oregon.

32. *THE FAMILY* of Adis Romer of Chico, California was about to take a trip in their "Silver Streak". That's Adis wearing the snappy cap standing behind his sister.

33. *STEAM TRACTORS* were big in the 1930s, as photo sent in by Sherrill Carroll of Big Spring, Texas attests.

31. Firstborn

32. Are We There Yet?

33. What's the Big Wheel?

34. Early Convertible

35. Biplane Brothers

36. Laces, Belts and Bows

34. *MODEL T's* were often subject to remodeling at the hands of young men. Jim Shelley of Rockville Centre, New York is next to his brother Will, who was behind the wheel in 1931.

35. *HIGH FLYERS* Eugene Walsdorf (left) and his brother, Jerry, were hoping for a ride over Wisconsin Dells, where their dad took this shot in 1929. Eugene, who sent the picture, now resides in Encinitas, California.

36. *ALL SPRUCED UP* and pretty as a picture were James and Johannah Clausing in 1914. Janet Wielhouwer of Grand Rapids, Michigan sent shot of her dad and aunt.

37. *AT THE WHEEL* in 1938 was her grandmother, Mary Jane Munn, says Iva Smith of Texarkana, Texas.

37. Spinning in the Grass

38. Hold on, There!

39. Brooklyn Beauties

38. *HER COUSIN,* Ivan McNeil, kept running away from the photographer in 1912, recalls Ruth Temming of Holly, Michigan. Ruth finally took matters into her own hands.

39. *FLAG DAY* 1945 was reason enough for Patricia Wagner's family to get dolled up. Patricia, now of New York City, peeked out of the carriage on the right.

40. *SHOCKING STOCKINGS* were the pride and joy of Elizabeth Simonton back in 1925. Betty, as she was known then, is from Seminole, Florida.

41. *TWIN SISTERS* of the Miller family were a handful for the rest. Elva Miller of Belvidere, Tennessee sent the photograph of her children taken in 1958.

40. Bee's Knees

41. Lucky Seven

42. Grandma's Girl

43. Two Towheads

44. Contact, Sport

45. That's a Mouthful

42. *FAMILY POSE* in 1896 included Mary Dick's grandmother, the little girl in front. Mary, of Canoga Park, California, says that today she looks just like her grandmother.

43. *BIG BROTHER* Albert McGraw smiles with pride alongside his little brother, Alfred Jr., in the 1926 photo Albert sent from his home in Anderson, Alabama.

44. *FLY-BOY* Richard Seres and sister Viola, the flight attendant, struck pre-flight pose for a traveling photographer in the late '20s. Richard now lives in Yreka, California.

45. *A LICKIN' GOOD TIME* was had by Howard Rusthoi, as sister Vi watched him clean up the icing after Mom baked a cake. Howard now lives in Alameda, California.

46. Ragtime Memories

47. Young Love

48. Lean on Me

49. Automaker's Namesakes

46. *HOT TIMES* were had at Virginia Gardens in Chester, West Virginia when James DeMar Miller played piano with his band. James' son Richard, Vero Beach, Florida, provided the 1926 photo.

47. *STAIR-STEP ROMANCE* was blossoming in 1925 when Bob Lichty cuddled with Rosemary Houser. Bob sent the photo from Vacaville, California, but reports he lost track of Rose.

48. *GREAT-GRANDPA* John Chatterley had a hold on Max (left) and Garth Heap on Fourth of July 1918. Suzanne Harris, Pinesdale, Montana, shared shot.

49. *THE GASS TWINS,* Henry and Ford, were held by their mom and sister for this 1916 picture. Henry now lives in McPherson, Kansas.

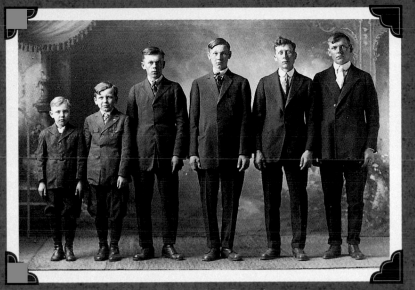

50. Step Up, Brother

51. Lacy Ladies

50. *BIGGER AND BIGGER* grew the Wedeking boys. Helen Wedeking of Clarksville, Iowa provided the picture taken in 1924. Her husband is the little guy on the left.

51. *THREE SISTERS,* Anna, Eve and Teresa Potts, posed in their finest for photo sent by Rosena Burkart of Cincinnati, Ohio.

52. *MILK WAGONS* drove themselves with horses like "Molly" in the traces. Irene Mieras of Rochester, Minnesota shared this 1924 photo of her milkman-dad, Harry Cowles.

53. *WORLD WAR I* veteran Lloyd Lane could rest in Germany in May 1918—the war was over. Lloyd's picture was shared by his daughter, Carolynne Wulf of Springville, New York.

53. At Ease

52. Never a Quart Low

54. Hart-Warming

55. Pickin' and Grinnin'

54. *THE HART FAMILY* lined up in 1928, with parents John and Nancy at the head of the group. Tot on the end is Dorothy Hart Lama, Lindsay, California, who sent the photo.

55. *STRUM SOME!* The Smith Entertainers were all the rage during the Depression in Medina, Ohio. Lillian Smith Young, who still lives there, shared the family photo.

56. *BONNETS BALANCED BEAUTIFULLY* on a sunny day, Mary McCarthy of Lexington, Massachusetts and her two younger sisters posed in 1915.

57. *TOUR CAR DRIVER* Charles West guided visitors through the Garden of the Gods in Colorado, says granddaughter Pat Owsley of McCall, Idaho.

56. Bundled-Up Babies

57. Don't Back Up!

Chapter Six

Mother's Love Was Special

Mother's Love Was Special

When the television cameras come in close on an athlete who is resting on the bench after making a great play, you know what he's going to yell: "Hi, Mom!" Not "Hi, Dad" or "Hi, Uncle Harold". In his moment of triumph, he knows who to salute—it's Mom!

In recent decades it's been fashionable in some circles to devalue the importance of being a Mom. What counts, some say, is for a woman to go out there in the business world and duke it out with the men to demonstrate her intelligence and worth.

The truth is that it takes a lot more to be a successful Mom than it does to become president of a major bank or a Fortune 500 corporation.

And if you asked most successful businesspeople how they achieved so much, they'd instantly say it's because of...their Mom.

What Is a Mother?

Never mind whether Mom was a gourmet cook or could whip up a ball gown from the old curtains. Never mind if she sometimes forgot to dust or left piles of unfolded clothes on the dining room table for days. None of those things are what being a Mom is all about. But this is:

Mom is the person who believes in you when no one else in the world does.

Mom is the one who convinces you that you can slay dragons and climb tall mountains, when down inside you're sure you can't.

Mom is the one who binds up your bumps and scuffs, especially the ones inside where no one else can see the hurt.

My mom would never let me settle for being second best at *anything*. It wasn't a matter of winning. She just believed it was sinful not to use *all* the talent and abilities that God had given you. Anything less than your best was cheating yourself, cheating your friends and family and cheating God.

"You're better than that," she'd scold.

Wrong Was Never Right

She also made clear the distinctions between right and wrong. And wrong was always wrong, no matter how I tried to rationalize it. No child of hers was going to grow up a liar, a cheat or somebody who took shortcuts that perhaps were *legal,* but sure weren't *right.*

The best thing she did, though, was to let me go when it was time to leave the nest. It grieved her, I know. But from the time I left home she never volunteered advice, told me how to raise my children nor sniped at my spouse.

I guess she figured she'd done the best she could, and I'd find my way with the moral compass she had provided. Not that I always lived up to her standards, but I'd like to think she was never ashamed of me.

Mom never made chairman of the board of General Motors. She had a bigger, more important job to do. No one could have done it better.

Now turn the page and read about some other great Moms who touched lives and, in the end, made the world a better place.

—*Clancy Strock*

For Us, Home Was Where Mother Was

By Edith Miller, Bakersfield, California

WHEN I WAS SMALL, Mama was always full of song, despite the fearful challenges she faced. I'm so glad to have memories of a mother who took the time to rock me to sleep and sing me lullabies in her clear, sweet voice.

During the Depression, we usually lived out in the country, wherever we could find an old place that was run-down and deserted so we didn't have to pay rent. I don't recall us ever living in a place with running water. But Mama made each

---

"Mama kept her fears to herself..."

---

place a home, and it never disturbed us that we moved so often. Home was where Mama was.

We couldn't afford to buy books, but she made up stories for us and created picture books with old pieces of oilcloth and photographs cut from Sears catalogs.

She invented games to take our minds off the cold nights and the shortage of food. When the dinner dishes were cleared away, she played tag or hide-and-seek with us

among the great cedars and evergreens in the long Montana twilight.

In the evening, Mama taught us the multiplication tables as we sat around the coal oil lamp. Then she'd read us books and magazines our older sister

WASHDAY. Edith Miller's mother scrubs her family's laundry in a washtub outdoors. "As a child, I thought Mama was exceptional," says Edith. "In my memories, I still think so."

brought home from the library. By the time I started first grade, I knew my "times tables" and could read.

Mama used cast-offs to make all our clothes, as well as our dolls' clothes, beds and furniture. She turned apple and orange crates into small chairs and made most of our household furniture as well.

Whatever fears Mama suffered, she kept to herself. I remember waking and seeing her standing at the window in the dark. "Mama," I'd ask, "can't you sleep?" Though sometimes she'd turn to me with tears glistening on her cheeks, her reply was always reassuring. "I was just looking at the stars," she'd say. "Aren't they pretty?"

She never let on, by word or deed, that she might be worried or scared. It was only after I grew up that I had any concept of the worries she endured, and the heroism she displayed.

Mama is gone now, but I hope that somewhere she is skipping around great cedars and teaching little angels to play hide-and-seek. I'd like to think of her holding a small one in her arms, singing the same lullabies she sang to me.

Shrewd Mom Knew the Value of an Education

THE QUALITY I remember most about Mother is the value she placed on education. She taught us to respect our teachers, made sure our homework was done and never let us stay home from school for any frivolous reason—we had to be sick.

Mother came from a family of Irish immigrants, and she knew education would help us get ahead.

When I was a high school sophomore, I started to slack off and received a "D" in Spanish. Mother made me put on some old clothes, then took me to an employment agency and registered me to do housework. If I didn't appreciate the value of an education, she said, this was what I could do!

Of course, Mother never would have followed through on her threat, but it put the fear of God in me. My Spanish grades skyrocketed!

My brother remembers Mother best on a ladder, a paintbrush in her hand. Aside from painting and papering, she built a concrete walk, a stone wall and a grape arbor. She also was comfortable laying linoleum and doing electrical work and plumbing. Her handyman skills could have put many men to shame!

I'm terribly proud to have had a mother who knew what was truly important in life and who gave us all a happy home to remember.

—Doris Reynolds
Foxboro, Massachusetts

BRUSHING UP. Alice Conway's mother, Katherine Curley, thought nothing of painting the house herself. Alice, of Highwood, Illinois, shared this 1920s photo.

Mom Kept Us on the Right Track

By Paul Barber, Volcano, California

OUR sweet mother would tell my brothers and me, "If you work in the garden all morning, you can swim all afternoon."

That was a bargain to a 10-year-old like me, because the adventures we had at the ol' swimmin' hole far outweighed the discomfort of a hot summer morning in Mom's garden.

We swam at an abandoned limestone quarry outside of Huntington, Indiana, and we always skinny-dipped. This was during the Depression, and no one we knew even owned a swimming suit.

One day my brother, our friend Gerald and I were walking along the railroad tracks on the way to the quarry. When someone yelled, "Last one in is a rotten apple!", we all started racing.

I began undressing about a half mile from the quarry, and before long, I was completely naked and winning the race.

My bare feet flew over the rough rocks on the railroad right-of-way and I felt like a regular Jim Thorpe, until I passed some empty boxcars parked at a siding. Suddenly a hand shot out from between two cars and nabbed me!

It was the railroad detective! He'd been told to put an end to pesky kids swimming naked where passengers might see them. Wow, was I scared!

After retrieving my clothes, the detective told me he was taking me to jail. First, though, he took me home to face my mother.

After explaining that he'd caught me wearing nothing but a "beanie" on my head, he said to her, "If you give him a good whipping, I will let him go." Mom said, "All right, I'll do that."

When the detective left, Mom sat me down for questioning. I was preparing myself for a spanking when I noticed a twinkle in her eye. "So…all you had on was that little beanie?" she asked, before bursting into uncontrollable laughter.

Just then, Gerald and my brother walked in (they'd hid when I got caught).

Soon all of us were laughing so hard that we kids were rolling on the floor!

Mom really understood us. How I wish the kids of today could have a mother like her and enjoy life like we did back in those Depression days!

Minutes Dragged by When Mama Was Away

MY father died in 1930, leaving Mama with five children just as the Depression was starting. She had no way of making a living, so she took what was left of the insurance money and moved us to a farm.

Mama bought a sow, some chickens and seven milk cows to keep us going. We had no transportation, so a kind neighbor took our milk along with his when he went to the creamery in town. Mama sometimes went along to buy what we needed—or could afford.

Those days when Mama went to town passed slowly for us kids, because we knew Mama would bring us a treat. We did our chores and tried to stay busy. As the time neared for Mama to return, we'd watch eagerly for the truck to turn into the driveway.

When we spotted it, we'd shout, "Mama's home!" Whatever else she bought, she always had a sack of candy for us.

That was long ago, but I can still hear the shouts of "Mama's home!" and taste that sweet candy.

—*Arlene Shelton*
Shawnee, Oklahoma

Mother's Songs Lifted a Neighborhood's Spirits

MY FONDEST MEMORY of growing up in Queens, New York is of my mother's singing. Heaven knows what there was to sing about during those Depression days, but she sang all the time. I'm sure there were occasions when she sang through her tears.

Her voice was a lot like Ethel Merman's, so strong and clear as she belted out songs like *Melancholy Baby* and *I Cried for You*. Despite the bread lines and soup kitchens, there was Mother singing out loud for all the world to hear.

She'd sing while cleaning, cooking and even as she stirred the huge pot of Argo starch that kept my homemade cotton school dresses looking crisp and neat. Sometimes when she stopped singing, someone in the next flat would call out, "Sing some more!"

Looking back, I admire my mother so much. During those seemingly hopeless years, she lifted the spirits of so many discouraged people with her lovely voice.

—*Rhoda-Katie Hannan, Kings Park, New York*

Her Vow Fed the Hungry, One Person at a Time

By Petula Marshall
Florence, South Carolina

THE DAY the banks closed, Papa had been to town and come home late. When we sat down to eat, he was very quiet. His health had been bad, and we were sure he was just tired.

After dinner, Mama finally asked, "Lee, what's wrong?" Papa took out his billfold, laid 49¢ on the table and said, "This is all the money we have in the world. President Roosevelt closed the banks today."

Mama asked how long they'd be closed. "No one knows the answer to that," Papa replied. "Maybe forever."

Mama just sat there, dumbfounded. Then she said, "Well, Lee, we're not going to worry about this. Our Lord will see us through. We've been in tight spots before, and we'll be okay now.

"We're lots better off than most people," she added. "We own our farm. We have cows for milk, chickens for eggs and our hogs are growing fine. We have sugarcane, so we can make syrup and even sugar. And we have our gardens and fruit. So we just won't worry!"

That night, Mama made a vow to herself and God that as long as the Lord gave us food, she would not turn any hungry person away. Our house was near Highway 1, the main route from New York City to Miami, so we knew hungry, unemployed people were al-ready out there. We'd seen them walking that road for months.

Once we started feeding those travelers, more and more of them came, sometimes in crowds. One day we fed 19 people. Not a day passed that we didn't feed someone.

Sometimes we got low on food, but we never ran out. All our neighbors knew about Mama's vow, and just when we started to wonder where to turn for the next meal, they'd bring something—a bushel of potatoes, dried butter beans, a side of pork, some canned food.

Mama kept her vow, and we kept feeding those hungry strangers until they simply stopped coming. Perhaps the formation of the WPA, CCC and other work-relief programs had a hand in that.

My mother—what a woman! She died peacefully at age 94, leaving a legacy of living for others and planting seeds of salvation for the Lord.

Hobos Could Count on Her for a Helping Hand

DURING THE 1930s, hobos often knocked on our back door to ask for a bite to eat in exchange for repairing a lawn mower, sharpening a kitchen knife or fixing an umbrella. Mother always fed these poor souls and often helped them in other ways.

One hobo I recall was hungry, nearly blind, and he sold poems printed on cards he carried in a white cotton flour sack. Mother bought one of his poems for a dime, then fed him. When he finished eating, he asked if he could leave his bag in our yard while he went to town.

Before the old man was even out of the yard, Mother had begun sewing him a new bag of blue-and-white-striped ticking. She knew that material would be easier for him to see, and she added a shoulder strap to make the bag easier to carry.

When the old man returned, Mother gave him the bag, and he cried with joy when she helped him transfer his poems and belongings from his dirty old sack into the brand-new one.

She reminded us, as she often did, of the words of St. Francis: "It is in giving that we receive." We believed her. And we wondered when the old man would find his next meal, which Mother had hidden in his new bag, along with some coins for coffee.

—*Norma Hendrix, Ripley, Tennessee*

NURTURING NATURE. This woman reminds Petula Marshall and Norma Hendrix of their own mothers, who unselfishly shared their family's food with many homeless and hungry people.

Mother's Love Made Treats Even Sweeter

By Jo Huddleston, Auburn, Alabama

WHEN I WAS a fourth grader, I often stopped at Lou's Cafe on Main Street on my way home from school. Mother worked there part-time as a waitress to help our family make ends meet during World War II.

I can still picture Mother, her pretty face turned toward the wooden screen door, beaming as I walked inside with my best friend. The door would barely flap shut behind us before Mother came over to hug me. Then she'd seat us at one of her tables, knowing that would probably cost her a customer who would have left a tip.

Pencil poised above her order pad, she'd wait patiently as we lingered over the familiar ice cream flavors listed on a wooden board behind the lunch counter. I usually ordered one scoop of chocolate and one scoop of vanilla, with the vanilla on top.

As Mother placed the cones in our hands, she'd urge us to lick around the sides first so the huge dips she gave us wouldn't slide off.

When she could, Mother took her afternoon break with us, letting us talk about whatever we pleased, smiling at me and reaching across the Formica-topped table to pat my hand.

A mother now myself, I can better understand her love—the nurturing I welcomed as a child, the sacrifice that paid for my ice cream cones with precious tip money, the unselfishness that kept her on her feet, waiting tables, so I could have a special treat once in a while—like my blue raindrop costume for the school play.

I live a great distance from Mother now, and she can't reach across the miles to pat my hand. But my childhood memories serve me well. They confirm her love for me…even though she can no longer give it in ice cream cones.

MOM COULD DO ANYTHING! Jo Huddleston's mother worked hard as a waitress in the early '40s. Somehow she found time to make Jo this dress so she could be a raindrop in the school play.

Mom Left This Bully with Egg on His Face!

EVERY AFTERNOON, my mother went to the grocery store to buy the makings for that evening's meal. All the years I was growing up, her routine was the same: change stockings, put on sturdy walking shoes and a clean house-dress, pull her hair into fluffy buns over her ears and walk to the store.

But as my sisters and I got older, she occasionally let us fetch some small item. One cold day in 1936, when I was 10, she needed half a dozen eggs and asked me to go.

Coal Was a Prize

The kid next door, a lumbering bully who always teased me, was sledding in front of his house as I started out. But he was in a good mood and offered to accompany me and look for coal on the way. The Depression was in full swing and everyone had coal furnaces, so if you found a lump of fuel that had fallen from a delivery truck, you took them home.

We walked to the store and I bought the eggs and carried them out in a paper sack. We started for home, laughing as we collected bits of coal.

Then we both saw it—a chunk of coal so wondrous it made our eyes bug out. I grabbed it first, but the bully pushed me hard, and the lump fell and landed at his feet. He snatched it up and shoved it into his pocket.

Then he sat down and took it out to examine it more closely, and that's when all reason left me. I may have been smaller, but I was feisty, and that chunk of coal was not a treasure to be given up lightly. I lifted the bag of eggs high and smashed it over his head!

Music to Her Ears

As egg whites, yolks and shells streamed down his face, he started to cry, then yelled, "I'm telling my mother on you. You're gonna get it, just you wait!" He grabbed the sled rope and headed for home, leaving me standing in the street, wondering what punishment would await me.

As I approached our house, I saw that the bully and his mother were already on our porch. I hid in the bushes and listened intently to their tale of my crime. Finally, as I crouched there in the cold, I heard my mother speak words that were like music to my half-frozen ears.

"Well," she said, "if that big lummox can't defend himself from a little thing like her, then he deserves egg on his face." With that, she quietly closed the door. (Mother was always a lady!)

Later, she did chide me just a bit for wasting those eggs, but not for the deed itself. She understood my dignity was being challenged, and that I had a principle to defend! —*Dorothy Meilenner, Milwaukee, Wisconsin*

Mother Made Our World Wonderful

By Phyllis Gailis, Hemet, California

THE FIVE OF US began our trek through life in a three-room house that was hardly bigger than a bread box— or so it seemed at times. The Depression was upon us, and we heard about it often. But we had a special person who guided us through troubled times.

Our mother started telling us about the world and all its charms when we were very young. While we sat on the porch in the dark night, she told us how the angels lit the stars and showed us the wonders of fireflies.

When a storm came out of nowhere, she'd walk all of us out to the porch and tell us never to be afraid. If we woke from a frightening dream, she'd come into our room and comfort us. If we suffered some disappointment, she would soothe us. "No matter how bad things get," she'd say, "everything will turn out right."

Though we were poor, she always told us, "If anyone comes to your door hungry, you are never to turn them away. You share what you have." She did just that, many times.

She was not a scholar and couldn't help us with our schoolwork, but she was the wisest person I've ever known. As we grew, each of us knew we could never fail—because she told us we wouldn't.

Mom made our world wonderful.

Friends Were Always Welcome To Share Mom's Good Cooking

MOTHER AND ME. Mary Williams climbed onto the running board of the family's 1933 Plymouth to give her mother a hug.

I'M SO THANKFUL for my wonderful parents! They were always there for me no matter what, and they made my friends feel welcome, too. If it was mealtime, my friends were always invited to eat with us.

I can remember Mother pounding the daylights out of a piece of steak, then frying it in an old iron skillet. It was so good! What I'd give today to taste one of Mother's delicious dinners, especially her homemade beef and noodles, her creamy coleslaw and her tart flaky pies. She never followed a recipe for any of these things—she just knew how to do it.

Even though we didn't have a lot of money, I can't remember that I ever really wanted for much that I didn't have. We were a close family, and Mother let me know I was loved very much. To me, that is riches more valuable than money.

—*Mary Williams, Newark, Ohio*

Although she's been called home, she'll never be truly gone; she gave us simple pleasures we'll remember forever. When I need an extra hug, I can stand on the porch and feel her near.

Shopping Trips with Mom Had Sweet Payoff

By Nell Geissel, Seattle, Washington

EVERY AFTERNOON around 3 p.m., Mother would contemplate her supper menu. We were usually short "just a few things"—maybe a loaf of bread or some sugar. Then she'd say, "We need to go to the store."

First we'd stop at the bank for cash. I don't remember ever seeing my mother pay for something by check. When utility bills were due, she'd stop at the bank, then walk to the telephone, gas or electric company office to pay her debts with real money.

The bank was halfway between our town's two grocery stores and next to The Sweet Shop, where we often stopped for a treat. Mother always ordered a chocolate soda. My favorite was an olive-nut sandwich, made of chopped green olives and peanuts, held together with mayonnaise and spread on soft white bread. It was so good!

Then it was on to the store. No matter what was on our list, we always bought too much to carry home comfortably in our willow basket and canvas bag. Groaning under the weight of our provisions, we stopped often to rest our arms and visit with neighbors along the way.

Cart Made Trips Easier

As I grew older, Mother eagerly embraced a new invention—the metal shopping cart on wheels. I hated it. One of the worst mortifications of my teen years was walking beside Mother as she pushed that rattling cart!

Of course, I didn't *have* to go with her anymore—with a cart she could bring the groceries home by herself. But I didn't want to miss a trip to The Sweet Shop...or a chance to see the cute carryout boys. I was particularly taken with a redhead who worked at Kroger's. When he was working, I sometimes went to the store two or three times a day!

Mother noticed how much I seemed to like Kroger's and asked the manager if he had a job for me. He did, and I was ecstatic! For the first time, I had my own paycheck—and I got to see more of the cute redhead!

I'm not sure if things worked out as Mother had planned. That redhead and I were eventually married. Some 40 years later, I still enjoy shopping but don't have to worry about a cart. Thanks to Mom, I have my own carryout boy!

Whole Busload of Friends Didn't Faze Her Mom

By Debbie Wadley, Paoli, Oklahoma

MY FONDEST MEMORIES of growing up in rural Oklahoma are the overnight visits by school friends. There were six kids in our family and I don't think a week went by without one, or even all of us, having friends over.

Most of the time Mom knew when we were going to invite someone, but once in a while, we'd surprise her. For instance, one Friday afternoon the school bus pulled up in front of our house and it emptied out right there!

Each of us kids had invited two or three overnight guests, and we were in for a houseful! I'll never forget the look on Mom's face when we all piled off that bus. Even the bus driver started laughing when he saw her mouth drop open.

But dear old Mom pulled through. First, she had us go outside and do our chores while she figured out how and what she was going to feed us all.

We milked the cow, gathered eggs, fed the chickens, slopped the hogs and helped Grandfather round up sheep. Then we played a game of baseball—we even had enough people to make up two teams! We had a great time playing ball until it got dark.

Meanwhile, Mom was fixing up a good old-fashioned wiener roast. Our grandparents lived across the road, so my grandmother picked a watermelon and put it in a washtub with ice to keep cold.

Dad got a big bonfire going to roast the franks, and Mom made the works for all 18 of us kids—and Grandma and Grandpa, too! After eating and resting awhile, we dragged out the old box-springs and mattresses we stored in sheds to use in the summertime when it was too hot to sleep in the house.

We set these up in the yard and just slept under the stars. There were beds scattered all over the yard. Of course, we didn't get much sleep since we were all giggling, telling "scary" stories and pestering each other.

The next morning after we'd finished the chores, Mom made pancakes for the whole bunch. Around noon, parents started coming to pick up their kids and Mom even helped get some of them home.

After everyone was gone, she called us all together and threatened us within an inch of our lives if we ever pulled that stunt again!

We never did, of course, but we also never forgot the fun of that night. It was one of the best times I ever had growing up, and I'm sure many of those long-lost friends probably think about it from time to time.

I know their parents did, because, every once in a while, I'd run into one of them and they'd remind me of the night Mom took in a whole busload of unexpected guests.

HOT DOG! Once again Mom saved the day at the sleepover of Debbie Wadley and her five siblings by having a wiener roast like above.

She Refused to Let Salad Snafu Block First Day of Business

WHEN MY HUSBAND'S parents started a delicatessen in Brooklyn, New York, they worked almost all night to prepare for the next day's opening. To lure customers, they offered a free pound of potato salad with the purchase of a pound of frankfurters.

Mama Block made the best potato salad in the world, but by 2 a.m. she was rushed and tired. She had spent hours cooking, peeling and cutting potatoes, and when she reached for the oil to pour over them, she picked up floor wax instead!

You can imagine the scream that followed, and then the tears of anger and exhaustion. Then Mama dried her eyes and started on another huge batch of potatoes, going through the whole routine once more—with one exception. This time, she looked very carefully when it was time to add the oil! —*Helene Block, Mars, Pennsylvania*

DRESSED FOR WORK. Helene Block's mother-in-law wore a long apron to work with her husband in their delicatessen. The couple operated many delis over the years, but the opening of their store in Brooklyn was especially memorable!

Easter Finery Made Her Feel Like a Princess

I WAS INVITED to an Easter party when I was a child. I told Mama how much I wanted to go, but I didn't have a nice dress to wear. With eight children to feed during the Depression, there was never any money left for clothes.

Mama didn't say anything, but when I came home from school the next day, she had a surprise for me. She'd taken an oversized hand-me-down dress and turned it into the prettiest party frock I'd ever seen! She had even made me a pair of anklets to match. I felt like a princess!

Mama was a saint in my eyes; her love and talents knew no bounds. I thank God I was able to return some of that unconditional love by taking care of her in her last days. —*Betty Sagen Whitefish, Montana*

MAMA'S PRIDE AND JOY. Betty Sagen (second from left in the front row, with her brothers and sisters) remembers how her mother, Lulu May Hoffman, went to any lengths to make her children happy. When her mother grew older, Betty displayed her love by caring for the woman who cared for her.

"Lard Bucket Picnic" Thrilled Youngsters—and Young at Heart

A PICNIC was one of our favorite things, and Mother was always ready with some novel way to have one.

Remember the old lard pails with handles? One of the best picnics I can remember was when Mother packed individual lunches for all five kids in lard pails, then sent us up into the great old maple tree by the front door of our farmhouse.

Our perches provided shade and a breeze on that sweltering day, and the little buckets served as hanging baskets that could be suspended from a branch when we needed free hands for climbing. We've referred to that event ever since as "the lard bucket picnic".

Did I say five lunches? Make that six—because Mother climbed up to join us, proving she was just as much a kid as we were. I do seem to recall, though, that she perched in the lowest fork of that magnificent tree!

—*Alice McDonnell, Tucson, Arizona*

Children Were Jewels More Precious Than Diamonds

MAMA MET DADDY in church, where she'd been playing the organ since she was 13. Daddy thought she was beautiful, with her golden curls, bright blue eyes and fair skin, but she didn't think much of his looks—she said he grinned like a cat!

That all changed, of course, once she discovered how kind and loving he was. They were married in the same church, right after Sunday services, with the whole congregation attending.

As our family grew, Mama saw to it—with Daddy's help—that we never missed Sunday or midweek services. Our big, busy household included seven children and the aunt and uncle who'd raised Mama as a child. But Mama was never too tired to say "I love you", hear our prayers or sing a song. Her favorite was *Count Your Blessings*.

My mother never had a diamond, but

WELCOMING AROMA. Dlores DeWitt was welcomed home from school by the wonderful scent of her mother's fresh-baked bread.

she and Daddy used to say they had the best gems imaginable—seven children and our aunt and uncle ringed around the table, holding hands and asking a blessing on the food that Daddy raised and Mama prepared. —*Mary Eberhart Louisville, Kentucky*

Prize-Winning Cook Made Sure Children Never Felt Deprived

MOM'S FRESH-BAKED BREAD was the best in the whole wide world! We loved to come home from school to a house filled with that delicious aroma. My father-in-law later said he'd rather have a slice of her bread than a piece of cake anytime.

All Mom's cooking was good. When she entered her baked goods at the county fair, she always won first prize. Some of the ladies used to ask her when she was going to stop entering so the rest of them could win for a change!

Mom also made all our clothes, mostly from flour sacks or old clothes that she tore apart and "made over" so they looked brand-new, and in the latest style. She sewed, cooked and canned many long hours after all the rest of us were asleep.

Because of Mom's love and devotion, none of us ever felt we were deprived of anything. Mom may have known we were poor, but we never did.
—*Dlores DeWitt Colorado Springs, Colorado*

Talented Pianist Hosted 'Little USO'

By Patricia Collins, Bend, Oregon

MAMA had arthritis for as long as I can remember. She could do light house chores until she got tired, then she had to sit down. There she'd remain until some one came to help her up.

When I was small, we lived across the field from our grammar school, and my teacher would periodically let me dash home and help Mama out of her chair.

Despite this, I have no memory of hearing her complain. She loved company, always had a smile for everyone, and offered a broad shoulder to friends with burdens to bear.

Happiest at Piano

She also was blessed with a great talent for piano. Once, while playing at a friend's house, one of the guests was surprised to learn she didn't have a piano of her own. Within a week, a beautiful upright was delivered to our door!

Mama spent many contented hours at that piano. During World War II, she was happiest when the house was filled with young servicemen who sang and danced as she played. We entertained so many of these young men that our home in Merced, California became known as "The Little USO"!

She may have had to give up a lot during her life, but Mama filled the lives of all who knew her with happy memories. It's such a compliment when someone tells me, "You remind me of your mother."

CHRISTMAS CONCERT. Patricia Collins' mother plays a holiday tune on her piano on Christmas Day in 1948. She played often for servicemen who stopped at their home in Merced, California during World War II.

Her 'War Work' Enlarged Household by Six!

By Harriet Hodge, Glencoe, Illinois

IN THE SPRING of 1944, I returned to my mother's home in Kansas City, Missouri with my 2-year-old son. I'd been staying with my husband as the Navy transferred him throughout the States, but now he was being shipped overseas. Housing was in short supply because of the war.

When I got to Mother's home, I found my sister was already living there with her 2-year-old daughter. Her husband, a Navy doctor, had just been shipped out, too. And there was one more coincidence—each of us was expecting another child!

Mother was just magnificent through it all. She shepherded my sister and me to and from hospitals, waiting patiently while we had our babies. Within months of our arrival, she had four grandchildren under the age of 3 in the house!

Mother helped with the children and did the grocery shopping, taking charge of all seven food rationing books. She'd been allotted only enough heating oil for a single person, so she spent a whole day at the ration board to request and obtain enough oil to keep the babies warm.

After the war, whenever we reminisced about the bedlam our presence created in her house, Mother always replied, "I didn't mind. I considered that my 'war work' and I was glad to do it."

THE MORE THE MERRIER! Harriet Hodge's mother needed a contraption like this for four young grandchildren staying at her house!

Mother Made Naptime Special

WHEN I WAS a small child, my cradle was often a bright green rowboat tied to the dock near our summer cabin.

When it was time for my afternoon nap, Mom nestled me in a soft blanket she'd spread on the bottom of the boat, then sat beside me on the dock. As I watched the soft, white clouds slowly change shape overhead, she'd sing or tell stories and I drifted off to sleep, gently rocked by the water.

With the fresh sea air and the feel of the sun-warmed blanket, I often wished that little boat would sail away with just my mother and me!
—*Andrea Peterson Cerritos, California*

SUNNY SMILES. Mother always had a way of bringing a smile to a child's face—this Iowa mom and her happy little one provide proof.

Mom's Face in the Window Led to Warmth of Home

ONE OF MY FAVORITE memories of Mother is of the days I'd trudge home from my one-room school and see her peering out the kitchen window, looking for me. If she wasn't there, I worried that something bad had happened.

On those rare occasions when she and Dad went to town, the house would be cold—not only because the fire in the wood stove had gone out, but because the warmth of her presence was missing.

—*Phyllis Haynes*
Kalispell, Montana

Her Green Thumb Colored Papa's Vegetable Garden

NO DOUBT ABOUT IT, Mama had a green thumb. She loved plants of all kinds. Our house was full of them, and our yard was a profusion of shrubs and flowers. You never knew what would come up, or where.

Once she planted a climbing rose next to a holly bush. The two intertwined, so it looked as if the holly bush was blooming with roses. That unusual sight made the local paper.

Mama's favorite trick, though, was to wait until Papa planted his small vegetable garden behind the back porch. When he wasn't around, she'd stand on the steps and cast a mixture of flower seeds gathered from last year's blooms.

When the flowers came up, Papa knew perfectly well how they'd gotten there but would pretend to wonder how it had happened. Mama would just grin and innocently say she couldn't imagine. "Maybe the wind," she'd offer.

They played this little game year after year, watching Mama's colorful maverick flowers bloom so proudly among Papa's cabbage, carrots and beans.

—*Marjory Cunningham*
Torrance, California

Mother's Comfort Soothed Her Broken Heart

ONE OF THE strongest and earliest memories of my mother is of a night in 1931 when we went to the movies. I don't remember what the film was called, but it was about Eskimos and their sled dogs.

Two dogs were pulling a sled carrying two men, when suddenly they all disappeared into a hole in the ground. They howled all the way down. Small as I was, I realized they had died and began to cry—big, heartbroken sobs.

Mother finally had to take me home, and I cried the whole way. Those poor dogs. Those poor men!

ROSY GARDEN. This photo reminds Marjory Cunningham of her mother's green thumb and colorful spirit. Each year, her mother made certain that fragrant flowers grew among her husband's mundane vegetables!

When we got home, my mother held me on her lap, rocking back and forth, cuddling me to her breast. As she stroked my hair, she hummed softly and told me over and over that it was only a movie; it wasn't real. I finally fell asleep in her arms.

Mother took good care of me throughout my life, but that moment made a lasting imprint on my heart and my memory.

—*Millie Whittaker*
Metairie, Louisiana

Day Started Before Sunup For Busy Mother

MY MOTHER WORKED so hard for her family of 10.

She rose each day at 4 a.m., then started heating water on the coal stove for the day's cooking, baths and laundry.

Mother washed clothes on a washboard with a piece of lye soap and a bottle of bluing, then wrung everything out with a hand wringer. She ironed all the clothes with flatirons heated on the coal stove.

Picture all this happening on a hot summer day—the coal stove roaring away, no fans and no such thing as air-conditioning!

Mother sewed a lot, too—clothes, quilts, fancy pieces to sell. She made most of what we wore, using feed sacks, fabric linings from old cars and anything else she might come upon. We were as happy with what she made as if we'd gone shopping.

Mother stayed so busy all day every day that the poor tired soul would sometimes doze off right in the middle of something. After a minute or two, she'd wake up, go right on with whatever she was doing and never miss a lick.

Mother always took good care of us when we were sick. She was the only doctor we ever knew. I could write all day about my mother and never say enough good things about her.

—*Donald Boyers*
Warsaw, Kentucky

Mother's Sacrifice Filled Their Lives with Music

By Clarice Keiser, Tucson, Arizona

MOTHER WAS a pillar of strength in our lives, but only after we matured did we realize all she had done for us.

Mother was widowed at 36, in the middle of the Depression, with five children ages 1 to 8. She left our farmhouse and went to live near her parents in northern Minnesota.

Our new place had no electricity, no running water and no bathroom. The bedrooms were unfinished, and in winter we'd wake to see frost on every nail

---

"We'd gather around the piano, singing in four-part harmony..."

---

head in the rafters where a ceiling should have been. There were only two bedrooms; Mother and one of the girls slept in the living room on a cot.

The boys carried in wood to keep the stove and range going. One day my brother Dick, then 6, went out to the woodpile and tarried so long that Mother went out to check on him. She found him playing tunes on sticks he had arranged in the snow according to their tones!

Mother promptly sold her watches, rings and whatever else she could spare and bought a secondhand piano. There was no money for lessons, so she put a

A SONG IN HER HEART. Clarice Keiser's mother sacrificed greatly to fill her children's lives with the joy of music. This 1932 photo shows her with (from left) children Leland, Dick, baby Genene, Donna and Clarice.

chart behind the keys to label them and gave us a beginner's instruction book. Three of us learned to read music, and it's a skill I enjoy to this day.

We barely had enough to eat, but Mother made sure we had our music, including tickets to concerts. In the evenings we'd gather around the piano, singing songs in four-part harmony.

In later years, Mother bought instruments for us to play in the school band, and we participated in all the music festivals, fairs and parades.

Mother's brothers came over often to sing with us, too. They were like substitute dads, teaching us games and giving us clothing their own children had outgrown. Mother's close-knit family and her enduring faith in God helped her survive a difficult life.

Mother died at age 92, but the old family piano remains in my living room, a symbol of her sacrifices for her children and her vision of what could be. Mother's gift of music will last us all our lives.

BATHING IN MOM'S LOVE. Judy Carpenter's mother gave her a backyard bath. Judy, who now lives in Whitefish, Montana, says this photo was taken in 1937.

Mom Had the Perfect Remedy

I DIDN'T MIND being sick when I was young, because that's when I had Mom all to myself! All that undivided attention always made me feel so much better.

If I had a stomachache, she'd bring warm milk with butter and cinnamon to my bedside—always with instructions to "sip slowly".

Hot tea with honey and lemon eased a sore throat, but some colds required a special cough medicine. Mother filled a bowl with chopped raw onion and poured a cup of sugar and a little lemon juice over it. Then she put a smaller plate on top of the onion mixture and weighted it down with a stone.

This concoction was stirred every hour until it produced a thick, sweet syrup, which we were given by the teaspoon. It not only quieted the cough but helped make us sleepy.

I also remember getting chicken noodle soup, bowls of ice cream and Jell-O, rubs with Vicks and hot cloths on our chest. Sometimes we even got to sleep with Mom. She made us feel so special, it almost seemed a shame to get better!

—*Delores Managan*
Appleton, Wisconsin

Mother's Lessons Lasted a Lifetime

By Robert Bickmeyer, Troy, Michigan

I THINK OF MOTHER often. She never stopped teaching my sister and me, and her lessons are a constant reminder of her influence in our lives. She was more than a mother; she was a teacher.

The lessons started early—good manners and consideration for others. When we crossed the street, she'd offer her arm to me so I could escort her. On the sidewalk, she whispered to me to walk on the outside until it became second nature.

When I was older, I couldn't go out on Saturday mornings or listen to the radio until I'd done my chores, be it scrubbing the kitchen linoleum, picking up ice, removing coal ashes from the cellar, cutting hedges, shoveling snow, painting or washing dishes. Chores always came first. Knowing your work was done really did make play more pleasurable, just as Mother said.

Mother taught me about money, too. "Pennies make dollars," she preached. "Save them until you have enough to really do something worthwhile...save some and spend some." Again, she was right.

I learned to care for myself and my surroundings, to eat properly and to fight my own battles. A few times Mother watched through the window, fighting the impulse to run to my aid, as I scuffled with a boy down the street. She knew there were some things I had to do for myself. She taught me not to run from a fight.

Even in adulthood, Mother didn't stop teaching me. When I was 50, she told me, "You'll always be my little boy." Now I'm 64, her grandchildren are 35 and 33—and I understand exactly what she meant.

I wish Mother knew how often I still think of her. But maybe she does. Maybe she's still looking over my shoulder, as she always did...as all good mothers do.

HAPPY THREESOME. Robert Bickmeyer beamed between his parents, John and Ida, in this 1951 photograph. Robert says his mom "wasn't perfect—just the best darned mother that there ever was".

Mom's Dollars and Sense Provided Family's Extras

By Lou Ella Weber Salem, South Dakota

IT IS AMAZING how many ways Mom managed to make and save money so we could have just a bit more than the necessities.

She worked long and hard, sewing all our clothes, cutting our hair and cooking everything we loved. Yet she still found time to work for the church and visit friends and relatives. We always had lots of company and had such good times!

Every spring, Mom would buy about 30 rooster chicks for my sister and me to raise during the summer. In fall, we sold the roosters and used the proceeds for school supplies, saving a few pennies to buy some of our favorite candy.

Mom also bought about 500 chicks every spring, which supplied us with eggs and meat. Those laying hens were Mom's pride and joy, but they also helped us buy groceries and clothes. When we bought a farm in 1943, Mom had saved enough from selling eggs to buy all new kitchen cabinets for our new house!

Sometimes when we kids were cleaning the henhouse, we'd wonder if all that work was worth it. Then we'd see the pride in Mom's face, and we knew it was. We weren't only helping the family get by, we were making Mom happy.

LED BY EGGS-AMPLE. Like this farm woman near Wayland, Iowa, Lou Ella Weber's mother raised chickens each spring. She sold the eggs to help buy groceries, clothes and even kitchen cabinets.

Mama's Bonnet Foretold Our Day

By Pauline Wight, Rogers, Arkansas

MAMA ALWAYS wore a bonnet. She had two: a pretty pink one, starched and ironed, for visiting the neighbors; and a dark gray one, of soiled chambray, for work. With 10 kids in our family, there was plenty of work...and Mama wasn't shy about making sure we all did our share.

We always watched to see which bonnet Mama reached for. Our destinies rode on her choice. The dark bonnet meant only one thing—Mama had found some big job for us to tackle.

"Those green beans are crying to be canned," she'd announce. "All right, you kids, let's get busy!"

After what seemed like an eternity of picking in the hot sun, we'd lug our baskets to the shade of an oak tree to snap the beans.

While everyone else was sitting in a circle, snapping beans and seemingly having a good time, I was set in front of a No. 2 washtub full of hot suds and an endless row of mason jars.

"Mama, why do I always have to wash the jars?" I whined.

"Because you can get your hand inside and the other kids' hands are too

---

"Mischief was like the measles— highly contagious..."

---

big," Mama said as she used the bonnet to fan herself after finishing a cooker of beans on the big wood stove.

For a 10-year-old, an afternoon of washing jars seemed like a year at hard labor. I vowed that later on, at supper, I'd clean my plate and drink all my milk in an effort to make my hand outgrow the mouth of a mason jar.

Sitting at my solitary post, I'd see an occasional bean fly through the air when Mama's back was turned. Someone would yell, someone else would smother a giggle and Mama's gray bonnet would smack the culprit on the backside.

Whenever one of the boys remarked that he wished we didn't have any beans to can, Mama's answer was the same, "They'll taste mighty good next winter

DARK FORECAST. This woman wears her working hat to fix another home-cooked meal. Pauline Wight's mother also wore her dark bonnet when she meant business...and the kids knew they would be recruited to help!

when it's cold and the snow is flying."

Of course, every day wasn't a "gray bonnet day". There were many afternoons when the pink bonnet came out— and that meant that Mama was going visiting. She usually took one of us kids with her; the one with the cleanest face or one who'd been especially good (that was seldom me).

But I didn't mind—there was more going on at home when Mama was gone than at the neighbor's anyway. Before she left, Mama gave us our orders:

"Now, you older kids look out after the little ones. Stay away from the well and the pond. Don't be climbing in the barn loft. One of you take a cool drink to Dad in the field, and all of you stay out of mischief."

Mule Wasn't Mentioned

With 10 children in a family, seven of them boys, the word "mischief" was a lot like the measles—highly contagious.

Mama hadn't said a word about the new mule, so as soon as the pink bonnet was out of sight, Joe climbed a persimmon tree and I drove the mule under it so he could jump on his back.

On the way to the field with Dad's cool drink, we found a big anthill, and by the time we'd drowned all the ants, there wasn't much water left in the jug.

Back at the house, there was a boxing match going on in the backyard and I got a ringside seat in the old tire swing. When Clyde pulled back the swing and let it go, I got a black eye intended for Lawrence.

By the time Mama's pink bonnet came bobbing back over the top of the hill, everything was in chaos—kids were yelling, dogs were barking and Dad's new mule was scared out of his wits.

Mama calmly hung up her pink bonnet, put on the gray one and began to restore order by paddling everyone within reach.

PITCHIN' IN. Like these folks, Pauline Wight helped with family chores, including picking beans for canning.

Her Strength Got Children Through Difficult Times

WE CHILDREN leaned on Mom for everything. She was tenderhearted, but she was strong for all of us when we faced trouble and heartache.

There were 12 children, but only two—my sister Betty and me—were still at home when Daddy died. Mom sold the farm, and the three of us moved to a two-room apartment in town so she could work at a bakery to support us.

Mom worked long and hard making doughnuts, and at night, she'd slip quietly in so as not to wake us. But her work wasn't over. We'd always hear her moving around in the kitchen, sometimes canning food until the wee hours of the morning.

Mom missed Daddy a lot, but she did the best she could. I speak for all 12 children, not just Betty and me, when I say that Mom gave up a lot for us. Mom is at rest now with our father, but the memories the two of them gave us will linger forever. —*Peggy Ratliff*
North Tazewell, Virginia

Mother Made Sure Kids Ate Vegetables

MY BROTHERS and I hated squash, any kind of squash, with a passion. But during the Depression, Mom and Dad grew plenty in our vegetable garden

"HOPPY" TIMES. This picture reminds Linda Walsh how her mom played the title role for each holiday, like Easter.

despite our feelings about it.

One day, after we'd all once again spurned her squash at dinner, Mom firmly stated: "One of these days, you will all eat squash *and ask for seconds.*" We roared with laughter at that, because there was no way we'd ever eat squash!

A few days later, Mom served pie for dessert and oh, how we loved her pies. We eagerly dug in, then every one of us asked for more. After each of us polished off our second piece, Mom sat back and chuckled.

"Remember when I said you'd eat squash and ask for more? Well…you just did!"

We were astounded to discover that the delicious confection was actually a combination of squash, eggs, sugar and other ingredients baked in Mom's usual fantastic, flaky crust.

If we hadn't been so stuffed, we would've eaten thirds. Moms know everything, don't they?
—*Barbara Page, Weatherford, Texas*

Mom Made Holidays And Every Day Special

HOLIDAYS were always special at our house, thanks to Mom. On Easter, she would make sure to leave a trail of shredded carrots to the "hard-to-find" Easter eggs. We all thought the Easter Bunny left the trail as he ate the carrots we'd set out for him.

At Christmastime, Mom would make Santa's footprints beside the Christmas tree by dipping my dad's work boots in flour (it never occurred to us to wonder why the snow didn't melt!).

But the nicest thing Mom did for me took time and patience. I loved seedless white grapes, and they tasted so much better without the skin. With a paring knife, she'd carefully peel the skin off enough grapes to fill a bowl for me—I had no idea how good I had it!
—*Linda Walsh, Odessa, Maryland*

Wise Mother "Kept Watch" on Time

BACK in the '20s, we'd occasionally

VOW WAS SQUASHED. Barbara Page's mom made pies like this woman and tricked her into eating a vegetable she vowed never to eat!

let our old windup clock run down. But our wise Mother knew how to determine the time of day even when there were no phones, radio or television.

She'd pick up the old *Farmer's Almanac*, check the time the sun was due to set, then station one of us kids to watch the horizon. When the sun disappeared, our clock was set.

The time may not have been exact, but in those days, a few minutes one way or the other didn't really make much difference. —*Catherine Rogers*
Danville, Arkansas

Family Shared Memories Over Mama's "Button Box"

REMEMBER mama's "button box"?

My mom would get hers out on rainy days, and we kids would pick out our favorites as she told us stories of how they came to be there. During the Depression and the war years, buttons weren't bought, but salvaged from favorite outgrown or worn-out garments.

We shared many close times, thanks to that old button box! Mom has been gone many years now, but her button box is still being shared with new generations of children on rainy days.
—*Maybelle Volz*
Lakeville, Massachusetts

Mom and Children Enjoyed Special Times

By Barbara Martin, Dallas, Georgia

MY FATHER died near the end of World War II, leaving a widow of 22 and two small children. I was 5 and my brother was 3.

Mother had to find a way to support us, and she was thrilled when she found a job with the telephone company as a long-distance operator.

It was her first job, though, and she had mixed feelings: She liked the job, but she also wanted to be with us. Still, we knew who came first in her life. She told us we were her number one priority and that she wanted Daddy to be proud of us. Our job was to be good and help look after each other.

My grandparents moved in to help Mother, so there was always an adult around to care for us while Mama was at work. Saturday nights, though, were reserved as "our special time".

On Saturdays, Mother worked a double shift and came home late. My brother and I were allowed to wait up for her if we followed one rule. We had a large front porch with a swing, and the rule was that, as long as we stayed on that

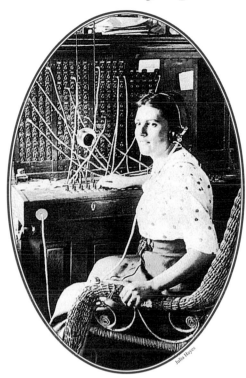

CALLED FOR MOM'S SUPPORT. Like this woman in 1914, Barbara Martin's widowed mother worked as a phone operator to support her family.

swing, our special time could continue.

While we waited, the two of us cuddled together and giggled with anticipation. When we finally saw Mother coming down the street, it was one of those happy moments you never forget. She always brought us hamburgers and small bottled Cokes.

"How Was Your Day?"

The three of us would eat together alone in the kitchen while she told us about the funny things that had happened at work. Then she'd ask about our day and we'd discuss our problems with her.

Saturday was the only night of the week that Mother slept with us. Before we fell asleep, she'd tell us funny stories about mean old stepmothers and wonderful stories about our father and their times together. I will never forget those stories and "our special time".

Later, when Mother started dating again, she nearly always took us along. She'd tell prospective suitors, "The three of us are joined at the heart, so if you want one of us you get all three." We were so lucky to have Mildred Payton Sharpe for our mother.

Mom's Imagination Made Childhood Exciting

FOR ME and my brothers and sisters, childhood was exciting because so often Mama turned the drudgery of work into fun. If she needed something in a hurry she'd say, "Fly like a bird!" and we would...without a second thought.

Hoeing with us in the hot, dry fields, she'd encourage us by promising little treats like an apple at the end of the row. Mama taught us to pick cool, green leaves to stuff in the crowns of our straw hats as protection from the sweltering sun.

Drank from "Goblets"

She also made food and drink taste divine by conjuring up a word picture to fit any situation. After downing cold water, she'd remark, "Nectar from the gods", and we would imagine that we were drinking from a Roman fountain.

With her vivid imagination, she could make drinking buttermilk in the kitchen seem like we were sipping from silver goblets at King Arthur's round table.

And oh, what wonderful bedtime stories she shared! The end of a perfect day was having Mama tuck you into bed with that familiar saying: "Snug as a bug in a rug."

It continues to amaze me how she found time to give each of us so much individual attention yet still promoted family togetherness. The methods she used to settle sibling rivalry required the wisdom of Solomon and the patience of Job.

I've often thought that if Mother had headed the United Nations, there would have been no more wars.

—*Eunice Elkins*
Clarkton, North Carolina

PICTURE PERFECT. In 1922, 3-year-old James Oswald and his mom pose for a photo in their Sunday best. Today James lives in Chicago, Illinois.

One Last Letter from Mom

By Arlene Baldino, Nutley, New Jersey

MY MOTHER and I had a very special relationship—maybe that's the reason why, when I was very young, I gave her a nickname. That childlike name was "Mosk".

Like a carefree child, Mosk used to romp with me and my brother. Many an hour we spent wrestling on the floor, chasing each other around the lawn and up trees. For my mother, enjoying her children always took precedence over housework.

Not having a college education herself, Mosk was determined that her children would receive one. She put both of us through school and even gave me an extra year of study in France. While in France, I received a letter from her nearly every day. Inside would be a most welcome dollar bill (which I dubbed a "George") that I'd exchange for five francs.

Her letters were just like her personality: bubbling with energy and unrestrained by anything as conventional as punctuation. Whether 10 lines or 10 pages, a letter from Mosk was one long sentence of uninterrupted thought and emotion.

Reading her letters was almost as good as having her right there in the room with me, and those notes, with the "Georges" tucked inside, sustained me through several long, bitterly lonely months of homesickness.

Though I knew she was greatly saddened by my absence, only once did I receive a letter without Mosk's usual good humor—and that was the one in which she told me that my dog, "Sweetie", had died.

A few years later, I went abroad again for the summer. Mosk, true to form, sent me her warm and loving letters with "Georges" enclosed. No matter where I was, her words would arrive to fill me with the warmth of home.

Then, suddenly and without warning, the source of that warmth was extinguished forever! Soon after I returned home, a heart attack took our mother from us at the age of 55. She only had time to look at me and say, "I'm sorry, darling", as if she were apologizing for the heartache she knew her death would cause.

In the days following her death, I went from numbness to rushes of despair. Sorting out her clothing to give to charity was difficult, but a favorite hat presented a special problem: I couldn't stand to have it around, but the thought of someone else wearing it was unbearable. Finally, one Saturday, I took it out to the barbecue that my father had built and burned it to ashes.

A week after the funeral, I returned from work in my usual dismal humor, dreading to go to the mailbox to pick up the daily pile of sympathy cards. But when I pulled out the day's mail, I stared with disbelief at the envelope on top. It was a letter from Mosk!

How Could It Happen?

It was the last letter she'd written me during my trip to Europe. That letter had been forwarded through countries all over Europe, always just missing me. Now, here in my hand, was a message from one whom I had loved so much and whom (I thought) I had lost forever.

It was a typical "Mosk" letter, a long run-on sentence with one last "George" inside (that is one dollar bill I will *never* spend!). Though that last letter had nothing extraordinary in it, its timing brought home a truth that I shall carry in my heart forever: Someone who is loved can never be completely taken from us by death!

As long as we allow them to, they will find a way to reach us and to say, just as Mosk said in this letter and in every other letter she ever wrote to me: "No matter how far away you are, my dearest, at this moment, and for all time, because of love, I am with you!"

LOVE LETTERS. Like this woman, Arlene Baldino's mother faithfully mailed numerous letters to Arlene who was studying abroad. Each letter was filled with love, laughter...and life.

FAMILY FUN. Marge Donaldson of Tucson, Arizona had many cherished moments with her kind mother and father. That's Marge sitting in the wagon with her brother Fred. Behind them, left to right, are sister Barbara, father Carl, mother Ruth Ann holding baby Carol, and brother Floyd.

Chapter Seven

Pets Were Part of The Family

Pets Were Part of the Family

NO QUESTION about it...pets were considered to be part of the family. And sometimes that included helping with such chores as tending livestock, guarding the homestead or even "baby-sitting" the children. Folks hold dear to their hearts the special memories of these feathered and furry companions.

I was 3 years old when my grandfather decided I needed a dog of my own. At least that's the family legend—I don't recall the event. But I sure do remember "Laddy". He was a fine collie, just like the dog Albert Payson Terhune wrote about.

Laddy was my friend, playmate and confidant. He also at times was the only one in the family who had the foggiest idea where I was. I had an entire farm to roam and would go AWOL at unexpected times. But my parents never worried. They'd just whistle for Laddy and watch where he came from.

We were inseparable. When the whole world (Mom and Dad) turned against me, I could pour out my grievances to Laddy and he was there to lick away my tears. If I craved adventure, he was eager to help me hunt down tigers or stalk rustlers.

At that same time, we had a white Angora cat named "Frosty". He was our "house cat"—as opposed to the hoard of yowling, undisciplined "barn cats" who only showed up at milking time to beg for a squirt of warm milk direct from the cow.

Frosty was a pampered, ungracious prince. He made it clear that we were privileged to have him for a boarder. He also made it clear that we were never to presume a friendship which could never exist.

Frosty taught me everything I ever needed to know about cats. Dogs truly like people; cats merely tolerate them.

Ming the Terrible

When Laddy moved on to Dog Heaven, he was replaced by an adult chow dog given to us by friends who were moving to another state. His name was "Ming", in honor of the terrifying villain in the Flash Gordon stories.

I remember Ming's tenure as the period when we were deprived of the company of insurance salesmen, seed corn peddlers, county agents and all other uninvited guests. Not one of them would put a foot on the ground when Ming came to greet them. His unflinching glare and the low, thunderous growl rumbling in his chest cowed the bravest of them.

We stayed in the house. The salesman stayed in his car. It was simple as that. Truth to tell, Ming was friendly to a fault. Had a burglar come in the middle of the night to ransack our house, Ming would have joyously shown him where the silverware was hidden.

If You Knew Susie...

During high school days I had yet another pet and close friend. Her name was "Susie". She was a Poland China pig.

I purchased Susie in a pregnant condition. She was the Eve of my eventual pig enterprise. Susie and her offspring produced scores of pigs and, later, financed my first year or two at college.

The trouble was, Susie and I became friends. She followed me around the farm like a friendly puppy, grunting and oinking her innermost thoughts. How do you send someone like that off to Oscar Mayer? Take my advice: Never get too attached to a pig.

Whether it's a dog, a turtle, a pig or a parakeet, I think every kid needs a pet while growing up. If you don't believe me, just turn the page and read dozens of reasons why.

—*Clancy Strock*

BOY'S BEST FRIEND. Through the years, no friendship has been able to match the special bond between a boy and his dog.

We Played Tag with a Turkey!

By Barbara Bradley, Oroville, California

TURKEY TROT. Unlike that big bird above, Gobbler Jim rarely stood still. Barbara Bradley recalls a turkey that took after anyone who happened into the yard—but it was all in good fun!

ONE OF MY BEST childhood playmates was a turkey we called "Gobbler Jim". My brother and I even played tag with him!

Gobbler Jim reigned supreme in the farmyard, and whenever we ventured outside, we'd dance a teasing jig to get his attention. Jim would spread his wings and begin the chase. Delighted, we'd run to the outhouse and slam the door.

Jim would stretch his neck high, circling the old privy, waiting for his prey

> "He assumed anyone who came into the yard was there to play!"

to emerge. We'd peek through the cracks in the plank walls, waiting until he circled to the rear before we'd dart back out. Then Jim would be back on our heels again, jabbering and gobbling.

Squealing with joy, we'd race around a bit, then dash inside to start the game once more.

Gobbler Jim would play this game for as long as we wanted. If we wanted to stop, we ran for the woodshed connected to the house and flung the gate closed behind us. Jim seemed to understand when the game was over; he'd simply strut off, chest inflated, to survey his domain.

We tried this game with our rooster once when Gobbler Jim wasn't around, but the rooster was satisfied just to banish us from his space. As soon as we got inside the outhouse, he went back to pecking and scratching.

One time my brother tried to play the game alone. Gobbler Jim blocked the privy door, and my brother had to seek sanctuary in the chicken coop!

He was only 2 years old—small enough to squeeze through a tiny opening meant only for chickens. Jim paced back and forth in front of that hole, waiting for him to come out.

My brother was stuck in the chicken coop until dinnertime, when Grandma came to his rescue. He was a mess! Grandma just laughed and held him at arm's length while she hustled him to the creek for an unscheduled bath.

Gobbler Jim didn't want to play tag just with children. He assumed anyone who came into the yard was there to play! He circled everyone who came into the yard, trying to get a game started.

Anyone who visited the outhouse could count on Jim to keep a constant vigil. And when they came out, he'd circle again, pecking at their backsides as they scurried out of his way.

Everyone seemed puzzled by this behavior, but my brother and I watched with amusement and wonder. "Big people" knew so much—but they didn't know how to play tag with a turkey!

'Eggie' Made One Terrific Baby-Sitter

By Marie Cochrane
Mt. Vernon, Illinois

NEVER LET DOWN HIS GUARD. Pet dog Eggie (shown with Marie Cochrane and brother Bobby) acted as the boy's personal bodyguard.

OUR FAMILY had a Border collie mix when my brother and I were kids. He was named "Egbert" by my mother's youngest sister, who was living with us when a neighbor presented her with a puppy.

"Eggie" became my brother's constant companion. If Mother lost track of little Bobby when he was playing in the yard, she just called for Eggie and watched which direction the dog came from, then followed him to Bobby. The dog seemed to know he was supposed to lead her to his young master.

One day when Mother couldn't find Bobbie and called for Eggie, Eggie didn't come. Naturally, Mother was concerned. Then she heard a low rumbling sound coming from the pasture on the other side of the house, and what she discovered gave her quite a scare!

Another neighbor kept a large herd of white-faced cattle in that pasture. There, sitting with a semi-circle of cows around him, was my little brother—while Eggie, true to his breed, busily patrolled the line of cows. Each time a cow took a step toward Bobby, warning growls rumbled from Eggie.

Mother carefully crawled between the strands of barbed wire surrounding the pasture and slowly walked toward the frightening scene before her.

"Git! Git on out of here!" she cried. And "git" they did!

Eggie stayed close to Mother as she picked Bobby up and carried him to the safety of the yard, where he was told to never go into that pasture again.

Eggie, on the other hand, was heaped with praise. Mother was convinced he had saved Bobby's life, and our dear dog was more precious to us than ever.

The Day It Rained Cats and Dogs

By Suzanne Saltsman
Guerneville, California

THE BEDRAGGLED little puppy stood forlorn and alone on the city sidewalk in Wichita Falls, Texas. The pup cringed against a brick wall, shying away from each passerby—until my daddy walked past.

For some reason, the puppy leapt from his hiding spot and followed Daddy down the block. He walked straight to the butcher shop, bought a pound of hamburger and fed the pup right there on the sidewalk. After taking her home, he cleaned her up and named her "McTavish".

As the years went by, I recall Daddy saying to us kids, "You know, I've had McTavish longer than I've had your mama!" It was true; McTavish accompanied Mama and Daddy on their first date.

Daddy and Mama were sitting in the front seat enjoying the drive-in movie, with McTavish in the back. Every time Daddy tried to put his arm around Mama, McTavish would stick her head between them!

One day, not too long after I was born, there was a heavy rainstorm. Daddy took McTavish for a walk along a nearby creek bed, which was filled and rushing fast. Suddenly, for no apparent reason, McTavish leapt into the water and began to swim furiously.

Dad ran along the creek trying to keep up with McTavish, but he soon lost sight of her. Daddy was worried she would drown... but not for long.

Soon McTavish came running back up the path to him – and she was carrying a half-drowned kitten!

Daddy took the kitten home, and McTavish raised her along with her own litter of puppies! The two remained close companions as long as McTavish lived.

PURRFECT PAIR. McTavish and rescued kitten became family, not only to the Saltsmans but also to each other!

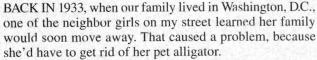

I Helped 'Nipper' Find a Home

By Philip Cox, Sun City Center, Florida

BACK IN 1933, when our family lived in Washington, D.C., one of the neighbor girls on my street learned her family would soon move away. That caused a problem, because she'd have to get rid of her pet alligator.

She'd bought "Nipper" at a five-and-dime in Florida while vacationing. He was just a little thing then, about 6 inches long, and she'd been allowed to keep him in the bathtub of a guest room.

By the time I got Nipper, he'd grown to about 18 inches, which to me still seemed like a baby.

When I brought Nipper home, my father said I couldn't keep him. He said somebody might get hurt, that I'd need a permit...and most likely the gator would freeze in winter, because he *wasn't* coming in the house!

Made Other Arrangements

Nothing I said would change Dad's mind, and he said the zoo was the place for Nipper. Since I was responsible for this, it was up to me to make the arrangements. When I called the zoo, they said they'd gladly take Nipper, but there wasn't any pickup service.

A buddy and I decided why wait until Saturday for Dad to take us? We could bring Nipper to the zoo on the bus.

To be safe, we taped the gator's mouth closed. We found one of my sister's doll bonnets to put on his head, and we snugly wrapped Nipper in an old army blanket and tucked his tail inside. Then we set off for the bus stop.

"Baby" Was Well-Behaved

We were less than a mile from the zoo entrance when a woman on the bus remarked, "What a good baby you have there," and peeked through the top of the blanket.

There was a brief silence followed by a hair-raising scream. The bus driver slammed on the brakes, pitching the passengers forward and scaring the daylights out of everyone!

In all the commotion, my buddy and I managed to sneak out the back door of the bus with Nipper. We crossed the road, made a mad dash to the zoo, said good-bye to Nipper and grabbed the first bus headed toward home!

When I got home and told Dad what happened, I wished I hadn't. Though I spent the next several months in the doghouse, I guess it was worth it—I've had the memory for over 60 years.

'Pet' Was a Good Listener for Young Bride

By Val Marie, Puyallup, Washington

AS A YOUNG BRIDE, I went to Idaho to live on a small farm with my husband and his family. It was 1952, the Korean War was on, and this would be the loneliest year of my life.

My husband was sent overseas with the Army. My in-laws worked during

PICTURE THIS. Val Marie was keeping an eye on her in-laws' place when their Guernsey cow strolled past the picture window and right off the farm!

the day, so I was at their home alone, with only our baby for company.

One day I had just put the baby down for a nap when I saw our only cow, a Guernsey named "Pet", walk past the picture window and down the driveway. She glanced at me in the window once,

---

"I'd visit her in the barn and pour out my heart..."

---

then trotted up the drive, ignoring me. I panicked and ran out the door after her.

I ran. She ran faster. (Little did I understand the bovine mentality!) Finally I gave up and returned to the house, too concerned about the baby to pursue Pet any farther. I hesitated to call my mother-in-law at work and worry her, but waiting seemed worse. Still, that's what I did.

Two hours later, I was standing at the window holding the baby and wondering how I'd explain the cow's disappearance. Suddenly, here came Pet,

ambling back up the driveway, tail swishing nonchalantly.

I didn't know whether to scream, laugh or cry! Pet had been visiting "the girls" at the farm next door and was now ready to return to her field of cornstalks.

During the long, lonely months that followed, Pet and I got to know each other better. When the sky was starry and cold, and my anxieties and fears about my husband seemed so great, I'd go visit her in the barn to hug her, kiss her big soft nose and pour out my heart. She always seemed to hear and understand.

But as nice as she could be, she still loved to take off and visit, and it seemed no fence was secure enough to hold her. We often had to drive her home from the neighbor's fields of wheat or rye. She was plainly not befriending me on the same level I was befriending her!

I somehow had a soft spot for her, though. Later, when we bought more milk cows, I was always gentler with her than the rest. After all, she was a great listener!

Grandmother's Ducks Were Lucky

THE INCIDENT with the ducks happened sometime around 1898. My grandparents were homesteading then near Maxwelton on Whidbey Island, Washington, where the Indians gathered for a yearly potlatch. Money was scarce and barter was the common form of exchange.

One time, Grandmother made a trade for eight fertile Pekin duck eggs. The ducklings hatched. Grandmother raised them and was quite proud of the large white ducks that greeted her every morning at the back door.

One morning she went out to feed them—only to find her beautiful ducks lying dead in the backyard. What a terrible loss!

Grandmother knew she couldn't feed her family ducks that had died of some mysterious illness, but being a thrifty homemaker, she decided to pluck all the choice feathers for pillows. This done, she sadly directed my father to carry them out to the far side of the garden.

The next day, Grandmother postponed going out to feed

EVERYTHING'S DUCKY. These ducks have their feathers— unlike those owned by Marla Clark's grandmother!

the chickens, knowing her Pekin ducks would not be there to great her. Imagine her surprise, then, when she opened the door to be greeted by eight *nearly naked* ducks!

It seems that Grandfather had made cider vinegar the week before and dumped the squeezed pulp toward the back of the garden. The Pekins had found the fermented pulp and feasted on it until they were "dead" drunk.

Because this happened in October, when the nights in Puget Sound grew cold, Grandmother worried for her featherless ducks. After some thought, she got some Siwash socks Grandfather wore under his logging boots, cut off the toes and made slits for their wings, then pulled them over the ducks' heads.

That winter, Grandmother's Pekin ducks sported the gray and red "body stockings" until their feathers grew back, and Grandmother began each day to the quacking of Whidbey Island's most stylish ducks.

—*Marla Clark, Portland, Oregon*

FAST FRIENDS. Wolf, a German shepherd, was Dale Dunn's pal throughout his childhood, helping him with chores and errands by pulling a sled or wagon in harness. This photograph was taken in 1934.

Versatile Shepherd Was Full of Surprises

By Dale Dunn, Riverside, California

THE BEST DOG we ever had was a German shepherd named "Wolf". He was a good watchdog, a natural at herding and hunting, and he even pulled a sled and wagon in harness!

We got Wolf when he was a puppy, and he was always friendly around us. We didn't realize what a good watchdog he was, though, until one hot day when our neighbors came by the farm

---

"Our visitors were sitting under Wolf's watchful eye..."

---

for a Sunday visit in their 1928 Chevrolet. We weren't home, and when our friends stopped the car, Wolf wouldn't let them get out!

The car needed to be hand-cranked to start again, so when we got home several hours later, our visitors were still sitting there under Wolf's watchful eye. As soon as Wolf saw us, he trotted off as though they weren't even there!

Wolf was also a good livestock and hunting dog, and he caught fish for us. When the northern pike spawned in a wide, slow-moving creek near our place each spring, Wolf waded out into the shallow water and caught them, then brought them up to us on shore.

Wolf helped with my chores and errands, too, by pulling a sled or wagon in harness. It was my job to bring in water from our well, which was a long way from the house. I'd fill a couple of 8- or 10-gallon cans, load them onto the sled or wagon, then let Wolf do the rest.

Although he'd do this job, Wolf didn't like it much. Sometimes he would hide behind the barn or shed with his big ears up, listening to see if

I'd finished pumping. When I saw what he was doing, I'd scold him and he'd come right to me.

Wolf also pulled me on the sled or wagon when I was visiting neighbors, running errands or collecting for Easter Seals. Most of our neighbors were several miles away, but Wolf would trot tirelessly over miles of roads and trails. Once he was in harness, he never tried to break away or chase anything.

We didn't train Wolf to do any of these things—he just went wherever we did and helped as best he could. He was a strong, healthy dog, and I don't think he went to a vet or had a shot in his entire 14 years.

Backward Approach Foiled Grandpa's Fierce Watchdog

MY GRANDPA had a huge German shepherd named "Ranger", and we all treated him with respect. Whenever anyone pulled into the farmyard, Ranger would lie on the porch and growl. No visitor would even get out of the car until Grandpa told Ranger to be quiet.

One day a neighbor bet Grandpa $20 that he could come through the kitchen door without Grandpa saying a word to Ranger. The bet was on.

Neighbor Was Sneaky

The next morning, Ranger was lying on the porch in front of the screen door when the neighbor drove into the farmyard. We watched from the kitchen window as the neighbor laid his hand on the front gate. Ranger growled threateningly.

Then the neighbor turned around and walked *backward* through the gate, across the yard and onto the porch.

To our amazement, Ranger moved out of the neighbor's way so he could come through the door. He backed into the kitchen, then gleefully collected his bet from Grandpa!
—*Randy Maydew
Albuquerque, New Mexico*

Chatterbox Crow Always Had the Last Word

By Lori Westrich, Jacksboro, Tennessee

"PETE" AND I joined the family the same summer. What made him different was that he was a pound and a half of black feathers and mischief—a talking crow who lived in our cherry tree!

My first memories of Pete go back to when I was 3 years old. Mom would send me out to play, and that pesky bird would bite my ankles, chase me around the yard, steal my toys and stash them in his tree. Then he'd fly down and squawk, "My toys, my toys."

Mom said Pete and I fought worse than siblings!

Grandma Would Be Purple

Pete loved to vex my grandma, too. She hated her name, Josie; no one called her anything but Grandma. Except Pete.

Whenever she visited, he'd pull at the hem of her dress and fly onto her head. When she tried to retaliate, he would escape to his tree, squawking,

"Ah, Josie, ah, Josie" over and over until Grandma was purple with rage.

Although Pete often stirred up trouble, he was also a great protector of his human family. If suspicious-looking strangers came into the yard, Pete alert-

---

"Pete stashed my toys in his tree..."

---

ed the dogs. And when the occasional snake slithered past, Pete flew around it, just out of striking reach, calling until Mom or Dad came to kill it.

Like a child, Pete loved attention. When we picked up a kitten or pup, he'd lie at our feet or fly onto our knees and demand to have his head scratched. If my sister was painting my fingernails, Pete would interrupt, holding up one foot, then the other, for *his* coat of nail polish!

Pete shared our lives for 19 years, except for one brief period when he disappeared. The headline in the local paper read: "Pete Henson Missing—Reward Offered". Most everybody in

the surrounding counties knew about Pete, but no one had seen him. We were heartbroken.

One day my sister was walking through town and heard Pete call to her. He was in a cage in someone's house! She fetched the sheriff, and the owner of the house admitted he'd stolen Pete. The thief went to jail, and Pete came home with my sister in a taxi.

Added to Vocabulary

Mom and Dad called everyone they knew to say Pete was back, none the worse for wear—or so we thought. One Sunday afternoon, the minister stopped by, and Daddy took him out to see Pete. To Daddy's horror, Pete chose that moment to show off the new words he'd learned at the thief's house—curse words!

I thought Daddy would die on the spot. But the preacher had a good sense of humor and was chuckling when he left.

As Pete got older, his feathers gradually turned white, but he continued to wreak havoc until the day he died. His grave is marked by a seedling taken from his cherry tree.

AS THE CROW FLIES, Pete was never far from Lori Westrich's childhood home. He ruled his domain from a cherry tree in the yard. This old photo of Lori and Pete shows him in one of his quieter moments.

Their Pet Sang Like a Canary... When He Wasn't Singing Opera!

OUR CANARY, "Dickie", was an opera nut. Six days of the week, Dickie sang the usual bird songs, but on Saturdays, when we listened to operas on the radio, he seemed to think he was an Italian tenor!

He listened to the soloists and matched them note for note, although he was always about four notes behind. The neighbors often stopped by to hear him sing.

As much as Dickie loved opera, he hated Doc Matthews, a local preacher whose services were broadcast every Sunday. We never knew why he disliked Doc so much, but anytime we listened to Doc, Dickie would sulk and refuse to sing another note until the following Saturday! —*Bonnie Fitch Lakewood, Washington*

This Pigeon Fancied People!

By Margaret Werner, Lake Havasu City, Arizona

OUR MOST UNUSUAL PET was a pigeon who thought he was a human!

We lived in Waukesha, Wisconsin at the time, and local pigeon fanciers often released their birds near our house. But one pigeon didn't fly off—she stayed in our garage, made a nest for herself and laid some eggs!

After the eggs hatched, our son, Bill, found one baby who hadn't left the nest. He put the bird in a box, brought him into the house, fed him and loved him. At night, Bill put the box on the floor next to his bed, and he'd stroke the squab's feathers until they both fell asleep.

New Playmate

Bill named his buddy "Charlie". He walked around the house with Charlie perched on his shoulder, and they'd watch television together.

Later, Bill introduced Charlie to the neighborhood boys, who all loved him. Whenever they played football, Charlie would fly down and sit on the ball when it landed!

Charlie loved to be with people. When Grandpa met him for the first time, Charlie flew right out to meet him and sat on his head! If we got into the car to go somewhere, Charlie would ride along on the hood as

PLEASED TO MEET YOU. When Charlie the pigeon met someone he liked, he broke the ice by perching atop that person's head!

OH NO, YOU DON'T! William Luck of Richmond, Virginia says he couldn't resist taking this photo on a Sunday in 1953. His 3-year-old son, Ronald, had a pet chicken that he'd raised from hatching. That morning, Ronald overheard his folks suggesting a Sunday dinner of fried chicken. At that, Ronald dashed into the yard and guarded his pet with his life. "We had other stock to choose from," says William, "so his precious pet was spared!"

far as the corner, then fly back to the garage to wait for us until we got home.

The only problem was when the children left for the two-block walk to school. Charlie would fly along with them, and when they entered the building, he'd flit from one window to another, trying to find them!

On the last day of school, Charlie was invited to visit, and the local newspaper sent a photographer. Charlie walked in that building proud as a peacock, hopped up the steps and flew right onto Bill's desk!

Dogged Retriever Made Sure Rafter Had Weathered Rapids

By Roger Bowen, West Branch, Iowa

WHEN I WAS 9, my folks and a couple of friends went on a weekend trip to our favorite creek. I brought along my raft, which was made of old inner tubes and had a pine plank to sit on.

My golden retriever, "Snubs", stayed on shore with my parents while I launched the raft above some rapids. As I approached the faster water, Snubs began barking as if to warn me of the danger.

I made it through the rapids okay, but Snubs wanted to be sure, so she leaped into the water and swam out to me! After a couple of tries, I got Snubs into the raft behind me and we sailed on down the creek together.

KING OF THE WILD FRONTIER? Roger Bowen looked a bit like Davy Crockett as he glided down a creek with his golden retriever in '37. He fashioned his cap from an old cowboy hat, and his mom added the foxtail on the back.

In a Pinch, Dog Could Spot Packards and Fords

UNCLE GEORGE had a dog named "Cuddles" who sat on his lap and looked out the window whenever we went for a ride in his Packard.

Uncle George always told us that Cuddles was particular. Her favorite cars were Packards, but she liked Fords, too. And it was true! Every time we passed a Ford or Packard, Cuddles would bark. She never barked at anything else.

I thought Cuddles was the smartest dog in the whole world—until years later, when I discovered that every time we passed a Ford or Packard, Uncle George would pinch her tail!
—*George Lash, Mentor, Ohio*

Long-Awaited Pup Was a Living Doll

WHEN I WAS 4 back in 1932, I wanted nothing more than a puppy. But every time I asked, Mother would say, "Oh, Jean, we just can't afford to buy one right now." Still, I kept wishing.

Every weekend, Mother, Daddy and I would drive from our home in Oak Park, Illinois out to a farm in the country to buy fruit and vegetables. On one trip, what should run out from under a truck at the farm but a tiny puppy!

She had a white body and a black and brown face, and she looked a little like a bulldog. It was love at first sight.

Mother, her voice trembling, asked the farmer how much he wanted for the dog. "Oh, I guess 50¢," he replied. Well, what could she and Daddy say? "Snubby" was ours. She slept on Mother's lap all the way home.

A couple of years later, we began spending our summers at a small apple farm Daddy had bought. There were no children for me to play with, but I was very content with Snubby and my dolls.

I'd dress Snubby in a kimono and lay her in my doll buggy, where she'd fall asleep. I'd set an alarm clock to go off every 15 minutes. When it sounded, she'd raise her head and open her mouth so I could give her a spoonful of "medicine"—a taste of water.

That sweet little dog lived to be 13 years old, and I'll never forget her.
—*Jean Elliott, Claremont, California*

Clever Collie Was More Than Just a Pretty Face

"RUFFLES" was a beautiful golden collie, but she was more than just a pet. She was a dear friend—and smart, too!

One morning while I was combing

A DOLL OF A DOG. Jean Elliott's girlhood pal, Snubby, took her naps in a doll buggy, but dutifully woke every 15 minutes for a dose of "medicine".

my hair, the comb flipped out of my hand and fell to the floor. Curious to see just how smart Ruffles was, I called her. She came trotting down the hall.

"Ruffles," I said, "I dropped my comb. Would you pick it up for me, please?" She looked at me, looked at the floor, picked up the comb and put it in my hand! I talked to her all the time, but she'd certainly never been asked to pick up a comb before! —*Ruth Boteler, Black Mountain, North Carolina*

Uprooted Farm Dogs Yearned for Home

IN THE FALL of 1929, we moved to a house in town, 14 miles from our farm, and brought our dogs, "Ol' Shep" and "Bob". Shortly after the move, we gave Bob to a friend of my brother's who lived 35 miles from the farm.

One day Ol' Shep came up missing. Dad thought he might have gone back to the farm, so he wasn't surprised to find him there when he checked on the cattle a few days later. Shep wiggled out of his old "scoot hole" under the granary door as soon as he heard Dad's truck!

What did surprise Dad was seeing Bob follow Shep into the farmyard!

We later learned both dogs had disappeared the same night. Bob must have come by our place in town and taken Shep to the farm with him, because that was Shep's only visit "home" until we all returned in the spring.
—*Celia Yoder, Blackwell, Oklahoma*

TRUE-BLUE "TIPPY" guarded pies when Thelma Marshall was growing up. "Whenever Mom put a freshly baked pie on the windowsill to cool, she'd tell Tippy to watch it," recalls Thelma, of Warren, Ohio. "After that, no one would dare get near it!" Tippy is shown above with Thelma's brothers, Gordon, Lloyd and Kenneth.

Acrobatic Cat Entertained Family for 20 Years

By Evelyn Corzine
New Port Richey, Florida

IN 1950, a family in our church decided to part with their cat, and our son Scott asked if we could adopt it. Our older son, Jack, wanted a dog. We told him we'd get one for him when the cat died. Little did we dream that wouldn't be for another 20 years!

When we went to pick up "Teamer Tom", his owner showed us a mealtime trick he'd taught him. The owner extended his arm at shoulder height—and Teamer leaped over it to "earn" his dish of food! Scott was thrilled—how many other boys had a performing cat to show off to their friends?

Teamer quickly became part of the family, traveling with us each time my

---

"When Teamer Tom saw me arrive at the station, he squalled like a baby!"

Navy-man husband was transferred—about every 2 years. During one move, we stopped to stay with friends in South Carolina and briefly left Teamer in the car with the window cracked a couple of inches. When Scott went to check on him

later, Teamer was mysteriously gone.

We hunted for hours, but Teamer never turned up. When we had to leave the next morning without him, Scotty was in tears. About 10 days later, Teamer finally returned to our friends' home, and they shipped him to us by train. When Teamer saw me arrive at the station to pick him up, he started squalling like a baby!

Teamer didn't like to travel, but he adjusted. We tried leaving him in a kennel once or twice when we went on vacation, but he wouldn't eat or drink anything until we returned. So he became a well-traveled cat. We estimate he logged about 30,000 miles on the road with us!

Leaps Got Lower

As the years passed, Teamer started to show his age. Those mealtime jumps grew more difficult, so we began holding our arms lower and lower. Eventually he would just stare at an outstretched arm and then walk underneath it. After that, we simply concentrated on keeping him comfortable and happy.

When Teamer's health and vigor declined even further, the vet advised putting him to sleep. At 21, Teamer had already outlived any cat the vet had ever heard of. Scott was grown and married by then, but Teamer was still

very much his cat, so we asked for his permission. He asked us not to do it.

Teamer died in his sleep a couple of weeks later, in Scott's old bedroom. It was like losing the fifth member of our family. He left us with many memories, and thinking of him still brings a lump to my throat.

TWENTY-YEAR TENURE. Teamer Tom (pictured at left with Evelyn Corzine) was top dog (or in this case, top cat!) in the Corzine family for 20 years. He hated to be left behind, so he traveled across the country with the entire family. Evelyn estimates he rode about 30,000 miles in the family car!

Growling 'Watch Cat' Tipped the Hand of Midnight Prowler

I'LL NEVER FORGET the night we discovered our cat, "Toby", was a "watch cat"!

It was midnight, and we were all sleeping soundly. Suddenly Toby jumped into an open bedroom window, growled like a dog and bolted down the stairs. Then he sat in the living room and continued to growl.

Dad got up quietly and peered outside to see what had spooked Toby. For just a flash, he saw a hand moving quickly up and down, as if someone were brushing away a mosquito.

Dad tiptoed downstairs, got the shotgun and hid outside until he spotted the prowler. "Who goes there?" Dad yelled. The man started running. "Halt or I'll shoot!" Dad hollered.

The man leaped the pasture fence like an antelope. When Dad fired into the air, the prowler doubled his speed, splashing across the creek and crashing through the willows.

The next morning, Dad discovered the man had been in the cellar and crawled around under the house. He was probably looking for a whiskey still—if he'd found one, he could have reported it to the authorities for a $1 reward.

That might seem like a lot of trouble to go to for a dollar, but a buck went a long way in the '20s!

—*Rosemarie Patterson*
Tacoma, Washington

Grandma Loved Her Pet Piglet

By Dennis Harmon, Ozark, Missouri

FOR 50 YEARS, Grandmother started her day by baking biscuits…so the mere fact that she was now sharing her daughter-in-law's kitchen seemed no reason to quit!

I was 8 when Dad's mother came to live with us and started The Great Biscuit War. Mom staked her territory and kept right on baking biscuits of her own, which put Dad in the touchy position of trying to stay neutral. (We kids didn't care, as long as there was plenty of gravy!)

Things were getting stressful until "Piglet" came along. He was born blind and rejected by his mother, and Grandma couldn't stand to see him starve. So she brought the tiny pink piglet into the house to bottle-feed him.

Dad put up a feeble protest—until he realized how soothing that pig was to Grandma's spirit. With Grandma's bottle-feeding, Piglet quickly outgrew his litter mates and progressed to biscuits…of which there was an *endless* supply.

My sister and I loved that animal almost as much as Grandma did. Piglet was like a faithful dog. Though he couldn't see, his hearing was incredible. Grandma kept the surplus biscuits in one of Mom's stoneware canisters, and if we ever rattled that lid, Piglet was right there begging and squeaking.

Piglet even had an old shoe he loved playing tug-of-war with. He'd also drop that shoe on my face in the middle of the night when he needed to go out.

Dad Wasn't Hog-Wild

Dad eventually banished Piglet from the house, because Grandma's pet had grown to 300 pounds. Piglet remained outside on the porch with a nice comfy pallet.

The day I'll never forget was when Dad hired Lou Zuplo to hang new wallpaper in the house.

We all went our own way that day while Lou went to work. Sometime during the day he made the mistake of looking for sugar to put in his coffee…and started rattling the lids of Mom's stoneware canisters. Unable to resist that sound any longer, Piglet burst through the screen door!

Two hours later, Dad found Lou standing in the kitchen sink waving Mom's bread knife, screaming half in Italian and half in English that the hog was trying to kill him.

Piglet, not meaning any harm, was still squeaking and begging for a biscuit!

BACON BISCUITS. Like the woman above, Dennis Harmon's grandmother was a biscuit baker extraordinaire. Leftovers went to Piglet, who loved them. He grew from a small fry, like the pig in photo at left, to more than 300 pounds.

Goat's Antics Sent Him Through the Roof!

WHEN MOM brought us home from school one afternoon, we found our goat stuck in a friend's car!

The friend had parked next to the woodpile, and "Goatie" loved to climb—so he jumped onto the wood, then onto the car roof. Unfortunately, the roof was made of canvas, and all four of Goatie's feet went right through it! When we arrived, he was still hanging there, his legs kicking inside the car.

Mom called for help, and after a lot of struggling we got Goatie back on the ground. Dad got some patching material to fix the roof—but not until he'd threatened to run Goatie into the woods and let the cougars have him for supper!

—Rosemarie Patterson
Tacoma, Washington

Chapter Eight

The Old Home Place

The Old Home Place

Dad, my Grampa Strock and a carpenter named Jim Capp built the house my parents moved into after they were married in 1920. It was one of those square two-story frame houses with a porch across the front that you still see today on thousands of Midwestern farms.

It was a solid, unspectacular house and something of a novelty for those days, because it was wired for electricity and had an indoor bathroom and hot water radiators.

The kitchen stove burned kindling and corncobs. It was a blessing in the winter (a great place to thaw out chilled feet after walking home from school) but a curse in the summer. It also had only two speeds when it came to cooking—too hot or not hot enough. Mom even managed to burn gravy on that stove.

Eventually it was replaced with a kerosene stove, which was less hospitable in subzero weather but made the kitchen habitable during scorching Illinois summers. However, it had a terrifying way of shooting flames up to the ceiling when a pan boiled over.

Front Porch Hilton

In the dreadful summer heat of those Dust Bowl days, the old home place got a little too hot to bear. We either slept on the front porch or in the front yard. Mom took the porch swing at one end of the porch, while Dad slept on a steel cot at the other end.

There also was a canvas army cot and a huge feather tick, stuffed with feathers my Grandma Strock had plucked from her flock of geese. My sister and I argued endlessly over who would get to sleep on the feather tick. The loser got the army cot.

Our home was a magnet for Mom's relatives, all of them city-dwellers. It was where the clan gathered for holidays, birthdays, anniversaries and Sunday get-togethers. In summer there was a marathon croquet tournament in the front yard, mostly because Grampa Stevens insisted on it. He was the family champion, and the rest of us were just cannon fodder for his deadly accurate shots.

It was a given that there would be homemade ice cream, made with genuine cream from our dairy cows. The kids turned the crank until they were tuckered out, knowing their reward would be to lick the beater later.

The Best Safety Net

How I miss those wonderful family gatherings at the old home place! They were full of love and mutual support during tough times. Today we talk about "safety nets". Back then the family clan was all the safety net you needed. And you didn't have to fill out forms nor stand in long lines to get its benefits.

From the day Mom moved into that house, she was perpetually drawing up plans for how she would remodel it. She'd had no say-so in the original design. Grampa Strock was not one to consult women about anything and she never quite got over it.

The old home place still stands, but it doesn't look the same. The trees Dad planted are giants now. The farm buildings are gone, and the house is part of a suburban development.

The folks who bought it did a lot of remodeling. It's pretty much the way Mom always figured it should be.

—*Clancy Strock*

HOME SWEET HOME. This clapboard home likely kept generations of country folks secure—and gave them memories to last a lifetime.

Guy Bumgarner

Loving Hands Cleared Land for Home

By Jack Snowdy, Reserve, Louisiana

IT ISN'T EASY to say good-bye to "the old home place". There are lots of memories tied up in that house, which started out as just a cottage in 1942.

That was the year my father borrowed a few hundred dollars to buy the land in Olla, Louisiana. It was so thick with pine trees and saplings that you couldn't walk a foot in any direction without bumping into one.

Clearing the land was a family affair. My father, mother, sisters and I, along with several other relatives, worked every day for months, cutting down thousands of feet of pines and stacking them in ricks for the logging trucks to haul away.

As a farmer's son, I was used to breaking ground in new farm fields, but this was hard work, and I was glad to see the last log loaded and hauled away.

Within a month, the shell of a house was finished and we were able to move in. A carpenter uncle came to live with us, and he worked on it with my father and me for the next year.

Finally one day my uncle loaded all his tools into his car and said we wouldn't be needing him anymore. The house was completed at last.

House Was Security

My parents had been hit hard by the Depression, and they were very proud to own a home. We children were glad that we'd no longer have to move

HOMEMADE MEMORIES. Jack Snowdy and his entire family helped build this homestead by cutting trees, clearing the land and doing carpentry work.

from rented house to rented house.

We planted a huge garden and grew enough produce to share with our neighbors. I found a job as a clerk in a supermarket and saved my earnings to pour a winding sidewalk to the front gate. I, too, was proud of our home, simple though it was.

Through the years many folks came through our front door—visiting schoolmates, friends from church, countless relatives and acquaintances.

And all of us children left home through that door, going our separate ways in the world, leaving our parents to take care of the place.

They stayed until the day my father died, and his body was carried through that same front door for burial in the family plot in a rural cemetery. That's when my mother left, too. She moved away to live near one of my sisters.

The home place is up for sale now. But it's so hard to say good-bye.

Brooklyn Home Held Flapper Parties

By Sara Riola, Lakewood, New Jersey

IN THE 1920s, city homes were large, sprawling places with all sorts of nooks and crannies to accommodate large families and other guests who came from far away for lengthy visits. There were pantries and linen rooms, sewing rooms, dressing rooms and telephone rooms.

Our home in Brooklyn, New York was like that, and all that space came in handy when my parents hosted parties, which they did quite often when I was growing up.

A live band played in an alcove off the living room, and the adjoining sun room was opened to provide ample space for party-goers to dance.

We children were allowed to sit on the upper stairs, quiet as mice, to watch the early arrivals. It was so exciting to see the ladies in jeweled headbands and headpieces, skirts of ostrich and marabou feathers, short flapper dresses and high heels!

Took to the Floor

Soon the wonderful dancing began, and everyone took to the floor to do steps like the Black Bottom and the Charleston.

After each party, a few friends even stayed on for breakfast. I can still see my mother in her party pearls and short feathered skirt, serving hot coffee and happily whipping up her buttermilk biscuits in the kitchen.

HOSTS WITH THE MOST. Frances May and Ralston Hewitt frequently hosted parties in the 1920s at their large home in Brooklyn.

It's a Joy to Recall the 'Swing Era'

By Jim Thorley, Munster, Indiana

BACK IN the '30s, the greatest piece of furniture around the house was not the icebox or the kitchen table or even the new flush toilet for that matter—it was the front porch swing.

It usually hung suspended from hooks in the ceiling and could seat two adults comfortably, or seven fidgety kids uncomfortably.

On summer evenings when supper was over and the dishes were done, Dad would put a toothpick in his mouth and pick up the evening paper. Mother would hang up her apron and grab her sewing basket or sock-darning gear.

Together, they'd go out to sit on the swing. Meanwhile, we kids would straggle out one at a time to sit on the steps and peer around the neighborhood to see what kind of mischief was going on that would require our help.

One or another of us kids was continually getting up and going back into the house on one errand or another. This made the screen door bang shut twice on each round-trip. Finally losing patience, Dad would yell, "Quit slamming that door! Either stay in or out!"

Kids Settled Down

Not wanting to be trapped inside, my brother and I would sit back down on the front steps. All up and down the street, porch swings were occupied and swinging sedately to and fro. Conversations between neighbors, from porch to porch, had to be conducted in a louder-than-normal tone.

"Sure was a hot one today, eh, Bill?" my father would shout over to our next-door neighbor.

Mr. Howard would politely remove the cigar from his mouth and say, "Sure was, Mark, and the paper says it's supposed to be even hotter tomorrow."

Not to be outdone, Mrs. Howard, furiously fanning herself with a Burns' Funeral Home fan, added, "My washing dried faster than I could hang it up!"

Further enlivening the evening, a car came down the street. Conversation ceased as all eyes turned to follow it around the corner two blocks down. After a number of guesses as to the car's owner and possible destination, quiet reigned once again.

Chatted with Strollers

Often on those warm evenings, a couple would stroll by with the husband gallantly pushing a baby buggy. As the strollers passed each house, small tidbits of information were exchanged with each porch swinger.

"Nice evening for a walk."

"Yes, the air will make the baby sleep well."

"Don't keep the little fella' out too late, though…this night air, you know!"

The conversations weren't nosy or bossy—just neighborly with ample helpings of good ol' porch swing philosophy.

As darkness gathered, all that could be seen on porches was the occasional glow of a struck match. If a thoughtless kid turned on a porch light to look for his chewing gum, an adult would immediately yell, "Turn off that light! Do you want every mosquito in the neighborhood to know where we are?"

After a while, my dad would get up from the swing, yawn and stretch and say, "Well, let's go in. Another day tomorrow." Then, he'd go inside and tune in the old Atwater Kent. Pretty soon, we'd hear the haunting strains of "Poor Butterfly" from *Myrt and Marge*.

Us kids always hung back a little while before going in, hoping to see a falling star in the night sky. Now was the time when young couples, coming home from the library or the ice cream parlor, took over the porch swings.

Together they'd sit, holding hands and swinging slowly in the dark. Before long, Mother would go the door and tell my sister softly through the screen, "You'd better come in now, Ruth. It's getting late."

Alas, as a piece of furniture, the porch swing will not go down in history with the likes of a Chippendale cabinet or rolltop desks, but perhaps it should. After all, it symbolized an era: not exciting, but good, simple, honest …and peaceful.

PERCHED ON THE PORCH. When the day's chores were completed, folks like Jim Thorley's family would emerge from inside their homes and sit on their front porch for an evening of relaxation and friendly conversation.

FAMILY TIME. The Carters (left to right, Virginia, Gene, Charles and Alice) enjoy their front porch in Shawnee, Oklahoma in 1918.

Front Porch Saw a Lot Of Living

By Virginia Elliot, Naples, Florida

I WAS 12 when we moved to our new home. Mama quickly proved her mettle to the neighbors by sweeping the walk daily, planting her annuals neatly, hanging starched white curtains behind the vinegar-polished windows and dolling up the porch with fresh cushions on newly painted wicker.

I wasn't considered old enough to date or go to church socials or band concerts alone. So, while waiting for Mama and Papa to escort me, I'd perch primly on the front porch, starched, curled and beribboned, with my "Mary Janes" shining like black glass.

As the kids old enough to go out alone walked by, they'd give a friendly wave to the "new kid". I'd shyly wave back and smile brightly—especially at one particularly cute boy.

Did It Have to Be So Noisy?

By the end of the second week, the kids were stopping by for me and my parents didn't have to "go with" any more. That porch had been my showcase!

I think what I miss most today is the cushy, squeaky old glider that used to sit on the porch (I received my first kiss on one with poppy-printed padding). The summer my parents let me have a beau, they moved the glider to a strategic spot directly in front of the bay window of their bedroom.

During the day, Mama would rest on the porch between her chores of setting bread to rise, washing clothes, ironing or waxing woodwork. Her idea of rest was to have her pretty hands flying as she shelled peas, snapped beans, mended socks—or rocked back and forth with a mason jar full of milk in her lap.

Grandpa Welcomed Visitors

When Grandpa became too feeble to live alone, he moved into the downstairs bedroom. The space in front of the bay window was cleared so he could welcome passing folks to the porch.

They'd gather around a low table and Grandpa would hold court through

FOR ALL TO SEE. Like this little girl, Virginia Elliot's mother took pride in the family's front porch and decorated it with flowers and pretty wicker chairs.

the screen, exchanging wise chatter about how kids, cars, preachers and politics would never be the same again. Even my friends enjoyed his tales of

---

"Our front porch holds a special place in my heart..."

---

pioneering and his exaggerated yarns of outhouse tipping and runaway horses at Halloween.

On Sunday evenings we'd take turns hand-cranking ice cream and pouring lemonade—after the big midday roast, a "dessert supper" was all anyone could eat. Lucky neighbors passing by were always invited up to the porch while we kids fetched extra spoons, dishes and glasses.

That porch holds a special place in

my heart. But recently, when I asked an architect for a front porch on our new house, he looked at me as if I were crazy!

I forgave him because he was too young to know about porches. Still, just once more, I'd like to tend geraniums as the neighbors pass, and wave to toddlers learning to walk on the porch next door while my neighbor brings her peas over to shell with me.

I'd like to hear the swing squeak when my youngest girl gets her first kiss. I'd like to see my grandchildren coming down the street after school and know they're going to stop for lemonade and gingersnaps.

And I want a bay window from which my aged mother can share a piece of lemon cake as warm as her memories—memories that go back to a special time when a porch was part of every home.

COOKING UP MEMORIES. The kitchen was the center of activity for this family, as it was for Bonnie Fitch's family when she was growing up in the '30s. Bonnie says they cooked, sewed, relaxed—even danced!—in this multipurpose room.

Family Made Its Best Memories in Kitchen

By Bonnie Fitch
Lakewood, Washington

THE WARMEST MEMORIES in our old home were made in the kitchen. I can still see my mother darning socks at the drop-leaf table while Grandpa leaned back on a wooden chair, his feet resting on the open oven door of the wood-burning range, peeling an apple with his pocketknife.

He'd motion me to pull up a chair, then cut a slice for me and one for himself—how I loved that closeness!

The kitchen was long and narrow, with a large old sink, a zinc countertop and homemade cupboards and drawers. A built-in ironing board was at one end of the room, along with a windup Victrola and the old treadle sewing machine on which Mother had learned to sew when she was a child.

When I was 3 and started taking dance lessons, Grandpa built me an exercise bar in the kitchen. I practiced there for hours over the years, while the old Victrola played everything from *Shuffle Off to Buffalo* to *The Beach of Waikiki*.

I recall one disaster that happened in the kitchen. Mother was about to entertain a friend of her sister's. To get ready for her, Mother worked *so hard* scrubbing cupboards, washing windows and curtains, mopping and waxing the floor. The kitchen just sparkled!

About 20 minutes before our guest arrived, the worst happened. The stovepipe fell down!

It Was a Black Day

Soot covered *every inch* of the kitchen! Mother sent me running for our next-door neighbor, who helped Mother sweep and sweep. Still, soot was filtering down through the air.

Despite how furiously they worked, that kitchen still looked like the aftermath of a coal mine explosion. Finally, our neighbor scrubbed one chair for our guest to sit on, and she was very nice about the whole thing.

Today, the house's current owners will never know what that kitchen was like in the 1930s. Their children never had to haul coal or cut kindling to start a fire, make a cake from scratch or bake in an oven that required using your hand as a thermometer.

There wasn't an ounce of elegance anywhere in our kitchen. Yet, when the fire was crackling in the stove, it seemed the warmest, most secure place in the world.

Widower Kept a Dream Alive

AFTER my grandmother died suddenly in 1911, my grandfather continued to carry out their plans to build a new home. The house would culminate a dream they'd shared for a long time.

The house was to be built on the edge of their farm near Bolivia, North Carolina and would be large enough to accommodate their 12 children. Its design was very simple—a Southern farmhouse, typical of that day—and the building material was yellow pine cut from the surrounding woods.

The contractor who came to live with the family until the house's completion earned $1.25 a day, and his helper was paid 75¢. The mason's wages were $1.25 a day—and that included music lessons for two of his children!

The total cost of my grandfather's new home when it was finished nearly 2 years later was $1,100.   —*Earleen Shorey, Kissimmee, Florida*

BEAT THE HEAT. Folks at this home in Missouri probably sought shelter from the summer sun under the natural shade of neighboring trees. But Terry Curtis and his siblings took refuge in the man-made shade under their home!

Kids Kept Their Cool in Undercover Hideaway

By Terry Curtis, Austin, Texas

WHEN my children visited my old homestead in rural East Texas, they were amused to see the "miniature" house where I grew up. But they were even more tickled by the stories about the summers I spent *underneath* it!

The house sat on concrete blocks, with a crawl space beneath. It was so dark that Papa said it was "like crawling into a cow's third stomach", and it was at least 20° cooler than our parched yard. My brothers, sister and I escaped the scorching sun there every day, playing for hours in the soft, cool soil.

Our dogs, "Rebel" and "Queeny", and pig, "Smiley", spent most of their days stretched out under the house, too. The banty hens ventured in sometimes, spreading their wings as they nestled in the loose dirt. They'd watch us suspiciously for a few minutes, then nod off, muttering softly in their sleep.

The wood floors over our heads magnified the sounds from the house, so we always knew when Mama was pedaling her treadle sewing machine or starting supper. Papa was a telegrapher for the railroad, and we'd tap messages back and forth through the floor. He even convinced us we'd sent a real

Morse code message like: "We're under the house, Papa. Smiley is snorting in the dirt and Queeny and Rebel are scratching fleas."

We were shy as box turtles and withdrew under the house when the Watkins salesman or a neighbor came by. Visitors who saw us peering out from under the porch steps no doubt thought we were a strange bunch of kids.

She Had a "Litter"

Mama would tell them, "Yeah, I've got five pups under the house, four boys and one girl. You interested in tak-

ing one home with you?" We'd giggle and mimic the whimpering sounds that Queeny's pups made.

At suppertime, Papa would step onto the back porch and holler, "Come and get it before we throw it out to the hogs!" He didn't have to call us twice. We'd emerge from our den like ants pouring out of an anthill, dusting dirt off our trousers as we clambered up the back steps.

How nice it was to beat the heat and escape the world's problems…just by crawling under the house.

Her Childhood Home Hummed with Activity

MY PARENTS filled my life with love, music and laughter, and our small Oklahoma community was like an extended family. Friends and neighbors wandered in and out at all times of the day for coffee, conversation, bridge games or music. A friend who lived across the street said she'd never forget the sound of music drifting over from our place through the open windows on hot summer nights.

My parents entertained my friends as well as theirs. When I was in sixth grade, they not only hosted a messy taffy pull for my classmates, but sang, danced and entertained them, too!

There were slumber parties, club meetings, and girls and boys coming over to practice dance steps, listen to music and gossip. It seemed as though there was always something going on at our house!

—*Margaret Chesnut, Fort Myers, Florida*

We Were Scared on The Stairs!

By Miriam Smith-Ickes
Phoenix, Arizona

THE MECHANISM inside my camera snapped and buzzed, permanently recording a vision of the house where I grew up. My daughter and I stood across the street looking at the structure now occupied by strangers.

I'd come back to show her the place of my youth. We'd visited the graves of our ancestors and explored my old school and church. Now we'd come to the end of the trail: a green frame house that had stood for 100 years.

A flight of wooden stairs led up to the porch and the front door with its lace-covered window. Oh, those stairs —if only they could speak, what stories they'd tell!

I'd traversed them thousands of times with the lighthearted abandon of childhood. I'll never forget damp spring evenings. As the air filled with the aroma of lilacs and lilies of the valley, the steady swish of the backyard swing was accompanied by the twinkling of tiny fireflies.

Who's Got the Button?

Those were the evenings my sisters and I played games on those stairs. Soon neighborhood friends gathered, jostling for a space on the bottom step. Often, we played "Button, Button, Who's Got the Button?" Each time you guessed right you got to advance up

PRIVATE PLAYGROUND. Miriam Smith-Ickes recalls that porches were used for more than just visiting. They were also a place for kids to play games.

one step. Whoever reached the top first was the winner.

During the long balmy evenings of summer, someone might pass around a package of tender Necco wafers for a sweet treat (I was always happy not to get a purple one).

When the days grew shorter in fall, we watched for the first star to appear in the darkening sky so we could make a wish we knew would come true. Then our thoughts would turn to ghost stories, We were scared every time, no matter how often we'd heard the same stories.

There were some terrible tales told on those front porch steps. My sister Janet told the most wonderfully ghoulish story of them all. It was called "Johnny, Give Me Back My Liver!" and we never tired of hearing it.

I remember, too, the cold winters when the snow had to be shoveled or swept from those steps. I can almost hear once again the rhythmic *thunk, thunk, thunk* of the broom as it hit against the risers.

As I turned away from my childhood memories that day, my feelings were mixed. Too bad every little girl in the world doesn't have a flight of stairs on a wide front porch and plenty of sisters to share them with.

There are so many stories to be told, so many flowers to sniff—and trillions of stars to be wished upon. Wouldn't it be wonderful if every child had a chance to guess who's got the button so that they could reach the very top of the stairs first?

With Folding Tub, Hot Baths Were on Tap

OUR EIGHT-ROOM HOUSE was heated for years by a coal stove in the living room. We were excited when we finally got a furnace, but it created a problem, too—the register had to go where we'd always put our Christmas tree. We had to find a new spot for the tree, and it never seemed quite the same after that!

Our "bathroom" was a small cold-water room off the back porch. We didn't tarry there very long in winter, because it got mighty cold.

Sometime in the early 1940s, Mother bought a folding rubber bathtub from the Sears catalog, and we thought it was wonderful! We'd close all the kitchen doors, unfold the tub and pour in a couple of inches of hot water that had been heated on the stove. What a thrill that was!

—*Mary Williams, Newark, Ohio*

Trainman's Job Kept Family on the Move

By Patricia Turner
La Grande, Oregon

FOR MY SISTER and me, "home" in the 1930s and '40s was a little yellow house alongside the railroad tracks. And nowhere on earth could we have felt happier or more secure.

Dad was a signal maintainer for the Union Pacific Railroad, and we lived for years in quaint "railroad houses". They were always yellow with brown trim, and dotted the tracks every 10 to 15 miles.

One of our first railroad houses was at the bottom of a canyon, accessible only by train. My sister I were just 2 and 4 then, and I don't know how our mother had the courage to live in such an isolated spot. But this was during the Depression. Dad was one of the lucky few who had a job, and Mama would have gone anywhere to keep her family together.

Boxcar Was Moving Van

Jobs were awarded by seniority, so as new openings occurred, Dad applied for them and we kept moving up and down the tracks. Each place was a little better than the last. Mama was determined to get us settled in a spot that had a school, a decent road and a town not too far away.

Wherever we lived, a boxcar waited on a siding to transport our household goods for the next move. They were a far cry from today's padded moving vans—the furniture jostled as it made its way along the tracks, so mirrors broke and drawers lost their knobs. But it was free and got the job done.

KEEPING TRACK OF TIMES. Patricia Turner can't remember all of the numerous yellow and brown railroad houses in which her family lived. But special memories from that time are alive in her husband's photos (below) and friend's art (above).

By the time I was 7, we'd landed at Telocaset, a little village at the top of a sagebrush-covered hill in eastern Oregon. It had everything—a one-room school, a post office and neighbors. And *this* little yellow house even had an indoor bathroom!

That's where my life-long love affair with the railroad began. When you live near the tracks, the trains, engineers, brakemen, conductors and passengers soon become your friends. The clickety-clacking rails, the smoke and the whistling engines were so much a part of our lives that we didn't even notice them.

The trains were a comfort—the passengers were getting to their destinations on time, the freights were moving along and all was right with the world.

During 1943, we moved into town. As the years rolled by, the yellow houses disappeared, but my memory of that life will last forever.

A few years ago, my husband and I spent a night in our motor home in a state park with train tracks running through it. The next morning, the rest of our group complained they'd been unable to sleep because of the noise from all the trains. I hadn't even heard them.

Heating Register Pulled Triple Duty

OUR FARM HOME in the '30s had a wood and coal furnace, with one big register between the living and dining rooms.

When laundry couldn't be hung outside, Mother placed a big wooden clothes rack over the register and hung the clothes there to dry. In late afternoon, she often set pans or baking dishes with leftovers on the register to warm for the evening meal.

—*Lucille Stamper, Danville, Indiana*

COMFORT FOOD. Even during the Depression, Ann Champeau's grandma always seemed to have good food (like bacon and eggs!) sizzling in her cast-iron skillet on the trusty wood-burning stove like this one.

Life on Farm Was Simple—But It Was Home

By Ann Champeau, Norman, Oklahoma

DAD WAS a roughneck in the oil fields of Oklahoma, but was often out of work in the 1930s. Whenever money got too tight, he'd borrow a truck and take my brother, sister and me to my grandparents' farm for an extended visit. That's where I felt most secure—the place I called home.

It was a plain, simple place. The yard was bare from regular sweepings, and during the hot summers it was as hard and smooth as granite. (There were too many chores to do to have a grassy lawn that required mowing!) The only spot of cultivated beauty was a row of pink and purple hollyhocks that grew against the barbed wire fence.

The house stood 2 feet off the ground on spindly corner foundations, with raw-lumber siding that had turned a weathered gray. Inside, the rooms were sparsely decorated, but always scrubbed clean. The dim front room was wallpapered every 3 or 4 years, but used only when company visited.

The kitchen was the *real* "living room", where Grandpa read his newspaper, visiting grandchildren did their homework and Grandma knitted, crocheted and pieced quilts under the dim light of a coal oil lamp.

In the mornings, the kitchen was filled with the aromas of wood stove cooking—biscuits, eggs, home-cured bacon or ham sizzling in an iron skillet and homemade sausage from the smokehouse.

As soon as breakfast was finished, Grandma started cooking dinner—sourdough rolls or corn bread, fried potatoes and onions, fruit cobblers made with wild grape juice, and molasses cookies. Supper was usually fried mush with sweet sorghum molasses or a big kettle of oatmeal.

In summers after supper, we'd sit on the front porch until dark, shelling black-eyed peas and snapping green beans for the next day's canning. No one was idle except Grandpa, who spent the rest of the evening sitting on a rocker contentedly smoking his pipe.

Just before bedtime, we'd all kneel on the hard kitchen floor, heads bowed, for an hour or more of evening prayers. Weather permitting, my cousins, siblings and I slept in three double beds on the screened sleeping porch.

Our grandparents had the only bedroom. It seemed like a storehouse of wonder with its iron bedstead and quilt box, fabric scraps, spools of thread and twine, and the button-box odds and ends that were as precious to Grandma as jewels.

I went back not long ago; of course, the farm was nothing like I remembered. So I let my mind gaze back at the past, rejoicing again in all of the happy memories.

Family of 15 Often Had Extra Guests at Table

MY PARENTS moved to North Dakota, where they homesteaded a farm and raised 13 children, in 1908. Our little house always seemed full at mealtime—and not just with family members!

A branch of the Grand River flowed through our land, and it was an ideal spot for cowboys to stop for the night as they drove cattle to market. Whenever cowboys asked to camp there, Dad said, "Sure—and bring your other riders in for supper with us!"

They usually traveled in groups of six, but Mother always managed to feed them—and often threw in a pancake breakfast to boot.

—Albert Bowman, Rhame, North Dakota

Trees Help Him Recall His Roots

By Buck Young, Baytown, Texas

AS WE GROW OLDER, most of us feel the urge to return to our roots, the place where we started. We want to see if the old house or apartment building is still standing, if that special tree or brook is still there…if the place is as we remember it.

My journey took me to a slight rise of land called Pelly Hill. As I stood in the street, I could see it all in my mind's eye. There was the hill, with its limitless woods, thickets and bushes. There was the chain-link fence around the yard and the large citrus tree next to the front gate. (For years, we thought it was an orange tree—until it bore a single grapefruit.)

I saw the jasmine bush on the north side of the house, smelled the cloyingly sweet blossoms and saw the white petals wither when touched. I saw the gnarled cedar in the corner, remembering the day my brother planted it. I saw my favorite tree, the hickory that was so easy to climb, with branches that made a perfect base for a tree house.

I saw the one-car garage with the horseshoe nailed over the door, and the shed that held Mama's first washing machine. I saw the chicken yard out back and remembered gathering eggs from the henhouse and searching for nests in the tall Johnsongrass.

I saw the barn that held the cow, feed and hay, along with the Charles Atlas gym where we boys developed our own exercise program.

I saw the four-room white frame house where six children grew up. It was like a living thing, breathing life every day for so many years.

Then I opened my eyes. Everything that had seemed so immense to the boy looked close and cramped to the man. A mobile home sat on a small lot. Only the hickory tree and the crooked cedar remained. Everything else was gone— fence, house, barn, garage, woods.

But the memories are still there, and they are my reality. I knew and lived in this place with every fiber of my being, and the memories will be a part of me forever.

Wintry Day Filled with Warm Memories of Home

By Pat Smith, Baton Rouge, Louisiana

IT WAS WINTER in Lima, Ohio, and it looked like it might snow as I walked home from school. When I opened the door, the odor of Fels-Naptha soap filled my nose. Mother had been washing clothes.

Chunks of the hard brown soap plunged into the wash water as Mother sliced them off with a butcher knife. When the last load had been squeezed through the wringer for the second time, she'd take the agitator out and use the water to mop the whole house. One of us would follow her, laying a newspaper path, so we could walk from room to room while the floors dried.

Wet clothes hung everywhere on lines strung from the doorways. I worked my way through the newspaper walkways to the kitchen, where a big pot of navy beans bubbled on the stove.

My little sisters were drawing pictures on the fogged windows. Mother was making corn bread and giving my older sisters a sewing lesson with a box of used sweaters from our cousins. By cutting off the long sleeves at the

"Mother was giving my sisters a sewing lesson…"

elbows, then sewing up the edges, they could make short-sleeved sweaters with bobby socks to match.

My little brother ran in, yelling that Dad was on his way. Dad was a tool-and-die maker and got off the bus at 4:20 every afternoon. He came in, gave the baby a treat, then went to the bathroom to wash up, shave and entertain us all with his singing. Dad had a beautiful voice—before we were born, he had sung in minstrel shows.

When the beans were ready, we pulled the table out from the wall in our tiny kitchen. Four kids sat on one side and five on the other, with Mother and Dad at either end. For dessert, we had apricots sweetened with molasses. Mother was so proud of those apricots. We'd canned over a hundred jars from our two backyard trees that summer.

Suppertime was family time, when everyone came together to share events of the day and make plans for tomorrow. It was a time to complain…to exchange ideas…to enjoy each other.

Looking back now, I see that it was also a time to cherish each other and our home. Those simple meals gave us memories we would hold dear for the rest of our lives.

Chapter Nine

Family Holidays to Remember

Family Holidays to Remember

Every family has its own unique way of celebrating holidays, as the stories on the following pages remind us. You find out about it in a hurry when you marry.

For example, take the matter of when families open their Christmas presents. In our house, the *only* time was early on Christmas morning. There were few, if any, presents under the tree on Christmas Eve. During the Depression years when I was growing up, there was always the chilling fear that there wouldn't be any there the next morning, either.

The first person to awake on Christmas morning got the rest of the family up, no matter how early the hour. If it took banging on pots and pans or ringing a cowbell, so be it.

We trooped downstairs, plugged in the Christmas tree lights and there were the presents. Wow!

The Tradition Hung on

When my sister and I were little, we opened our presents on Christmas morn because, of course, Santa Claus dropped everything off during the night. As the years went on, our holiday-morning routine became part of our family tradition.

In some of our friends' families, the presents were always opened on Christmas Eve. To my way of thinking, that betrays a terrible lack of self-control. Yes, even a basic character flaw. Just watch. People who open presents on Christmas Eve are the same ones who first eat the frosting from their cake.

My family also had a special tradition for Easter morning. There were no Easter baskets on the dining room table. Instead, there was an envelope containing the first clue in an elaborate scavenger hunt mapped out by Mom.

The first clue might be something like, "If your ears are ringing, you must be getting close." Eventually, my sister or I would deduce that the next clue was sitting on top of the old hand-cranked telephone hanging on the wall in the den.

Search Continued...and Continued

Mom usually made us work our way through 10 or a dozen clues before we finally ferreted out our Easter baskets. We'd search upstairs and downstairs, and if the weather was nice, all around the farmyard.

Some traditions outlive their welcome, as Bernadine Chapman relates in her comical tale about Thanksgiving and roast duck on page 157. Others traditions must be imbedded in the genes. How else can you explain the Norwegian insistence on lutefisk at Christmastime?

As for my personal tastes come November, I maintain that no Thanksgiving meal is complete without creamed onions on the table. It's my own tradition...I don't intend to abandon it.

How we celebrate our holidays reflects our ethnic origins, our regional differences and our family traditions passed down through the generations. Sometimes, they're nothing more than accidental things we just decided were worth repeating.

They're what make holidays special...and they remind us that we're part of something even more special—it's called "family".   —*Clancy Strock*

OLD GLORY. Families showed their patriotism by elaborately decorating their homes on the Fourth of July, as this 1910 picture from Saundra Wiehe of Mt. Gilead, Ohio proves. Pictured are Saundra's mother, Mary Rachel (in the carriage), Saundra's two uncles, Kelsey and William, and on the steps (top to bottom), Saundra's great-grandfather, grandfather and grandmother.

Mom Made a Puzzle Out of Valentine's Day

I REMEMBER the time in the '30s when my mother made the valentine box for our third-grade class.

About a week before the classroom party, one of the moms would decorate a slotted "mailbox" and bring it to school. The time my mother volunteered, she covered the outside with ruffled layers of white crepe paper and glued on ruby hearts. The teacher claimed it was the best she'd ever seen.

Most kids only sent cards to their favorite classmates, so this became something of a popularity contest. It was always an exciting moment as the student "postman" approached one's desk with the envelopes, which were eagerly ripped open as gasps of surprise filled the room.

There were penny "joke" cards, which were playfully insulting to the recipient, and frilly cards, which expressed admiration. Often, these were mysteriously signed with a question mark.

Just before she delivered the box to school, my mom decided to surprise me by tucking in a valentine—a large fancy card that she'd signed with a question mark.

What puzzled me when I opened it, however, was the banner across the front of the card, which read "To My Hubby". Neither I nor my fellow students knew what a hubby was!

Mom had mistakenly addressed to me the card she'd gotten for Dad. Later at home, the whole family shared a good laugh about the mix-up.

—Mrs. George Gore, Cincinnati, Ohio

Mother's Creative Valentines Were Just "Bully"

DURING THE '30s, we used to get a wallpaper sample book in the mail every January. And that was when Mother and I always got ready to make valentines for the students in my country grade school.

Mother would make flour-and-water paste, then rummage through her scrap bag for bits of lace and rickrack. I got to choose the paper from the book. The ugliest pattern went to the bully who always picked on me, and the prettiest went to my best friends.

One year, the wallpaper book failed to come and Valentine's Day was only 3 days away. How I cried because there wasn't enough money to buy cards. I wouldn't have any valentines to pass out!

Of course, Mother came to the rescue. When I got home from school the night before "the big day", there on the table were chocolate fudge hearts. Each was painstakingly trimmed and had a student's name spelled out using a toothpick dipped in powdered sugar frosting.

I was so proud when I passed out my special valentines…and the bully was nice to me for the rest of the year!

—Inez Behringer, Spencer, Wisconsin

Handmade Valentines Came Straight from the Heart

MY HUSBAND and I were married at the ages of 16 and 17. He worked nights as an apprentice bus mechanic and I worked days at Woolworth's. When Valentine's Day came around, we had no money to buy cards, so I stayed up all night making him one. On the front I wrote:

We may not have a lot of money
To buy a card that's cute and funny;
But what we have can take the place
Of a paper heart with fancy lace.
We have each other, and that's the best.
Now open the card and read the rest.

Inside, I colored a large red heart and wrote "I love you". When he got home, I handed him my handmade valentine, afraid he would laugh at my childishness. But after reading it, he pulled from his pocket a small heart he had cut from a piece of sheet metal during his lunch hour!

In later years, we bought each other presents for Valentine's Day, but none has been as dear as those handmade gifts the first year we were married.

—Evelyn Wander
North Miami Beach, Florida

THEY PASS THE TEST OF TIME. Marlys Archer of Verdi, Nevada discovered these valentines that her mother had saved from the late 1920s. These special cards followed her parents throughout their marriage.

Bidding Was Spirited at Valentine's Day Box Social

By Audrey Van Lieshout, Sunnyvale, California

IT TOOK A REAL "norther" and sub-zero weather to make folks around home miss the Valentine's Day box social at Riverside School. Here was an opportunity for scattered farm families to escape the isolation of the long winter months and get together for fun and good eats.

Parents brought all the kids along, and the evening started out with songs and recitations by the students in grades one to eight. By the end of the night, everyone would be dancing to the lively accordion and fiddle music of the Jensen brothers. But the high point was the box social auction.

The women each brought a decorated box containing a supper for two, making a colorful sight arranged on a table in front of the auctioneer. The men would bid on the boxes, and the successful bidders would share dinner with the woman who brought the box.

It was supposed to be a "blind" auction, but the bidders were often tipped off by giggles, raised eyebrows and other prearranged signals.

It was understood that the husbands would make at least a "token bid" for his wife's boxed supper, but sometimes, the competition got pretty stiff. It was no secret some of the best country cooks were there—many of these gals had won blue ribbons at the fair for their pies, cakes, pickles and jams.

It was like a rite of passage for the

PRETTY PACKAGE. Audrey Van Lieshout hoped her Valentine's Day box would attract a potential suitor, but Grandpa's stomach growled loudest!

junior high girls to decorate a box and for the boys to venture their hard-earned pocket money on a bid.

The year I made my first box, I was hoping one of the eighth-grade boys would bid on it. I decorated it with fluted pink and white crepe paper and ribbon, and had made chicken sandwiches and potato salad. Also nestled inside was one of my mother's apple pies.

It was my Grandpa, however, who bid the highest on my box and would become my supper partner. He always claimed my mother was the best cook around...and I think my little brother tipped him off about the pie!

Cupid Took No Chances When This Couple Met!

ON VALENTINE'S DAY 1935, I went to a private dance at the invitation of a friend named Irma. She wanted me to meet a man named Russell and had invited him, too.

Early in the evening, there was a circle waltz. From time to time, the music would stop abruptly, and each couple would change partners with the pair closest to them. Irma, standing near the pianist, had the music stop every time Russell and I were close together. So, of course, we met!

Later, the men and women were asked to line up on opposite sides of the room. Then the women took off one shoe and tossed it into the middle of the floor. At a signal, the men dove into the pile. A man's partner for the next dance would be the woman whose shoe he'd grabbed. Russell got mine. Irma couldn't take credit for that.

After that dance, we were sent to opposite sides of the room again while a hostess stood between us, holding a bundle of long strings by their middles. The men grabbed strings at one end, the women at the other. Getting them all untangled was hilarious—and when we finished, there was Russell at the other end of my string.

At the end of the evening, the men and women selected valentine halves from two baskets, then matched them up to see who would be their refreshment partners. You guessed it—Russell and I had matching halves!

After that romantic evening, we felt we were meant for each other, and we eventually married.

Nearly 60 years later, I still have the valentine halves from that unforgettable Valentine's Day dance!

—*Elizabeth Sandeen, Cody, Wyoming*

Runaway Rabbit Made Convincing Easter Bunny

WHEN MY SON, Scott, was 5, his grandparents gave him a small white rabbit. Scott named him "Pinky" and took good care of him.

Pinky would eat almost anything and got so large we had to build a bigger pen for him. The clerk at the feed store said he'd never seen a rabbit that big. By the time Scott was 8, he was putting Pinky on a leash and walking him around the block for exercise!

One Easter morning, Pinky somehow got out of his pen. Scott was terrified we'd never find him. We searched our neighborhood, to no avail. Then we went out in the car and found Pinky a few miles from home, playing with a group of children. They thought he was the Easter Bunny!

That was a special Easter not only for us, but for others. Apparently Pinky had hopped around most of our small town before we found him, because at school the next morning, all the children were convinced they'd seen the Easter Bunny!
—*Mrs. John Heimann*
Madison, Wisconsin

Children Were Happy to Be "Strung Along" on Easter

MY MOTHER was widowed when the Depression began. It wasn't easy raising two daughters alone, I'm sure. I can remember her going to the grocery store, returning with one large bag and telling us, "This has to last a week, girls." We'd look at her and groan, but somehow we managed. And we never really wanted for anything.

Mother was a singer, voice coach and choir director and frequently sang at the Hollywood Bowl on Easter Sunday. That meant we couldn't have breakfast together, but she never failed to leave us something for Easter.

One year, she hid little Easter baskets filled with candy corn all over the house, linked to each other with strings. The first string was attached to our slippers to get us started. We followed strings all over the house, gathered our little baskets and then sat down to eat them for breakfast!

We had such a pleased, loving feeling inside, knowing Mother hadn't forgotten us even though she had to be away for a while.
—*Ruth Charters*
Sun City West, Arizona

Easter Custom Kept Children Well-Heeled

PENNIES WERE WORTH something during the Depression years, but my grandparents elevated them to golden treasures!

None of our baby shoes were bronzed; instead, they were in our grandparents' keeping. Every Easter, the shoes were returned to us—filled to the brim with pennies. What ecstasy! That was my bank account! I could never feel poor with those shoes full of pennies.

My grandparents saved carefully, penny by penny, to fill those six high-buttoned shoes. They always looked so proud when they brought them back to us!
—*Ruth Peterson*
McLean, Virginia

"Eppering" Was a Cracking Good Easter Tradition

WE CELEBRATED Easter by "eppering". These were contests to see who had the hardest egg.

We'd buy the hardest-shelled eggs we could find, then walked around the streets yelling, "Epper, epper, who's got an egg?"

To play, you cupped your egg in your fist so that only a small portion of each end was showing. Your opponent would tap it with his egg, trying to crack yours. Then you got a chance to crack your opponent's egg. If you cracked it at both ends, you got to keep it.

We also celebrated by displaying all our Easter decorations and baskets in the front windows so others could enjoy them.
—*Robert Braker*
Boynton Beach, Florida

BOY AND HIS BUDDY. A fluffy rabbit like this made one hectic Easter for Mrs. John Heimann and her family. See her story.

Easter Gift Shows Love for Generations

By Sue Schmidt, Portsmouth, Ohio

MAMA HAD four dresses to make for Easter, and time was running short. She and I went to Kobacker's Department Store to choose the material for my dress.

We climbed the stairs to the fabric section, and the scent of new material filled the air. A ceiling fan clicked overhead as Mama scanned the aisles before spying a sea-green dotted Swiss material on sale.

I sat in an oversized chair and turned the glossy pages of the pattern book. We finally picked a dress with a full skirt, puff sleeves, tiny pearl buttons and white lace around the neckline and sleeves...and a big bow that tied in back.

Saturday night before Easter, my dress was the last to be sewn, and Mama was almost out of time. She'd stayed up late the night before and worked most of the day. But she was determined I would have a new dress for Easter Sunday—and I did.

All four of us girls took part in the service the next morning. My new dress was the most splendid I'd ever had, and I beamed with pride. I was wearing lacy white anklets and black patent leather Mary Janes, and my hair fell over my shoulders in long, bouncing curls.

Wore It to School

On the Monday after Easter, children always wore their new clothes to school. I was *so proud* of my dress and told everyone my mama had made it just for me.

At recess, I ran to the sliding board, climbed to the top and shoved off, only to hear a loud *rip*. I looked down in horror to see my fairy princess dress torn in jagged pieces!

I sobbed as my second-grade teacher, Mrs. Rickey, attached the dress to the waist again with safety pins. I didn't think there'd ever be another day as bleak as this. I thought of Mama sewing for all those hours and tears dropped onto my writing paper.

"It's not so bad," my teacher consoled. "Maybe your mother can fix it."

At last, the bell rang. Maybe Mrs. Rickey phoned and told my mother about the incident—I'll never know—but as I stumbled from the bus and ran to the house, Mama took me in

ALL DOLLED UP. Sue Schmidt (shown in second-grade photo) remembers how her mother took a tattered Easter dress and outfitted her favorite doll (above). Sue still cherishes that loving gift after all these years.

her arms and kissed my forehead. "I know you would never do such a thing on purpose," she said. "It was an accident. Now, please...no more tears."

Months later at Christmas, I received a beautiful doll with long shining curls, wearing the same splendid dress of green dotted Swiss and a white petticoat. She was beautiful.

Eventually, I outgrew my dolls, married and left home. And many years later, Mama passed away. We were sorting through some things in her attic when my sister Glenda yelled, "Susie! You'll never believe this!"

Lying in the insulation and dirt was the doll—still wearing the green

> *"I told everyone that Mama had made the dress just for me..."*

dotted dress. Glenda and I hugged and cried, remembering our mother's love.

At home, I cleaned up the doll and carefully washed the dress, which became like new. I put the clothes back on her and sat her on a little stool near my fireplace.

Today whenever I look at her, I think of the wonderful Easter dress Mother made for me...and I feel her love once more.

April Fools' Trick Topped 'Em All

MY DAD was a practical joker and he loved to play April Fools' tricks on me.

One spring during my teen years, I was excitedly awaiting a new hat I'd ordered from the Sears catalog. It was pearl-gray straw with salmon-colored trim and had a cluster of imitation Royal Anne cherries on the side.

When I got home from school one afternoon and was told my order had come, I was so disappointed to open the box and find a plain black hat. I thought they'd substituted my order, so I got out the catalog to select another hat.

My younger sister was sitting at the kitchen table with me. "Opal," she reasoned, "this is April Fools' Day."

"I know it," I muttered, but kept studying the hats. (Mom told me later that she wanted to laugh out loud but didn't dare.)

After dinner, Dad strolled into the room wearing my nice new hat with the cherries on the side. He'd borrowed a hat of my grandmother's to fool me with!
—*Opal Carlson, Enumclaw, Washington*

Decoration Day Was Joyful and Solemn

By Dorothy LaFery, Madill, Oklahoma

IF THE DAY BROKE clear and beautiful on a prearranged Sunday in May, it was declared Decoration Day. Everyone from our community of Red Hill, Oklahoma would dress in their newest clothes and be at the cemetery by 10.

In recent years, Decoration Day has become "Memorial Day". In the early '20s, this holiday was a bigger event. Back then, people didn't drive to the cemetery after church to lay a wreath of artificial flowers on a grave and then leave.

It took *weeks* to prepare for Decoration Day. The ladies worked hard in their flower beds, made new clothes for the children and began preparing all the food that would keep without refrigeration. Some of the baked goods were wrapped in damp towels and stored in the cellar to preserve them.

Meanwhile, the men kept wood cut for the cookstove, went to the cemetery to clean grave markers and re-mound the dirt and did the shopping in town 20 miles away.

Come Saturday, big blocks of ice were purchased and covered with cotton picking sacks to keep them from melting. Barrels of water were loaded onto the wagons and some of the ice was chipped into them. Sugar and sliced lemons were added to the barrels for lemonade, and bales of hay were loaded for the horses.

The children scrubbed vegetables, fetched water and wood for cooking, helped pack dishes, silverware, table linens and sheets—then cut all the fresh flowers they could find, even wild ones, and stood them in tubs of water to be loaded onto the wagons. Some even made crepe-paper flowers.

With wagons fully loaded, the families set off for the cemetery. Each new arrival pulled up next to the other wagons outside the fence.

The preacher climbed into a wagon to quiet the greetings and loud laughter, and everyone took a spot on the ground or leaned against a tree. Soon, the only sounds were the

> *"In the early '20s, it took weeks to prepare for this holiday..."*

sweet chirping of bluebirds and the preacher's calm voice as he began his sermon. In the fresh morning air, the singing and prayers of the congregation sounded clear and beautiful.

It was nearly noon when the service ended and the men began to unload the boxes of food. The women spread sheets and table linens on the ground, and everyone helped set out food and silverware.

To hear all the "oohs" and "aahs" over the good country cooking, you'd think everyone had starved themselves!

After the blessing was spoken, the adults filled their plates and the children stood back to be waited on last. Through the clatter of eating and chatting, the ladies swapped recipes and blushed with the many deserved compliments as people exclaimed, "Who baked this?"

Friends and relatives who lived far apart found this a wonderful time to catch up on the family news, but all too soon it was time to clean up.

Everyone pitched in sorting dishes, sharing leftovers and loading boxes of dirty dishes, which no one looked forward to washing later.

We lined up by the tubs of flowers, two by two, as the preacher spoke: "And we hope none of us will join them, and that we may return to pay our deepest respects on Decoration Day next year."

We then gathered a bunch of flowers in both hands, and singing hymns as we entered the gate, scattered in all directions until every grave was decorated.

Although the flowers wouldn't last long, the cemetery was beautiful that sunny afternoon with vibrant color dotting the proud markers settled in the thick grass. It was a happy yet solemn moment, and the tears flowed for our departed loved ones, whom we bid good-bye for another year.

A TIME TO REMEMBER. Like these folks, Dorothy LaFery's family recognized Decoration Day by remembering departed loved ones—and by celebrating life.

Vicki Rozema

We Were Respectful on Decoration Day

By Mildred Heck, Prospect Heights, Illinois

WE ALWAYS CELEBRATED Decoration Day in our Ohio farm community in the 1920s. I never heard it called "Memorial Day" until I graduated from high school and started working in the city.

Decorating the graves of departed family members and neighbors was serious business; a barren or unkempt

> *"Arriving at the cemetery early was a show of good planning and ambition..."*

grave site was considered disrespectful. We kids kept a careful list of all the graves to be decorated, and counted and recounted the chipped canning jars we'd set aside to hold our bouquets.

The morning of Decoration Day, we finished chores extra early so we could start loading up the car. A basketful of jars was fastened to the running board.

The flowers, cut the night before and placed in tubs of cold water, were put in

the trunk and covered loosely with an old sheet. We kids balanced gallon jugs of cold tea between our feet, and Mother held the picnic basket on her lap.

We always left early to find a good parking place near the cemetery's only water pump. But arriving early was also considered a show of good planning, energy and ambition—sort of like being the first in the neighborhood to have your laundry flapping on the clothesline Monday morning!

We filled our jars, added the flowers and carried our arrangements throughout the cemetery, chatting with other relatives and neighbors doing the same. When we finished, we ate our lunch of pimiento cheese and peanut butter sandwiches, hard-boiled eggs, cookies and tea.

Around 2 p.m., there were a few speeches at the bandstand, then an hour of band music and more visiting. As soon as we got home, we got out of our Sunday clothes, kicked off our shoes and ran through the cool grass in our bare feet—the perfect end to a busy Decoration Day.

Children Picked Wildflowers for Decoration Day Bouquets

THE DAY BEFORE Decoration Day, we children would fan out over the Oklahoma prairie to pick wildflowers, then cut dozens of blooms from Mother's rosebush. We took them all to church, where they were placed in tubs of water to keep them fresh.

In the parade the next morning, all the flowers would be displayed on a "float"—a horse-drawn hayrack dressed up in red, white and blue bunting and American flags. Civil War soldiers marched behind the float, and a band played patriotic tunes.

The procession ended at the graveyard, where soldiers and our two local ministers gave speeches. The teenage girls of the community were responsible for decorating every grave with a bouquet and marking each soldier's resting place with a flag.

—Olive Stoval
Okemah, Oklahoma

They Picnicked Until The Cows Came Home!

By Donna Tanner, Ocala, Florida

NEXT TO CHRISTMAS, Independence Day was our favorite day of the year. The morning was filled with noise and commotion as our mother helped us dress in our new clothes and our grandmother prepared breakfast and a picnic lunch.

We always packed the same food—fried chicken, meat loaf, potato salad, banana coconut cake, and ice cream packed in dry ice. We also took a watermelon every year, but it never got cut. We were too stuffed to eat it.

UNEXPECTED "COWPANY". These folks enjoy a picnic in a secluded area. But at Donna Tanner's family picnic, the pasture was wide open for some uninvited guests who decided to join the party!

As soon as Grandma finished cooking, we loaded the car and drove to a state park, where we met several carloads of relatives. One year the men decided we would spend the day in the country, despite the yelps of protest from the kids. We watched the West Virginia scenery pass for what seemed like hours and grew ever more impatient and hungry.

To this day, we still don't know why we stopped at an open field. I suspect that my father, who was leading the caravan, just stopped there out of exhaustion. Everyone pulled off behind him, and tablecloths and food were spread on the ground.

The gloom lifted as we began to devour our dinner. We were so engrossed in our food that we didn't hear what was upon us until it was too late.

Suddenly everyone was screaming and scurrying. Our picnic grounds turned out to be a cow pasture, and several of them were heading right at us! The men tried to shoo the cows away while the women grabbed the food.

Our picnic was over before it even began. With long faces, we packed up for the long

"Our picnic area turned out to be a cow pasture—and they were heading toward us!"

drive home. There wouldn't be another Fourth of July for a whole year!

We'd driven only a mile when my father stopped the car next to a shallow creek and ordered us to take off our shoes and climb out. The next thing we knew, we were all wading in the creek and splashing each other—including the adults! Then we did something we'd never done on any other picnic. We actually ate the watermelon.

As we drove home in the gathering darkness, my mother said, "Well, at least we can remember this as the day we picnicked until the cows came home!"

Dad's Fireworks Display Drew Crowd Every July Fourth

THE FOURTH OF JULY was always a big day for me. In the morning, we went to town in Dad's 1929 Ford to watch the parade, then came home for a picnic lunch with relatives in the backyard.

The highlight was Dad's fireworks display. Folks came from all over the neighborhood to see his "shows", which included fireworks in the shapes of nursery rhyme and cartoon characters, and sparklers galore.

For the grand finale, Mom would put *Stars & Stripes Forever* on the phonograph while Dad set off fireworks in the shape of the American flag. It was a great thrill, and a memory I'll treasure forever.

—*Frances Olsen*
Mesa, Arizona

July Fourth Revelry Lifted Tired Spirits

By Richard Smith, Cincinnati, Ohio

OUR working-class neighborhood in Columbus, Ohio was an uneventful place 364 days of the year. But on the Fourth of July, it was the center of the universe as far as we kids were concerned!

We enjoyed a big celebration at the city park a block from my home. There were speeches, awards, a band concert and fireworks. For kids and adults alike, it was the high point of the summer—especially during the downtrodden years of the Depression.

Park Was Bustling

We kids ran to the park first thing in the morning to watch the workers set up the lights, sound system, seating and fireworks. We shot our cap pistols and set off firecrackers (legal in those days), playing cops and robbers around the temporary bandstand, while the public-address system blared out polkas and marches.

After noon, families began arriving from all over the city, toting blankets, folding chairs and picnic baskets. The program started in the early evening, with politicians giving speeches and presenting awards. Then the American Legion band performed with a few singers until darkness fell.

By then, thousands of people had filled the park. The lights were turned off and a loud "boom" overhead signaled the start of the fireworks—rockets, pinwheels, waterfalls and other colorful exhibits. The last display, an American flag, always brought cheers and applause.

Annual Traffic Jam

As the smoke cleared, we headed for home. But that wasn't the end of the evening! This was the one day of the year our neighborhood had a traffic jam, and we all sat on our porches to watch the loaded trolley cars and autos crawl past. Some of us lit up sparklers or other small displays as the crowds filed home.

At long last, the crowd was gone and the neighborhood was quiet. Everyone drifted back indoors, and a bunch of very tired kids went to bed. As hard as the Depression was on our families and others around us, the Fourth of July celebration always lifted our spirits and gave us hope. ✦

*I SCREAM, YOU SCREAM...*This boy creates a cool, creamy concoction as Daisy Prickett's father and brothers did on one "sweet" Fourth of July.

Cold Treats Were a Summer Luxury

ON THE FOURTH of July in 1932, it was terribly hot and it hadn't rained enough to make the crops grow. We lived a long way off the road on a sandy 80-acre farm, about 6 miles from town.

Dad was a widower, and he did his best to work that little farm and raise three children alone. Money was too scarce to waste celebrating, but he thought of an inexpensive way to observe this special day.

Early that morning, he told my two brothers to take their little wagon through the pasture to meet the iceman on the road. When that familiar horse and wagon appeared on its route, the boys bought a huge block of ice, carefully wrapped it in an old quilt, then covered it with a cotton sack so it wouldn't melt on the way home.

Living on a farm, we had plenty of fresh milk, cream and eggs. When the boys got home, Daddy and I had all of the ingredients ready and waiting in our metal half-gallon freezer.

There was plenty of laughter and anticipation, and that first batch of cool, sweet ice cream was everything Dad said it would be. We repeated the process two or three times that day and drank pitchers of sparkling iced tea while we waited between batches.

In those days, only a few families had wooden iceboxes, so anything made with ice was a true luxury. I'll never forget the delight of homemade cold ice cream sliding down my throat on that scorching hot day as we sat on our little front porch.

Children today who live in air-conditioned homes with such easy access to cold drinks and frozen treats can't possibly know the joy we experienced during our day of icy delight. What a wonderful way to celebrate the Fourth. —*Daisy Prickett, Dill City, Oklahoma*

The Night Halloween Pranksters Met Their Match

SIXTY YEARS AGO, Halloween was a night for real shenanigans. It wasn't unusual to see a farm wagon or a piece of machinery atop the one-room schoolhouse.

One year, a bucket of water was hung over the school door, and when the teacher opened it, she got drenched.

Another year, the teacher walked in and discovered two skunks had been let in the school, and they'd left their "calling cards" throughout. School was dismissed for several days, but we could still smell *that* prank for months afterward!

Dad Was Ready

But the best prank of all was the one that backfired. My dad was a bit of a prankster himself, and when a group of mischief-makers arrived at our house on horseback one moonlit night, he was ready.

The visitors tied up their horses at the end of the long lane leading to our ranch house, then began their stealthy approach. They skirted the ranch house, crouching low and trying to avoid the old

OUTHOUSE ANTICS. Photo reminds Kathryn McGaughey of the time her dad outsmarted some outhouse pranksters on Halloween.

machinery and barbed wire littering their path. Finally they neared the secluded spot where the outhouse stood.

But Dad was watching their every move from the shadows of the barn. Just as they were about to give the outhouse the heave-ho, he stepped from the shadows, lit a firecracker and tossed it into the air.

Horses Scared, Too

The blast was ear-splitting, and what followed was sheer bedlam! The young gents fled in such a hurry that they cleared the old machinery and barbed wire like Olympic hurdlers.

Meanwhile, their horses were so terrified that they broke away and galloped home riderless! The boys had to walk home, with nothing to show for their efforts but tired feet.

Halloween has changed since then…in our neighborhood, it's safe, sane and quite dull. I answer the doorbell, give little ghosts and goblins a treat and that's that. Still, I'm thankful I don't have to worry anymore about an outhouse being upset!

—*Kathryn McGaughey, Denver, Colorado*

This Mystery Guest Had Folks Bewitched

ONE HALLOWEEN, our teacher planned a costume party in the evening for the parents and students of our little one-room schoolhouse.

The day of the party, my father wasn't feeling well, so Mother decided to stay home and take care of him. They both insisted that we four kids go on to the party, though, and we had a great time bobbing for apples and singing along as a neighbor woman played the pump organ.

The party was in full swing when suddenly a witch, all dressed in black, "rode" through the schoolhouse on her broom, spreading chaos and cackling crazily. She made a scary sight with her pointed hat, hooked nose and warts all over her chin.

The witch then seated herself beside the organist, who was laughing so hard she couldn't continue playing. No one recognized the person behind the awful mask, and when she disappeared, everyone began speculating about who it could have been.

A few days later, my sisters and I stumbled upon a black pointed hat and the ugly, warty mask. Only then did we realize that the life of the Halloween party that night had been our mother.

—*Norma Chatelaine
Inver Grove Heights, Minnesota*

Dad's Trick Taught Greedy Goblins a Lesson

HALLOWEEN trick-or-treating was fun back in the '50s, and I'll never forget the time my dad turned the tables on two greedy goblins.

One warm Halloween night, my parents noticed that two of the same neighborhood boys kept coming back, over and over for candy. They even switched their costumes around to try to convince us they were first-time trick-or-treaters.

Dad wrapped some ice cubes in paper napkins, and when the boys rang the doorbell once again, Dad just smiled and placed a "treat" in each of their bulging paper grocery sacks.

Later that evening, as we stood on the porch listening to the chatter of children passing by, we heard those two boys suddenly groan when the bottoms of their paper bags soaked through and spilled their goodies onto the ground.

Dad and I both agreed…those boys learned a lesson in greed the hard way. They didn't know who gave them the ice cubes because they'd been to the same houses over and over that night… but I'll bet they knew why they'd been "tricked".

—*Ann Wooton Mounce
Science Hill, Kentucky*

Prank Turned Pastor into Devilishly Good Ghoul

By L. Merlin Norris, Mountlake Terrace, Washington

IN THE 1930s, the small country church I pastored was planning a Halloween party to "out-spook" all previous efforts. One person even suggested our "chamber of horrors" include a coffin with a fake body in it. But where would we get a coffin?

Suddenly I remembered that the local mortician had a coffin he couldn't sell. It was rose-colored, with a turquoise lining; he'd inherited it when he bought the funeral home.

The night before Halloween, under cover of darkness, we spirited the cas-

> *"There were continuous shrieks and gasps as they viewed my 'remains'!"*

ket into the fellowship hall and placed it midway through our chamber of horrors.

"Too bad that it lacks a body," I told my wife. "Any volunteers?" She declined with a laugh, then looked at me and said, "Good idea. You're elected!"

Why not? I still had some fake teeth and bulging plastic eyeballs from a college prank. I chuckled as I pictured myself in the coffin. "I'll put the fear of the devil in all of them," I laughed.

On Halloween night, my wife held the coffin steady while I crawled inside. I slipped the false teeth over my own, put the bulging eyes in place, donned a long black wig and smeared a bit of ketchup on my white shirt. My wife turned on the blue display light overhead, gave me a last look, then hurried off with a grin to join the rest of the group.

I hadn't realized how tired I was. The low droning of voices from the other end of the building was as soothing as a lullaby. I fell asleep.

The next sound I heard was a scream! I awoke with a start, looked through the tiny holes in my false eyes and saw the horror-stricken face of one of the town's most dignified matrons. After that, there were continuous shrieks and gasps as everyone viewed my "remains". I have to admit I enjoyed it!

After the last screaming guest departed, my wife told me, "You were a sensation. I think you made Christians out of most of them tonight!"

Many months later, I conducted a funeral service for a hobo who'd been riding the rails and died near the tracks.

As I entered the pulpit through a side door, I saw his coffin and did a double take. It was my rose-colored casket!

I looked to the back of the sanctuary for my friend the undertaker. He smiled and nodded; it *was* my coffin. I looked down at the stranger resting so peacefully on the turquoise lining and thought, "I was there first, my friend."

Urban Halloweeners Had Fun Without Trick-or-Treating

WHEN WE MOVED to a rural area of Pennsylvania, we were in for lots of surprises—including the way Halloween was celebrated. We'd never even heard of trick-or-treating!

In the city, we started our celebrations by filling old socks with ashes from the coal stoves. Then we'd fling them at each other, calling, "Ashes to ashes!" We wore old clothes for that, because we always came home covered with white ash marks!

Later, we'd dunk for apples. Mother would put apples in a water-filled tub, then we'd put our hands behind our backs, kneel over and try to pick up apples with our teeth. (I did this with my own children when they were small, and they still talk about it!)

Mother made our game even more exciting by slipping a coin into each apple. Usually it was a penny, but sometimes we'd find a nickel or a dime.

After we dried off, Mother would bring out a Halloween cake from the bakery, complete with a spinning witch on top. Inside each slice of cake was a prize like the ones in boxes of Cracker Jack. It was a wonderful evening, everyone was safe at home and the parents got to enjoy it, too.   — *Cathy Kuhn*
Milford, Pennsylvania

APPLE DUNKING GANG. Like these kids, the highlight of Halloween for many kids in the good old days was bobbing for apples.

Helping Others Taught Teen to Count His Blessings

By Michael Noggle
Oil City, Pennsylvania

OUR SON, "Bear", was big, rugged and afraid of nothing, and his world was one joyous adventure.

When he was 16, his confirmation class planned to deliver Thanksgiving baskets to the needy, and he volunteered me to drive. It was a great project, providing not only Thanksgiving meals but a generous supply of canned goods. I was glad Bear was involved.

Thanksgiving Eve, we drove to a run-down house in what had once been a pleasant neighborhood. A thin woman in a faded housedress and threadbare sweater invited us in.

The living room furniture consisted of a legless sofa and a few odd chairs. The only light came from a tiny TV and a

---

"Remember, we've all got plenty to be thankful for..."

---

bare ceiling bulb. A little girl about 6 and a boy a bit younger peered at us anxiously. Bear stood silently just inside the door, a strange look in his eyes.

"These first two boxes are for tomorrow's dinner," I told the woman. "Some of it'll need to be refrigerated."

We followed her into the kitchen and saw her refrigerator contained nothing but a quart of milk, two jars of baby food and half a loaf of bread. Bear looked anguished as he ran out for another box of food.

"We also brought some nonperishables, ma'am," I said when he returned. "Bear, will you…" But he was already gone. When he didn't return, I went out to check on him.

He was standing quietly next to the open trunk with tears in his eyes. "Anything wrong?" I asked gently. "No!" he said. He seemed serious, older, as we carried in the last four cartons of food.

"We really appreciate this," the woman said. Clasping Bear's big hand in hers, she continued, "It was so kind

LESSON IN LIFE. Michael Noggle's son—like this teenage boy—helped deliver food to the needy one Thanksgiving and in doing so learned a valuable lesson that he shared with the rest of the family.

of you. Please thank everyone for us."

As we drove home, neither of us spoke. Finally, we were back in the warmth of our own kitchen, where the welcoming aromas of bread, pies and other delicacies for tomorrow's big dinner hung in the air.

Bear said, "Dad, did you see how they lived?"

"Yes, Bear."

"But did you see that furniture? That little TV set?"

"Yes."

"And that empty refrigerator. Less than a quart of milk for two kids! I thought we'd be giving turkeys to people so they wouldn't have to eat spaghetti. That family had nothing! And right here, only 4 miles from where

we live!" His tears welled again as he asked, "You knew it would be that way, didn't you?"

I stared into my teacup, hoping he wouldn't see that my own eyes were wet, too.

The next day, as we gathered around our holiday table, a younger family member peeked into a serving dish and complained, "Broccoli cheese casserole? I hate broccoli!"

Bear growled, "Nobody says you have to eat it. Just be glad you have a choice." Then he smiled. "Remember, it's Thanksgiving, and we've all got plenty to be thankful for." He turned to me and gave me a hug. "Right, Dad?"

"Right, Bear," I said. "Every so often we just need to be reminded."

When Duck Took Wing, So Did Holiday Tradition!

By Bernadine Chapman, Lodi, California

IT WAS THANKSGIVING Day 1936, and the house was filled with the aromas of holiday cooking—including roast duck, which Papa boasted was his family's favored holiday meat. I didn't like it and became an expert at scooting mine around the plate or hiding it under the mashed potatoes.

"Mama," I pleaded, "why do we have to have duck again?"

"For generations, the Upjohns have served roast duck for Thanksgiving," she said, putting it on a platter. "It's their favorite. Besides, Aunt Eloise is here for dinner."

That settled, she marched the bird out to the table and placed it in front of Papa, who took a deep, appreciative breath. "Mmm," he said. "I just love the smell of roast duck. Where's Eloise?"

"Start grace, George," his sister called from the other room. "I'm coming."

Immediately after the "amen", Papa stood, rolled up his sleeves and ceremoniously raised the carving utensils high in the air.

With a swift downstroke of the carving fork, he pierced the duck's bulging breast. Just then Aunt Eloise

> *"The duck dangled on the end of the fork, catapulted across the room and landed on the dining room rug!"*

rushed into the room. A loud growl rumbled under the table, and my dog, "Skipper", leaped out and nipped at her ankle!

Aunt Eloise screeched and reeled backward. To keep from falling, she grabbed Papa's arm. As he struggled to keep his balance, the duck rose a foot off the platter, dangled precariously on the end of the fork, then catapulted across the room. It landed with a thud on the dining room rug.

We all stared at it silently as Aunt Eloise plopped into a chair. "It's all my fault," she said. "If I hadn't bumped into George's arm, this wouldn't have happened. Now let me think a minute."

Then her eyes began to twinkle. "Let's go down to that restaurant I saw on my way into town—the one

that's serving turkey dinners. I'd love to have a real Thanksgiving turkey for a change. My treat!"

"But, Eloise," Papa protested, "you're an Upjohn and you prefer roast duck."

"I may be an Upjohn," Aunt Eloise retorted, "but I can't stand roast duck!"

That was when I realized Papa was the only Upjohn who considered roast duck a family tradition. From then on, thanks to Skipper and Aunt Eloise, our traditional holiday meat was roast turkey…my favorite!

GONE TO THE BIRDS. This man reminds Bernadine Chapman of the pride her father had when carving the Thanksgiving duck—and of his shock when he discovered only he cared for it!

On Thanksgiving Morning, Children "Went Begging"

A TRADITION in my hometown of Glendale, New York in the 1940s and '50s was "going begging" on Thanksgiving morning. We'd dress up in old clothes and ring doorbells, asking, "Anything for Thanksgiving?"

We received fruit, nuts and pennies. Then we'd come home, wash up, change clothes and eat Thanksgiving dinner. — *Miriam Zalenski*
Fairfield, Connecticut

Spirit of Christmas Came in Cardboard Boxes

By Jeanne Malmberg, Norman, Oklahoma

I ALWAYS KNEW Christmas was near when I saw my schoolteacher-parents start lining up empty cardboard boxes in the dining room and filling them with food. When I asked Mother what she was doing, she'd say, "Getting ready for Christmas."

"But those aren't presents," I'd say. "It's just food."

"Food is a present if you don't have any," she'd reply.

One day I walked into the living room and saw her reading a letter. Tears filled her eyes as she looked up at Daddy and said, "He wants a toothbrush. Can you imagine a 7-year-old boy asking Santa for just a toothbrush?"

I popped off, "Who would be that dumb?"

Mother slowly turned toward me, her eyes blazing. "Jeanne, you're 6 years old, and I think it's time you learned a few things about what Christmas really means."

Daddy asked if I could keep a secret. I promised I could. And they proceeded to teach me about the true spirit of Christmas.

When our school's students wrote to Santa, Mother reviewed the letters to see which families need help. Then she and Daddy filled a box for each family.

"On Christmas Eve we put the box on their front porch, but we're very careful so they don't hear us," Mother said. "That's the secret you must keep. If you tell, you'll spoil the spirit of Christmas for us and them."

I vowed never to tell, and Daddy pulled me into his arms for a hug.

For the rest of the month, it was my job to see that each box had an equal share of canned food. Mother put the toys on a high shelf to keep me from temptation.

When Christmas Eve finally arrived, the day seemed to crawl by. I thought it would *never* get dark! When dusk fell, we

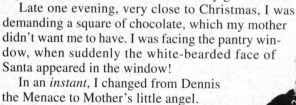

> *"I've warmed myself every year since with thankfulness for my parents..."*

drove almost to the first house and turned off the engine and lights. Daddy sneaked down the block and slipped onto the porch with the box while Mother and I watched excitedly and giggled as he made his way back.

At the second house, I wanted to deliver the box, but Daddy said that was his job. "All the dogs know me," he said. "That's why they don't bark."

Almost "Caught"

On our third stop, Daddy lost his balance and thudded against the porch railing. The front door flew open and a burly man stepped out. "Is someone out there?" he demanded.

Daddy crouched behind a cedar at the corner of the house. Then the man spied the box filled with food and toys. "Hey, Ma, kids, come look what's on our porch," he yelled. "It must have been Santa!"

Mother and I held our hands over our mouths, trying to keep quiet as Daddy crept back to the car. When we pulled away, we all exploded in laughter. Then we drove to the next house and the next, singing carols all the way until the last box was delivered.

I've warmed myself every year since with thankfulness for my parents, who carried the true spirit of Christmas in those cardboard boxes.

Years later, I discovered that everyone knew we were the ones making the deliveries. But they never figured out how my parents knew what toy each child wanted, and I never told. That was our little secret.

I Was Good, for Goodness Sake!

I'LL NEVER FORGET the day I saw Santa looking in our pantry window! This incident happened way back in the '20s, when I was about 5 years old.

Our house in Canton, Ohio had a large pantry with a window overlooking the backyard. Mother kept squares of Baker's sweet chocolate in one of the cupboards there, and I was occasionally given one as a special treat.

Late one evening, very close to Christmas, I was demanding a square of chocolate, which my mother didn't want me to have. I was facing the pantry window, when suddenly the white-bearded face of Santa appeared in the window!

In an *instant*, I changed from Dennis the Menace to Mother's little angel.

Sister Was Culprit

Years later, I learned the truth. My college-age sister owned a Santa costume that she used to entertain the neighborhood children. When she'd heard my tantrum over the chocolate bar, she quickly donned her Santa mask and slipped out the front door and around back to peer in the window.

For a long time after the incident, I truly believed "he knows if you've been bad or good, so be good for goodness sake!"

—*Thomas Russell*
Spokane, Washington

Santa Popped in with a Special Gift

I REMEMBER a special Christmas many years ago when I was a little girl. It was during the Depression and we were poor, like so many other families at the time.

My brother had helped a neighbor plant his garden during the summer and was given a few popcorn seeds. He planted them in a corner of our backyard, and they grew into tall cornstalks, each bearing an ear of popcorn.

Not Ready Yet

I continually asked him when we were going to pop the corn, and he would always patiently reply, "It's not ready yet."

On the day before Christmas, my brother volunteered to clean up the basement and take care of the furnace —if he could do it by himself. Permission was granted.

Christmas Eve, after we had our traditional Holy Night supper, the family gathered in the front parlor, which was only used on special occasions.

I remember Mother sitting in the rocking chair, singing hymns and carols from the prayer book she'd brought from the "Old Country". Father was smoking a cigar he'd been given months before and had saved for this special occasion.

We children were sitting on a threadbare rug on the floor and were admiring our little Christmas tree in the corner, when suddenly there was a knock on the front door.

Funny Looking Santa

When it was opened, there stood the funniest little Santa Claus I'd ever seen. He was short and skinny and wore a black and red plaid flannel shirt with a black tassel cap on his head. On his back, he carried a large sack with a big red cross on it...the kind we received

flour in from the Welfare Department.

With a hearty "Ho! Ho! Ho! *Merrrry Christmas*"—he bounded in and opened the sack. It was full of big, white, fluffy popcorn!

Instead of cleaning the basement, our little Santa had popped corn all day long by shaking the long-handled popper over the glowing fire in the big coal furnace that heated our house.

This sack of popcorn was my brother's gift to his family, and as I recall, I have never enjoyed more delicious popcorn than what we shared that night.

—Sophy Rozinsky
West Newton, Pennsylvania

Flickering Candles Made Christmas Glow

By Charlotte Tubesing, Stone Mountain, Georgia

I'LL NEVER FORGET Christmas of 1920. My mother, aunt and I walked from my aunt's home in Scappoose, Oregon along the canyon road to my great-uncle's house for a special event—the lighting of his Christmas tree.

Night was beginning to close in as we came upon the farmhouse, where glowing lamps had been lit and welcoming arms greeted us.

We walked into the living room with the others who'd come to share this moment and saw the fir tree in a dim corner of the room. It was so tall it almost touched the ceiling!

Tiny candles in metal holders had been snapped onto the branches, giving the tree a delicate uncluttered look.

With everyone assembled, we breathlessly waited as each candle was lit with a match. Brighter and brighter the tall tree glowed, until its candlelight bathed the dark corner of the room in a warm cheerful glow.

After a few "oohs" and "aahs", we stood in silence admiring the flickering light, but it wasn't long before someone said, "The flames are getting close to the tree's needles." One by one, the tiny flames were snuffed out.

Afterward, we three walked back to my aunt's house, and there under a small tree on the table was a beautiful new doll from Mother. Today I treasure that doll in the same way I remember that simple quiet evening, nearly 75 years ago.

OH, CHRISTMAS TREE. A tree like this one made Charlotte Tubesing's Christmas even brighter.

Christmas Tree or Gifts? Children Chose the Tree!

MY FOLKS weren't rich, but they usually managed to fill most of our desires for Christmas, including a freshly cut tree with all the trimmings. December 1943 found them struggling, however. With World War II under way, many items were rationed, and those that weren't were priced out of our reach.

In mid-December, our parents sat us down and said this would be a very slim holiday, and we had to make a decision. We could have the presents we wanted and no Christmas tree, or a tree and a few inexpensive gifts.

Without hesitation, all three of us answered, "It wouldn't be Christmas without a tree!" I'm sure that answer left our parents with lumps in their throats. That evening, we went searching for the prettiest tree we could find.

Christmas morning dawned without the usual hustle and bustle. We didn't expect any gifts, so there was no hurry to gather around the tree. Imagine how surprised we were to find it loaded with gaily wrapped presents!

Because a *symbol* of Christmas was more important to us than the gifts, our folks somehow managed to scrimp and do without so we could have presents, too. It was one of the merriest Christmases I ever had. —*Edward Bowser Arlington, Texas*

Robb Helfrick

A TREE, PLEASE! Edward Bowser and his siblings decided to forgo expensive gifts for a simple tree and had the best Christmas ever.

Someone Let the Cats Out of the Bag

CHRISTMAS at my grandparents' farm was always a big event, and to make it more exciting, the adults often borrowed a Santa suit from the local department store for Christmas Eve.

At the right moment, we were told to look out the window, and to our delight, we'd see Santa crossing the yard, waving and lugging a big pack over his shoulder.

We kids understood that some of the different red-suited fellows in the department stores were "Santa's helpers". But we were convinced that we were seeing the gentleman from the North Pole himself in our yard. The first shadow of doubt crossed my mind on a Christmas Eve when there'd been a big snow and the moon shone brightly.

Each person in the family had certain duties on the farm, and one of my aunts always fed the many cats we had.

To my surprise, when I looked out the window on this bright December night, I saw Santa crossing the yard with a long line of hopeful cats trotting at "his" heels. Apparently, it's easier to fool a child than a cat! —*Mary Turner Blountville, Tennessee*

Our Christmas Always Came in a Box

ON DECEMBER 1 of each year, my mother would give each of her eight kids half of an oatmeal box. In the '20s, they were long and rectangular.

Over the next month, we'd get busy decorating our boxes with wallpaper, ribbons, rocks, macaroni, buttons and beads.

Come Christmas Eve, we'd set our colorful boxes on the table, and the next morning we'd find them filled with homemade candy, nuts, oranges and sometimes gum. Since no two boxes were alike, there was never a problem telling which box to race to!

Mother and Dad are gone now, but all of their children have passed this tradition on to the grandkids and great-grandkids. They love it today as much as we did growing up.
—*Elenora Robbins, Pounce, Wyoming*

Big Brother Was No "Stinker"

WHEN I WAS 12, we were living on a farm in Iowa and money was not plentiful. My younger sister and I weren't expecting much for Christmas.

For weeks before Christmas, our older brother, John, was always sawing and nailing on something he told us was a "skunk box". He said he'd trapped a skunk and needed something to keep him in. Sis and I believed him.

Lo and behold, on Christmas morning we discovered that "skunk box" was really the most beautiful table and chair set, and it was just our size!

Many tea parties were served on that table, and I can still see Mother enjoying "tea" and trying to sit on one of the little chairs just to make us happy.

We didn't have much, but that Christmas is the happiest I can recall.
—*Lorene Thiede, Harlan, Iowa*

Christmas Was Fragrant In Sunny California

EUCALYPTUS, orange blossoms and apples...the fragrances bring back memories of Christmas on the farm in 1910.

Mama was widowed at the young age of 30. Papa died when I was 2 years old after having encouraged Mama to leave cold Minnesota and come out to California, "Where the birds are singing in the palm trees, and the orange trees have blossoms and fruit on them at the same time."

When Papa died, Mama had to support three children and tried to make it on her own by farming 20 sandy acres in Turlock, in central California. She traded eggs, fryers and home-churned butter at the grocery store for staples.

Money was scarce, so we had no decorations at Christmas. But that didn't stop Mama! She decorated our house with orange tree branches, with the fruit and flowers still on them.

Then she cut off a long branch of a eucalyptus tree, set it in a tub of wet sand and brought it into the house. Oh, the aroma! We decorated it with chains of colored paper made with flour-and-water paste, and garlands of threaded popcorn and cranberries.

For a holiday treat, Mama would somehow buy a box of apples. The delicious fragrance of that luscious red fruit wrapped in square tissues meant Christmas had arrived.
—*Vi Martinson*
Turlock, California

Special Present Stayed With Her for 43 Years!

MY MOST MEMORABLE Christmas was in 1941. I was 13 and had just started experimenting with makeup. In those days, you could send in magazine coupons for free samples of lipstick, rouge, lotions and powders. I had quite a collection of these samples and desperately wanted a vanity table for them.

We lived in Rock Springs, Wyoming. Mom and Dad were raising four kids, so it was hard for them to make ends meet. Dad worked days and went to school at night, but he somehow found time to make my vanity table—with only a pocketknife and a handsaw! He worked on it in the basement whenever he had a few spare minutes.

Mom and Dad were worried I'd go into the basement and spot it, so one day

Mom commented, "John, have you noticed how many spiders there are in the basement?"

"Yes," he replied, "seems like I kill two or three every time I go down there!"

That did the trick. They knew how scared I was of spiders!

By Christmas morning, it was finished—a glossy, handmade vanity table with a flowered skirt. It was one of the best Christmas presents I ever had.

I moved a lot in the decades that followed, but the table stayed with me for over 40 years. I'll never forget all the love that went into its creation.
—*Shirley Knight, Cedar Rapids, Iowa*

Parents Orchestrated Christmas Morning Magic

WE ALWAYS HAD a special ornament on our Christmas tree—a small, shiny red horn that you could actually blow. This was "the signal" Santa gave to tell us he was finished and on his way back up the chimney.

On Christmas morning, we four kids would wake early and rush downstairs to gather in the hallway, eagerly awaiting the sound. Then it would come—the musical blowing of the little horn!

My mother would throw open the

OPEN IT, MOM! "All attention was focused on Mother as she opened a special Christmas present from Daddy," recalls Blanche Comiskey of Franklin, Wisconsin. Blanche's mom, Mary Freischle, savored the moment in 1953.

doors and we'd all dash in to stare at the big decorated tree and all the gifts underneath.

Years later, we learned that it was my father who blew the horn, then tore madly out the other door through the dining room. Somehow, he still managed to rush in with us!

My parents' zest and determination to give their kids such an enchanted Christmas boggles my mind. As the years went by and we kids grew up, not one of the older children ever told the secret, so the full joy was saved for the youngest child.

I later used the same little red horn on my child's Christmas trees, and this favorite family tradition "plays on" as that shiny horn hangs on my grandchildren's tree today.
—*John Chase*
Rohnert Park, California

The Gift I Remember Most Was One I Once Gave

WHEN I WAS 8 years old in the early '30s, money was scarce. My two brothers and I were living with our grandmother at the time, and she gave us each a dollar and took us to Corpus Christi to do our Christmas shopping.

The dime store had never looked as enticing as it did that day. Clenching my crisp dollar bill, I selected my purchases: a plastic fountain pen for my cousin, marbles for my brothers and powder for Granny. I had about 9¢ left to spend when I realized I hadn't picked out anything for my aunt.

The nice clerk behind the counter sensed I needed help and led me to the material section. There she cut off a piece of green organdy and carefully explained how to make a dresser scarf by coloring flowers on each end of the fabric with crayons, then setting the pattern with a hot iron. I was so excited to try!

On Christmas Day, I couldn't wait for my aunt to open that gift...and when she did, tears welled in her eyes. My flowered scarf was the only gift she received that Christmas. Today, some 60 years later, she still has that dresser scarf!
—*Noma Pearce*
Fort Worth, Texas

'Mystery Gift' Moved Young Wife to Tears

By Nina Bunyea, Penryn, California

IN THE middle of the Depression, my brother-in-law, Roy, fell ill and was confined to a wheelchair. With no income and two boys to raise, he and my older sister cut expenses wherever they could.

They planted a garden, started canning and even turned off their electricity. My sister was embarrassed by their coal oil lamps, but the outlook was bleak. There was no room for pride.

Around that time, my father became the town postmaster and offered my sister a clerk's job at $28 a month. She took it, despite the stigma attached to women who left their homes and families for jobs.

It must have tortured Roy to take over the cooking, canning and cleaning, but he tackled them valiantly. He did the laundry on a washboard from his wheelchair and rigged up a device that allowed him to hang clothes out to dry. He even made sure his oldest son's school clothes were nicely starched and pressed.

Christmas had always been a magical time for them. Roy usually put a "mystery box" under the tree and teased

HOPE LIT THE WAY. Nina Bunyea recalls the Christmas that ended on a lighthearted note for her sister's family.

my sister mercilessly as she shook and rattled it, trying to guess its contents. She could hardly wait to open it on

Christmas. But this year was different. There was a mystery box, but *no one* was allowed to touch it.

On Christmas morning, my father and I joined them as they opened their gifts. My sister's "mystery box" was saved for last. We were so excited about seeing what was inside that we didn't even notice Roy *walked* several steps to hand it to her!

She tore off the paper, opened the box and found another gift-wrapped box inside—and another, and another. She finally ripped away a layer of newspapers to reveal the top of a Philco radio. "What a dumb gift," she said. "We have no electricity."

Roy just smiled and said, "Read the note that's with it." She began to cry as she read the words aloud: "Try the light switch." She did, and the whole joyful scene was bathed in light.

We watched in amazement as Roy walked across the room to her and said he'd found a good job… and yes, he could now spend several hours a day on his feet!

I was almost grown before I understood the tears. ❧

Rival for Dad's Attention Taught the Meaning of Christmas

WHEN I WAS growing up, my dad managed a Guernsey farm in Indiana. One summer, he was short of help and hired Little Joe—an orphan boy of 16 who'd been searching for work.

Dad brought Joe home to live with us, and they were together constantly. Being one of three daughters, I was aware that Dad sometimes spoke about his never having had a son—and now Joe was in our home.

I began to resent our new hired hand. I was jealous of all the store-bought clothes my parents gave him, while my sisters and I wore the homemade feed sack dresses Mother made for us.

Even worse, Dad and Joe spent many hours together out in the toolshed, and at night after supper, they'd disappear for hours more. I even found them whispering in the kitchen a few times.

When Christmas began to draw near, I was a very unhappy little girl, and I could hardly speak to Joe.

On Christmas morning, Mom and Dad ushered us three

girls upstairs and, of course, Joe tagged along. There was an old unfinished attic room next to our bedroom, so I was a little surprised when Dad and Joe opened the door to it and invited us girls to "go on in".

It was like walking into *House Beautiful*. There was a gorgeous new bedroom for us! It had three homemade beds covered in pretty feed sack spreads, three homemade dressing tables with ruffled gatherings and three new lamps —all just the perfect size for young girls.

I glanced back at Little Joe, standing there with Dad's arm on his shoulder…this orphan boy who helped Dad and Mom make Christmas special for me. There were tears rolling down his cheeks, and at that moment, I learned the true meaning of Christmas.

Joe became my good friend. Later, our family moved to Pennsylvania and Joe went on to college. We've lost touch now, but I will always remember our hired hand—whose helping hand touched us all.

—*Eloise Paull*
Clinton, Pennsylvania